Summer versus School II

Summer versus School II

The Balanced Calendar of School, Work, and Life

2nd Edition

James Pedersen
David Hornak
Jon Mishra

ROWMAN & LITTLEFIELD
Lanham • Boulder • New York • London

Published by Rowman & Littlefield
An imprint of The Rowman & Littlefield Publishing Group, Inc.
4501 Forbes Boulevard, Suite 200, Lanham, Maryland 20706
www.rowman.com

86-90 Paul Street, London EC2A 4NE, United Kingdom

Copyright © 2025 by David Pedersen, David Hornak, and Jon Mishra

All rights reserved. No part of this book may be reproduced in any form or by any electronic or mechanical means, including information storage and retrieval systems, without written permission from the publisher, except by a reviewer who may quote passages in a review.

British Library Cataloguing in Publication Information Available

Library of Congress Cataloging-in-Publication Data Available

ISBN 9781475873849 (cloth) | ISBN 9781475873856 (pbk.) | ISBN 9781475873863 (epub)

No generation of educators in history has been asked to do what Americans now demand of their schools. Each year the burden grows, and each day millions of teachers and administrators give everything they've got to meet the challenge. Their record of achievement is remarkable. But no matter how hard they work, or how often they are criticized, they cannot produce the results our nation needs. Not because they are arrogant, overpaid, or unionized. America's educators cannot teach all students to high levels, because they work in a system designed to do something else; select and sort young people for an industrial society that no longer exists.
~ Jamie Vollmer

Contents

Introduction		ix
1	History of School Calendars	1
2	Reexamining Time in Our Schools	31
3	Exploring Diversity in School Calendars: A Comprehensive Analysis of Various Models	43
4	Redefining Time: The Future of School Calendar Reform	57
5	Modified School Calendars Today	67
6	Current Research on Schools with Modified Calendars	117
7	Case Studies in Washington State	143
8	Strategies for Implementing a Balanced Calendar	161
9	Questions and Answers	169
Conclusion		183
References		187
About the Authors		215

Introduction

WHY DO WE NEED THIS BOOK?

One of the fundamental challenges of the American education system is its strict adherence to a fixed daily schedule of six to seven hours and a yearly schedule of 180 days. This approach, which heavily relies on time as the primary organizational factor for schools and curriculum, is based on several assumptions. It assumes that all students come to school ready to learn in the same way and follow the same pace of progression. It also perpetuates the belief that the educational calendar that served previous generations adequately should also be sufficient for today's children, despite considerable societal changes.

So, is *Summer Learning Loss* a real concern?

Every year, the media buzzes with discussions about summer learning loss. The premise is straightforward: during the summer break, American children, while enjoying leisurely activities like lounging by the pool, watching TV excessively, and playing numerous video games, tend to forget a significant portion of what they learned in the preceding school year. This phenomenon is particularly concerning for low-income students, who often experience a more pronounced setback in their academic progress.

During these summer months, without the structured learning environment provided by the school, many students experience a decline in their academic skills. This regression can be attributed to a lack of educational engagement and opportunities for intellectual stimulation. Without regular practice and reinforcement of concepts, students may struggle to retain the knowledge and skills they acquired during the school year.

Furthermore, the impact of summer learning loss is not evenly distributed across all socioeconomic groups. Low-income students are disproportionately affected, as they often have limited access to educational resources, such as multiple meals each day, access to instructional materials, and enrichment activities during the summer break. This exacerbates existing achievement gaps and can lead to long-term academic consequences.

Addressing summer learning loss requires a multifaceted approach. Schools can implement summer programs to provide continued academic support and enrichment opportunities for students. Families can also play a crucial role by encouraging reading and other educational activities during the summer break. By recognizing and actively combating summer learning loss, we can help ensure that all students have the opportunity to maintain and build upon their academic achievements year-round.

The current two 1/2-month break is a vestige from a bygone era and may not be relevant for today's students. However, adopting such changes would require giving up the American tradition of summer vacation, prompting a debate about the trade-offs between tradition and reform for student success (Pedersen, 2015). As we continue to debate the merits of a balanced calendar, a growing number of American schools are shifting to year-round calendars (Addison, 2023).

WHAT IS THE PURPOSE OF THE BOOK?

It seems like the only thing many people appear to agree on when it comes to the impacts of COVID-19 is the way people want to work. Whether it be shortened work weeks or work-from-home days, many people seem to enjoy the freedom of less traditional work hours. This has also found its way into school systems, where educational leaders are once again looking into ways of redistributing instructional time. With this thought in mind, the authors of the book felt that calendar reform, namely balanced calendars, is not only a niche group but one that is expanding every year. Therefore, the purpose of this book is to educate and dispel some of the myths of the balanced calendar as well as inspire possibilities that have not even been thought of yet.

WHAT DO WE HOPE YOU WILL LEARN FROM THIS BOOK?

We hope that you will find the intricacies, benefits, and possibilities of a balanced calendar as you explore this book. We hope that in the end, you will make an informed decision that will benefit the students and stakeholders in your schools and districts. It should also help those determining if they would like to implement a balanced calendar in their school or district. Some important things must be considered right from the beginning:

- A balanced calendar is not a miracle reform.
- It will not guarantee a failing district will become high-achieving.
- It will not make every parent or every stakeholder happy.

There is definitely an adjustment time that should be taken into consideration, but in many cases, those who have adopted a balanced calendar stay with it and cannot think of returning to a traditional calendar. But, with the proper planning, creating, revising, and reflecting, it could serve as a tremendous tool that could decrease learning loss and increase motivation and morale.

THE AUTHORS

David G. Hornak, Ed.D., has lived and worked in Holt, Michigan, for the past 30 years. As an employee of Holt Public Schools, he has taught young fives, kindergarten, first grade, and Reading Recovery. Hornak was promoted 17 years ago, as he became the instructional leader (principal) of Horizon Elementary. Horizon is a year-round school, which operates on a balanced school calendar. Hornak has presented hundreds of times to school boards, district officials, community groups, and PTO groups across the world regarding alternative calendar and wellness initiatives such as the *Walking School Bus*. His dissertation titled "The Impact of Summer Recess on Mathematical Learning Retention," which was selected in 2016 as the national dissertation of the year by the National Council of Professors of Educational Administration further supports the need for school officials interested in minimizing the summer learning loss to consider the balanced school calendar. In April 2015, Hornak was named Executive Director of the National Association for Year-Round Education. In July 2015, Hornak was promoted to serve as the superintendent of schools in Holt. He is addicted to serving others, especially his own community as well as those interested in learning more about the balanced school calendar. Hornak and his partner Anne are the proud parents of daughter Olivia and son Maxwell. To connect with David: davidghornak@gmail.com.

Dr. Jon Ram Mishra currently serves as an assistant superintendent for the Office of Superintendent of Public Instruction (OSPI) in Washington state. In that role, he provides leadership over elementary, early learning, and federal programs. He has been at the agency since June 2019. Prior to landing at the state agency, Jon has served as a school administrator at all levels in Oregon and Washington state as well as at the district level, including a stint as a superintendent of schools. Dr. Mishra has worked in districts ranging in size from less than 300 to greater than 17,000 students in his 33 years of service. Jon has presented at the state and national levels on various topics, including the balanced calendar approach; diversity, equity, inclusion, and belonging; instructional best practices; aligning systems for success; emergent technology; and effective implementation of professional learning communities. Jon and his wife, Loreena, have three children, Kaajal, Varsha, and Aakash. Jon is the son of Ram and Bijay Mishra. Jon's parents migrated from the Fiji Islands in 1965 to make a better life for their children. As a servant leader, Jon's hope is his work will leave a legacy of excellence.

Dr. James Pedersen is currently the superintendent for the Essex County Schools of Technology, which is an award-winning school district located in his home state of New Jersey. His career in education spans over 30 years and includes a variety of instructional and administrative positions. He has had the opportunity to teach as an adjunct professor at Montclair University, Centenary University, and Delaware Valley University. Pedersen has published and been cited in over 20 articles as well as two books focusing on education, *Rise of the Millennial Parents* (2013) and *Summer versus School: The Possibilities of the Year-Round School* (2015). His research and contributions to the research of school calendars have been a passion of his that was noticed by the educational stakeholders in Washington state who began their work on calendar reform.

HOW DID IT START IN WASHINGTON?

Four months after taking office in 2017, State Superintendent Chris Reykdal launched a long-term vision for Washington's K–12 public schools. Included in that vision was a redesign of the school year, building in research-based allotments of time for recess and lunch, educator collaboration, dual language learning, intensive learning time for students needing additional support, and more. Further, in 2019, Reykdal requested $10 million from the Legislature for a pilot of a balanced and/or extended school calendar. Although the Legislature did not act on the request at that time, in 2021, the OSPI leveraged its federal Elementary and Secondary School Emergency Relief (ESSER) to create a balanced calendar grant program.

In the spring of 2021, Kevin Chase, superintendent of ESD 105, convened a group of interested parties in his region to discuss the balanced calendar approach. He invited Dr. David Hornak, superintendent of schools in Holt, Michigan, and current Washington state balanced calendar consultant to begin the groundwork for implementing this reform. This idea made its way to the OSPI, and it coincided with the launch of COVID-19 ESSER relief funds. In the 2021 Legislative Session, the Washington State Legislature directed $200 million of state and federal ESSER funds to the OSPI exclusively for learning recovery. The balanced calendar initiative is part of this overall $200 million to launch a statewide effort. The project has been funded by ESSER funds during the 2021–2022 and the 2022–2023 school years and the intention is to extend funding into the 2023–2024 school year.

As mentioned earlier, Superintendent Chris Reykdal's vision included a redesign of the school year. It received funding in 2021. Key players at the beginning were:

- Dr. Jon Ram Mishra, then Executive Director of Special Programs and Federal Accountability at OSPI.
- Kevin Chase, ESD 105 Superintendent.
- Dr. David Hornak, Washington state balanced calendar consultant.
- Scott Seaman, Executive Director, Association of Washington School Principals.
- Jessica Vavrus, Executive Director, Association of Education Service Districts.
- Tim Garchow, Executive Director, Washington State School Directors Association.
- Sally McNair, Washington Education Association.
- Darcy Weisner, ESD 123 Superintendent.
- Dana Anderson, ESD 113 Superintendent.
- Phyllis "Bunker" Frank, Steadfast supporter of the balanced calendar and Former State Board of Education for Washington member.

Dr. Jon Ram Mishra from OSPI was assigned the balanced calendar project, connected with John Cerna, then superintendent of schools in Toppenish, and Mark Anderson, superintendent of schools in the Highland School District to talk about their modified/balanced calendar journey since these two districts were in calendar modification. From there, Jon connected with Kevin Chace, and the two of them devised a plan to further the efforts in Washington by engaging with multiple state and local agencies along with consultants Drs. David Hornak and James Pedersen to bring support and advice to participating districts.

HOW WE FIGURED OUT THE TOPICS COVERED IN THIS BOOK

The topics covered in this book were gathered from numerous presentations, conventions, discussions, and consultations from educators around the country regarding this topic, although a good portion of the most recent feedback is based on the work the authors are currently part of in the state of Washington. The feedback produced a variety of topics that cover pre-pandemic and post-pandemic views on time and learning as well as experiments with time from those experiences. This is also the continuation of the work first started by Dr. Pedersen's initial doctoral work on this topic, where he realized that the multi-track approach to calendar reform is not successful because all it does is address overcrowding. This book is also the follow up to his previous work, *Summer versus School* published in 2015.

HOW THE BOOK IS ORGANIZED

The book is organized in a manner that would assist both groups of individuals—those who have experience with balanced calendars and would like to know what is currently happening as well as readers who know very little about this subject. It is also beneficial for educators as well as non-educators who may be involved in the discussion process of implementing calendar reform.

The chapters cover the origins of school and summer vacations, proponents, critics, and other stakeholders' perceptions of balanced calendars. It also examines an overview of how time has been utilized in American schools as well as how reform is being implemented in current schools. Lastly, it provides current research on the topic, strategies for implementation, and practical experiences from schools in Washington state.

WHAT IS THE GOAL OF THE BOOK?

The goal of this book is to educate anyone interested in this topic to better prepare them to make an informed decision. It would be foolhardy to think that their work written here will convince an adamant critic.

But this is true for any type of reform—there is no magic spell that will solve all problems.

If the book can shed additional light on this subject, inspire other types of educational reform, or assist someone in making an informed decision, then the overall objective of the book will have been fulfilled. Lastly, it should be noted that the overwhelming support and assistance provided by the many educators of Washington have made this a truly rewarding experience for all involved.

Chapter 1

History of School Calendars

Many still believe that school summer vacations harken back to the age of agrarian calendars to a time when many, if not all, school-aged children worked on farms, preventing them from attending school year-round. Although there is some truth to this belief, the history of schools and their calendars is much more complex and has its roots starting back as far as 15th-century Europe, long before the colonists began settling in America.

As early as the Middle Ages, some European universities adopted a break schedule that included "short recesses at Christmas, Easter and Pentecost, and a longer vacation in summer" (Weiss, 2013). Generally, the year began around the middle of October and ended somewhere in the middle of June. Other educational institutions placed their breaks from the end of August to early October. During this time, the creation of summer and winter breaks began to take form and became standard practice for most institutions of learning. The winter and spring breaks were created out of religious obligations, while the summer break seemed to be created out of the need for leisure and travel for the wealthy.

In America, the two- to three-month-long summer vacation that many know today evolved between 1850 and 1913 when it was almost universally mandated in many schools nationwide. Although reasons for the growth of the summer holiday seem to vary, safety concerns regarding high temperatures during the summer months appear to be most common. During this time, summers were also used for teaching immigrant families the English language (Glines, 2009; Silva, 2007). In the past, continuing to the present day, these limitations of appropriate air-conditioned facilities were barriers to attempting to continue schooling during the hotter months (Pedersen, 2012). Ironically, however, summer vacation, as it is known and observed by a majority of people in the United States, as well as around the world, was not widely instituted until the late 19th century. Coincidently, this was also a time in history when one of the measurements of a good school at that time was the number of operating days that it was open (Weiss & Brown, 2005). Some other researchers on the subject have stated that the school calendar widely used in the United States today was, "a blend of the six-month agrarian calendar found in rural areas and the longer, 240-day calendar utilized in urban settings" (Dixon, 2011).

THE 1600S

Shortly after the establishment of the colonies in North America, colonists initiated efforts to address the need for educating their children. While their educational programs were founded upon the English schooling systems, they were heavily influenced by the local Protestant religions, with most, if not all, schools being situated within local places of worship. Not surprisingly, there was a notable lack of uniformity in school calendars during this era. These calendars were primarily tailored to meet the specific needs of the local communities, rather than being guided by pedagogical considerations. Additionally, the regulations regarding school attendance, duration, and scheduling were determined at the local level, leading to variations in the number of months and days in the school calendar from one area to another. Eventually, many regions then began to formalize their educational systems, most notably their calendars.

The school calendars, therefore, were based more on the needs of the local community than any pedagogical reasons. It was also found that the requirements for who was to attend schools, how long they attended, and on what days they attended were all set at the local level. Therefore, the exact number of months and days of the school calendar varied from one area to the next.

In rural American school districts, the timing of the school year was closely tied to the seasonal rhythms of agriculture, resulting in sessions held during both winter and summer (Fischel, 2006). Most schools during this period were single-room structures with one teacher responsible for approximately 30 children, ages 5–18, though class sizes could vary from 10 to 50.

For example, in *Summer versus School*, the author states, "as early as 1684, Massachusetts required 12 months of school for its students." The author adds that once the children were old enough to assist with farming demand, they "usually attended school only in the winter months when their labor was not needed at home. During the five- or six-month sessions, they learned reading, writing, and basic arithmetic" (Pedersen, 2015). Although many colonies took an interest in setting standards for their schools, Massachusetts stands out as a pioneer for education.

THE 1700S

At the outset of the 18th century, there were discernible and deliberate initiatives aimed at further formalizing educational institutions within the American colonies. While these colonies, and subsequently the emerging states, traditionally granted local municipalities control over the schools, including the formulation of school calendars, the seeds of uniformity in education began to sprout at both regional and state levels. The impetus for establishing a standardized duration for the school year was particularly evident in the state of Massachusetts, where comprehensive measures were undertaken to institutionalize the educational system, spanning from the colonial era through the postindependence period. This included addressing the crucial matter of lengthening the school session, which marked a pivotal step toward a more organized and consistent approach to education across the state. Much like in the previous century, however, churches were still the primary location for the schooling of the children (Kid's Corner, 2023).

As proponents of education began to gain momentum, interestingly, former President John Adams played a pivotal role at the state level in shaping the educational landscape through his contributions to the Massachusetts Constitution in 1780. A particularly noteworthy aspect of his involvement was the inclusion of a revolutionary provision that explicitly guaranteed public education for all citizens (Massachusetts, 2023). This was one of the first known laws of its kind that promoted public education and, in 1789, the state formally adopted a compulsory comprehensive education law that was the first in the country.

The significance of Massachusetts' commitment to public education did not stop there. In 1789, the state went on to formally adopt a groundbreaking compulsory comprehensive education law. This pioneering legislation was a trailblazer in the United States, setting the standard for compulsory education. It underscored the state's dedication to providing education to its citizens, setting an example that would be followed by others in the years to come. Concurrently, in neighboring Connecticut, state leaders were also at the forefront of educational progress, creating their legislation stipulating that towns with over 70 families had to have at least six months of school a year (Massachusetts, 2023). This legislative action in Connecticut further exemplified the growing recognition of the importance of education and the commitment to ensuring that it was accessible to the populace.

THE 1800S

In the early 1800s, students in major urban areas in the United States began attending school for at least 11 months a year. As the concept of education as a fundamental personal right gained traction, it became increasingly evident that a transformation in the labor landscape, particularly in industrialized areas, played a pivotal role in shaping the education and labor dynamics. The emergence of child labor laws marked a turning point, bringing about a significant shift in societal attitudes toward child labor practices that saw more restrictions on what age children could work and started to necessitate more breaks (Horn, 2022).

With the rapid industrialization of many regions, child labor had become alarmingly common, with young children toiling in factories and other labor-intensive industries. This practice not only raised concerns about the physical and emotional well-being of these young workers but also threatened their access to education. In response to these challenges, legislative measures were introduced to address the issue of child labor. One researcher found that children in rural farming communities who were enrolled in school in the 19th century typically spent five or six months in school—two to three months in the summer and two to three months in the winter (Horn, 2022).

One of the noteworthy aspects of these child labor laws was the establishment of age restrictions that determined when children could legally work. These restrictions resulted in more children attending school for longer durations during the school year, especially in the major urban centers. Some schools in urban areas increased their school calendars to 251–260 days of instruction in 1840, which usually spanned over 11- or 12-month calendars. In 1841, Boston schools operated for 244 days and Philadelphia implemented a 251-day calendar. It is interesting to note that many metropolitan schools at this time operated a very different school schedule that included instruction during the summer. Schools were open year-round but were not mandatory, and children came when they could. In 1842, New York City schools were open 248 days a year, dramatically more than the national average of 180 or so they are open today (Agraian, 2014). In 1842, Detroit schools were open roughly 260 days. New York's were open 245 days.

Meanwhile, during this time, many of these rural schools were only open about 6 months out of the year. Glines first wrote that the origin of the traditional school calendar based purely on agrarian needs was not entirely accurate (1995). At this time in the 19th century, districts organized their calendars around the needs of the community.

One researcher also noted that this time was when many states began to seek the need for a common school calendar (Dixon, 2011). This was sparked by the recognition of the need for a well-educated workforce. This prompted states to begin to implement education policies.

Consequently, school calendars became more formalized among the states. The work of Weiss and Brown (2003) also supported the evolution of summer vacation in North American public schools, including some places in Canada, as they evolved in the 19th and early 20th centuries. By the end of the 19th century, only one-third of the states still had not passed legislation regarding school mandates for children (Shammas, 2023).

THE 1900S

By the 21st century, the 180-day, 10-month calendar readily became the standard. However, in the 1900s, year-round programs were still being implemented in such places as "Newark, New Jersey (1912); Minot, North Dakota (1917); Omaha, Nebraska (1924); Nashville, Tennessee (1925); and Aliquippa (1928), and Ambridge (1931), Pennsylvania" (Gines, 1997). The main reasons these districts held on to this concept were attributed to assisting immigrant students, enhancing learning, introducing vocational programs, and accommodating the large influx of students. This would often be seen with a multi-calendar approach where students cycled through the year to accommodate more students and would be used in the 1970s in places like California and Texas.

Despite these few outliers, it was not long until school calendars across the country began to adopt very similar summer and winter terms, even in rural areas. Several factors including child labor laws and facility limitations added to the decrease in farming obligations for the students and contributed to the stardardizing of the school calendar. States around the country then began to enact attendance requirements for their students. For example, a compulsory attendance law was passed in 1919 in South Carolina that required mandatory attendance. Eventually, these things led to funding, teacher salaries, and teacher certification (Education, 2022).

As previously stated, the 1970s witnessed a resurgence of interest in reevaluating school calendars, driven primarily by the pressing issue of overcrowding in educational institutions (Wildman, 1999). During this decade, a considerable influx of students migrating across district borders posed logistical challenges for many school districts. To effectively cope with this influx, numerous districts took innovative measures to optimize the utilization of school facilities and resources.

This period also marked a significant shift in how school calendars were structured, with a specific focus on addressing overcrowding. In some instances, districts implemented novel calendar arrangements that divided the student body into groups, staggering their breaks to ensure that only a portion of the students were on vacation at any given time, while the others remained in session. This innovative approach aimed to maximize the use of school buildings, thereby alleviating the strain of overcrowding and enhancing the overall efficiency of educational facilities.

One such notable example of this approach was the introduction of the "year-round schooling" concept, which gained popularity during the 1970s. Year-round schooling divided students into distinct tracks or cycles, with each track attending school for a specific period and then taking a break while another track was in session. This method not only helped address the issue of overcrowding but also contributed to a more continuous and efficient use of educational resources, such as classrooms and teaching staff.

The innovative reconfiguration of school calendars during the 1970s exemplified the education sector's adaptability in responding to the challenges of the time, specifically overcrowding issues. These efforts played a pivotal role in enhancing the educational experience for students while optimizing the use of school facilities. The creative solutions implemented during this era set the stage for ongoing discussions and adaptations in school calendars to meet the ever-evolving needs of the educational landscape. In 1972, Ballinger and Kneese noted that California seemed to lead the way in the resurgence of year-round calendars, creating the first multi-track school in La Mesa, Spring Valley, and Chula Vista to address large increases in student enrollment (2006). Also, during that same year, educators from existing year-round schools formed the National Association for Year-Round Education (NAYRE, 2010).

It was not until the 1980s after such reports as *A Nation at Risk* (1983), *Prisoners of Time* (1994), and more recently, *Tough Choices, Tough Times* (2008) that prompted school leaders and policymakers to seek new ways to balance their calendars to diminish summer learning loss and improve student achievement. From the years of 1968 to 1970, year-round education was established in Missouri, Illinois, California, and Minnesota to accommodate the increasing student population (Glines, 1997). During this time, a majority of the districts that adopted year-round schools during the twenty years between 1970 and 1990 did so to maximize space (Hazleton, 1992).

THE NEW MILLENNIUM

The New Millennium saw the advent of recent educational innovations, including calendar reform.

In 2014, a significant trend emerged as at least 35 school districts, spanning over 10 states, announced either the implementation or consideration of a longer school day or year in select schools. This shift toward expanded-time schools has largely been driven by policies supporting the creation of new charter schools and granting new levels of autonomy to traditional district schools. This increased autonomy has empowered educators to restructure schedules, staffing, and budgeting, often resulting in significantly more learning hours for all students.

Moreover, in recent years, several influential federal programs, along with numerous state leaders, have advocated for expanding instructional time as a key strategy for improving chronically underperforming schools. These initiatives have been accompanied by additional resources to support the implementation of longer school days or years (Fzaberman, 2015).

The COVID-19 pandemic has also been a major impactful event in the new millennium. Never before has the world had to rapidly transition to remote learning in their schools. Many lessons were taught and learned during this time but perhaps the most evident one had to do with the digital divide. It was during this time that schools across the world found that students in areas that had access to technology and the internet fared much better than their peers. This widened the economic divide that had already existed between students who had resources and those who did not. This regression is often referred to as the *COVID Slide* and found educators looking for ways to ameliorate this slide like others in the past had done with Summer Slide regressions. This resulted in similar discussions regarding adding time to address the gaps as well as ways of experimenting with time that also included a newly found interest in calendar reform.

PROPONENTS

Advocates for balanced calendars champion their cause for a variety of reasons, each stemming from a distinct set of needs within their respective groups. It is crucial to emphasize that the rationale behind implementing a balanced calendar is inherently tied to the specific objectives of the groups supporting it. For instance, if the primary goal of calendar reform is to enhance student achievement, evaluating the success of such an initiative based on alternative criteria would be unjust. It is within this context that the proponents of balanced calendars articulate their varied but interconnected reasons that contribute to a more comprehensive understanding of their shared endeavor.

The array of perspectives supporting balanced calendars reflects the intricacies of educational priorities. While the specific motivations may vary, a common thread unites most of the proponents in the recurring themes of their advocacy.

One of the most prevailing points championed by proponents is the potential positive impact on student achievement. By redistributing breaks and vacations throughout the year, proponents argue that students may experience a more consistent learning trajectory, mitigating the effects of the traditional long summer break on knowledge retention. This emphasis on academic continuity is often accompanied by a focus on addressing learning disparities and providing additional support for students who may be at risk of falling behind. In fact, annually traditional calendar educators are required to reteach the curriculum from the year prior to each fall. This can amount to between 20 and 40 days of reteaching annually (Hornak, 2018), which cuts the number of instructional days available for the current curriculum each year.

Furthermore, proponents frequently highlight the benefits for educators and administrators, asserting that a balanced calendar can lead to improved teacher morale and professional development opportunities. The restructuring of the academic year offers educators the chance to engage in ongoing professional growth, fostering a dynamic and collaborative teaching environment.

In examining the shared viewpoints of proponents, it becomes evident that the push for balanced calendars is not a monolithic endeavor but a tapestry woven from a diversity of motivations. As conversations surrounding educational reform continue, these varied perspectives contribute to a nuanced discourse that seeks to address the evolving needs of students, educators, and the broader educational landscape. The continuing dialogue around balanced calendars serves as a testament to the complexity of educational reform and the importance of considering diverse perspectives to create a more adaptive and inclusive educational system.

Parents

Numerous studies have consistently reported positive feedback from parents following the implementation of a balanced calendar, highlighting several advantages that resonate within diverse communities (Horn, 2022). The widespread support for this educational shift can be attributed to a range of benefits, each contributing to an enhanced overall experience for both students and their families. Some of the recurring themes were:

- Flexible scheduling
- More vacation time
- Improved student attendance
- Reduced bus transportation time in rural areas
- Reduced stress

One of the primary factors garnering parental approval is the introduction of flexible scheduling. By reorganizing the academic year, balanced calendars afford families greater flexibility in planning vacations and activities. This adaptability not only accommodates the diverse needs of households but also promotes a more seamless integration of educational and recreational pursuits. In general, there has been a surge in positive sentiment regarding the adoption of the four-day school week. The key benefit lies in the enhanced opportunity for families to spend more quality time together. This newfound flexibility allows for a range of activities, including accommodating essential appointments such as doctor's visits and creating room for family trips.

The favorable reception of the four-day school week is largely attributed to its ability to align with the diverse and dynamic schedules of both work and family life. Families are finding that the condensed school week not only promotes a healthier work–life balance but also opens up windows of time for various personal and familial pursuits. Overall, the positive sentiments expressed about the four-day school week underscore its potential to positively impact the overall well-being and cohesion of families (Horn, 2022).

The provision of more vacation time stands out as another key element influencing parental favorability. The extended breaks interspersed throughout the academic year not only offer students the opportunity for rejuvenation but also allow families to engage in meaningful bonding experiences. This departure from the traditional long summer break is particularly appealing to parents who appreciate the chance to create lasting memories with their children during these interspersed breaks.

Improvements in student attendance represent a notable aspect contributing to parental satisfaction with balanced calendars. The restructured academic schedule has been correlated with higher attendance rates, suggesting that the continuous learning model contributes to a more engaged and committed student body. This positive correlation underscores the potential of balanced calendars to foster a more conducive learning environment.

In rural areas, where bus transportation poses unique challenges, the reduction in transportation time is a welcomed benefit for parents. The streamlined logistics not only enhance efficiency but also alleviate concerns about extended bus travel, contributing to an improved overall experience for students and their families.

Additionally, the reduction of stress is a commonly reported positive outcome associated with balanced calendars. Parents appreciate the minimized academic pressure on students, as well as the alleviation of stress related to long periods of inactivity during extended breaks. This reduction in stress levels is seen as conducive to a healthier and more balanced approach to education.

David Hornak, one of the contributing authors, aptly notes that parents value shorter summer breaks, as they observe their children becoming bored after approximately six weeks (Clarey, 2023). Furthermore, the ease of budgeting for childcare during these interspersed breaks is a pragmatic consideration that resonates with many parents, adding another layer to their positive perception of balanced calendars.

The multifaceted advantages of balanced calendars, encompassing flexible scheduling, increased vacation time, enhanced attendance, reduced transportation time, and stress reduction collectively contribute to a favorable view among parents. This alignment of benefits reflects a broader recognition that the adoption of balanced calendars can positively impact not only the educational experience of students but also the well-being and satisfaction of the families to which they belong.

Teachers

A wealth of research details the positive reception of balanced calendars among teachers with studies delving into themes such as burnout, retention, and recruitment. The findings from these studies shed light on the multifaceted impact of balanced calendars on the teaching profession.

In recent years, teachers have been confronted with escalating burnout rates, driven by a confluence of factors including economic challenges, stagnant salaries, and the added stressors brought about by the COVID-19 pandemic. This surge in burnout has raised concerns among educators and educational leaders, necessitating a closer examination of strategies to alleviate the pressures faced by teaching professionals. Balanced calendars emerge as a potential solution, offering a respite from the relentless demands of the traditional academic calendar and providing teachers with a more sustainable work–life balance.

Retaining experienced teachers within school districts has emerged as a formidable challenge for educational leaders. Economic constraints and workplace stressors have contributed to a notable turnover in the teaching profession. The implementation of balanced calendars presents an opportunity to address this challenge by creating a more supportive and nurturing work environment. As studies suggest, teachers who experience the benefits of reduced stress, more breaks, and additional time for preparation are more likely to stay within their districts, fostering a sense of stability and continuity in the educational workforce.

Recruitment of new teachers and the retention of veteran educators have become paramount concerns. With the teaching profession facing evolving demands, school districts have sought innovative approaches to attract and retain talented educators. Some districts have experimented with calendar reforms, including the adoption of four-day school weeks. This alternative scheduling has proven attractive to teachers for various reasons.

One of the primary reasons cited by teachers in favor of four-day school weeks is the prospect of experiencing less stress. The condensed schedule allows for longer weekends, providing educators with valuable time to recharge and engage in self-care activities. Additionally, the increased number of breaks embedded in the balanced calendar offers teachers the chance to step back, regroup, and return to the classroom with renewed energy and enthusiasm.

The extended time for preparation is another appealing aspect of balanced calendars for teachers. The traditional academic calendar often leaves educators grappling with limited planning time, impacting the quality of instructional delivery. The restructured calendar model provides teachers with the necessary breathing space to plan effectively, resulting in more engaging and impactful lessons.

Furthermore, the reduced stress for students is a factor that resonates with teachers. A balanced calendar can contribute to a more relaxed and conducive learning environment, promoting better mental well-being among students. Teachers recognize the potential positive correlation between reduced stress levels and enhanced student achievement, further reinforcing their support for calendar reforms.

In conclusion, the studies on teacher satisfaction with balanced calendars illuminate the intricate dynamics at play within the teaching profession. By addressing burnout, retention, and recruitment challenges, balanced calendars present a promising avenue for creating a more supportive and sustainable educational ecosystem. As districts explore innovative scheduling approaches, the potential benefits for both teachers and students underscore the significance of calendar reforms in shaping the future of education.

Administrators

Administrators, recognizing the positive impacts on both teachers and students, have increasingly embraced the concept of balanced calendars, acknowledging the potential benefits that extend to the realm of school leadership. In a reflective piece published in 2022, Daniel A. Domenech, the executive director of the American Association of School Administrators, delved into the challenges wrought by the pandemic and proposed strategic measures to address deficiencies in the educational system. Domenech notably emphasized the pivotal role that school calendars play in mitigating the disruptions caused by the pandemic, urging school leaders to reconsider and recalibrate their approach.

The upheavals in school calendars during the pandemic, marked by closures and openings in response to evolving circumstances, prompted administrators to seek innovative solutions. A prevalent practice involved utilizing summer months for catch-up sessions, allowing students to address learning gaps. However, Domenech raised a critical concern: the traditional long summer break, while a cultural norm, might inadvertently contribute to a loss of academic retention, particularly among disadvantaged students. As children indulge in leisure activities during the extended break, the risk of forgetting previously acquired knowledge looms large, exacerbating educational disparities.

Recognizing these challenges, administrators found balanced calendars to be effective in several key areas. One prominent benefit is the implementation of flexible scheduling, providing educators and students with a more adaptable framework that accommodates diverse learning needs and preferences. This flexibility fosters an environment conducive to personalized learning, allowing for tailored approaches that cater to the unique requirements of both teachers and students.

Administrators have also observed a reduction in teacher complaints, a noteworthy outcome associated with the adoption of balanced calendars. By aligning the academic schedule with the evolving needs of educators, addressing burnout concerns, and providing ample planning time, the grievances voiced by teachers have notably diminished. This improvement in teacher satisfaction not only contributes to a healthier work environment but also bolsters overall morale within the educational community.

Student achievement emerges as a focus for administrators advocating balanced calendars. The restructuring of the academic year aims to create a continuous learning experience, minimizing the potential for knowledge loss during extended breaks. By prioritizing consistent educational engagement, administrators believe that student achievement can be enhanced, narrowing the gap between academic levels and fostering a more equitable learning environment.

Furthermore, administrators appreciate that balanced calendars facilitate the implementation of new initiatives with greater ease. The restructured schedule allows for a more seamless integration of innovative educational approaches, providing the necessary time and resources for the successful implementation of initiatives that aim to enhance the overall quality of education.

Administrators have not only recognized the positive effects of balanced calendars on teachers and students but have actively championed this approach as a strategic solution to address the challenges posed by the pandemic and traditional academic structures. As the educational landscape continues to evolve, some administrators find that the adoption of balanced calendars aligns with their objectives of creating a more adaptive, equitable, and effective learning environment for both educators and students alike (von Hipple, 2019).

Students

Students represent another demographic that stands to benefit significantly from the regular breaks provided by balanced calendars. Despite initial concerns about extending the school schedule, students who have experienced a balanced calendar often express a preference for the more frequent breaks and reduced interruptions in their academic routine. Several aspects of this revised schedule contribute to heightened satisfaction among students, who find value in the following:

- Flexible Schedules: A notable advantage of balanced calendars, as perceived by students, is the introduction of more flexible schedules. This adaptability allows students to navigate their academic responsibilities in a manner that aligns with their individual learning preferences and lifestyles, fostering a more personalized and accommodating educational experience.
- Less Bussing for Rural Areas: Particularly beneficial for students in rural areas, the reduction in bus transportation translates to less time spent commuting. This not only minimizes the logistical challenges associated with transportation but also contributes to a more efficient use of time, allowing students to allocate their energy and focus more effectively during the school year.
- More Time to Complete Homework and Assignments: The additional time afforded by the balanced calendar model proves advantageous for students when it comes to completing homework and assignments. With a less compressed schedule, students have the opportunity to engage in more thoughtful and thorough academic work, fostering a deeper understanding of the material and potentially enhancing the overall academic performance.

As students increasingly appreciate the benefits of balanced calendars, it becomes evident that the positive aspects extend beyond the immediate academic structure. The flexibility, reduced transportation demands, and increased time for academic tasks collectively contribute to a more favorable and supportive learning environment. By acknowledging and amplifying the voices of students in discussions about educational reform, policymakers and educators can work collaboratively to create academic calendars that not only meet administrative objectives but also cater to the diverse needs and preferences of the students they serve.

Health Professionals

Several health studies, such as "Changes in Fitness and Fatness in Australian Schoolchildren During the Summer Holidays: Fitness Lost, Fatness

Regained?," have delved into the impacts of academic breaks on the well-being of schoolchildren. Building on this research, the advantages of adopting a balanced calendar extend beyond academic considerations and encompass broader health-related benefits.

One noteworthy advantage is the potential for increased physical activity. By restructuring the academic year, balanced calendars offer more opportunities for students to engage in regular exercise. The traditional long summer break often poses a risk of sedentary behavior, contributing to declines in fitness. In contrast, a balanced calendar provides consistent breaks, allowing for the integration of physical activities throughout the academic year. This not only supports the overall health and fitness of students but also helps mitigate the negative effects associated with extended periods of inactivity.

Furthermore, the benefits of a balanced calendar extend to the realm of mental health. The continuous nature of the academic schedule allows for consistent access to mental health resources. Rather than facing prolonged breaks without the support systems provided by schools, students can access resources and assistance when needed, fostering a more resilient and supportive environment. This proactive approach to mental health is particularly crucial given the increasing awareness of the importance of addressing mental well-being in the educational setting.

While health studies shed light on the potential fitness and fatness fluctuations during traditional academic breaks, a balanced calendar emerges as a proactive solution. The incorporation of more exercise opportunities and continuous access to mental health resources positions balanced calendars as a holistic approach to supporting the overall health and well-being of students. As educational systems evolve, considerations for health-related benefits become integral components in the ongoing discourse about optimizing the academic calendar for the betterment of students' physical and mental health (Olds, 2023).

Advocacy Groups

Advocacy groups have emerged as fervent advocates for the reformation of school calendars, reflecting a mounting concern over the limitations of our current calendar systems. Among these proactive organizations, NAYRE stands out as a stalwart champion dedicated to reshaping the traditional school calendar. NAYRE has undertaken a mission to provide stakeholders and the broader community with accurate, up-to-date research on year-round education and the concept of a balanced school calendar.

The unwavering commitment of NAYRE to advancing educational excellence through comprehensive school calendar reform is unmistakable. Rooted in the conviction that a reimagined academic calendar holds the potential to significantly enhance the overall educational experience for students and educators alike, NAYRE actively pursues this vision. The organization tirelessly engages in the compilation and dissemination of crucial data, striving to keep stakeholders well-informed about the benefits of year-round education and balanced calendars.

NAYRE's dedication extends beyond information dissemination; the organization actively promotes evidence-based practices and collaborates with stakeholders across the education sector. By fostering a constructive and informed dialogue about calendar reform, NAYRE seeks to catalyze meaningful changes that align more closely with the dynamic needs of our evolving society. The organization recognizes that the traditional academic calendar may not adequately cater to the diverse and changing demands of modern education.

In the pursuit of shaping the future of education, NAYRE places a strong emphasis on encouraging innovative approaches to calendar reform. By fostering an ongoing conversation that embraces diverse perspectives and ideas, the organization aims to create a space for dialogue, where stakeholders can collectively contribute to the evolution of school calendars. NAYRE envisions a future where educational timelines are not just a matter of tradition but are intentionally designed to optimize learning outcomes, support teachers, and meet the educational needs of students in a rapidly changing world.

In essence, NAYRE catalyzes change in the realm of education, advocating for calendar adjustments that go beyond tradition to align more cohesively with the ever-evolving landscape of societal and educational requirements. Through their multifaceted efforts, NAYRE stands as a beacon for those committed to redefining and optimizing the educational experience for the benefit of both current and future generations (2023).

Hornak has said that the balanced calendars still offer students and staff a break of six to eight weeks in the summer. They also get a week off in October, a week at Thanksgiving, two weeks around Christmas, a full week in February, a full week at spring break, and some time off around Memorial Day before ending in late June.

Hornak argued that year-round learning is more effective than the traditional school calendar in helping students recover from the disruptions caused by pandemic-related school closures. In addition to addressing learning loss often experienced during breaks, known as the "summer slide," Hornak believes that different students require varying amounts of instructional days, with some needing 150 days, others 180 days, and some even requiring 220 days or more of schooling (Clarey, 2023).

Yet another exemplary advocacy group making significant strides is the National Center on Time & Learning (NCTL), an organization steadfastly dedicated to revolutionizing and extending school time to augment opportunities and academic outcomes, particularly for students in high-poverty areas. NCTL's ongoing mission underscores a commitment to reshaping the educational landscape, striving to create an environment that fosters enhanced learning experiences for all students. In a noteworthy collaboration, NCTL has once again partnered with the Education Commission of the States (ECS), an organization with a primary focus on facilitating the exchange of ideas and knowledge related to educational matters among states.

This dynamic partnership has resulted in the creation of an enlightening snapshot of public school time in America, marking the third edition since its inaugural publication in 2011. By closely examining pivotal actions and initiatives that have unfolded at the federal, state, and local levels since 2013, the collective efforts of NCTL and ECS are directed toward propelling the national discourse on the strategic utilization of time within the nation's schools. The collaborative initiative seeks a transformative shift in how schools nationwide harness the power of time, with the ultimate objective of realizing a shared vision: delivering high-quality education for all.

The comprehensive exploration of public school time in America goes beyond being a mere snapshot; it signifies a milestone on the path to cultivating a more equitable and effective education system. The partnership between NCTL and ECS transcends conventional boundaries, aiming to address the entrenched disparities stemming from socioeconomic factors. In striving for a more inclusive and accessible educational paradigm, this collaborative effort aspires to bridge gaps and create a learning environment where every student, regardless of their background, has equal access to quality education.

This collaborative effort acknowledges that time is a critical resource within the educational sphere and seeks to optimize its utilization to benefit students on a national scale. By delving into key actions and initiatives, the partnership between NCTL and ECS aims to identify best practices that can be disseminated widely, fostering a culture of continuous improvement within the education system. In essence, the collaborative initiative acts as a pivotal stepping stone toward building a more resilient, adaptable, and responsive education system that can meet the diverse needs of students across the nation (Faberman, 2015).

CRITICS

Critics of balanced calendar reform often concentrate their objections on specific key areas, delving into focused areas of concern that collectively form the crux of their opposition. These critiques encompass various aspects, including financial implications, challenges related to existing facilities, resistance to change and disruptions to the established status quo, potential workforce reductions during traditional breaks, skepticism regarding the longevity and effectiveness of the reform, childcare complexities, and a perceived lack of comprehensive data supporting the proposed calendar adjustments. In exploring these nuanced points of contention, detractors aim to underscore the multifaceted challenges they associate with the restructuring of traditional academic calendars.

Costs to the District

Depending on the type of calendar being implemented, the restructuring of the academic year may necessitate adjustments in budget allocation, with opponents expressing apprehension about the associated costs and the impact on the overall financial resources within educational institutions. These financial concerns range from long-term facility plans and construction to creating pragmatic schedules that allow for flexibility. Facility limitations are a genuine obstacle for many schools. Critics also point to the need for adequate spaces and resources to accommodate the revised academic schedule and raise concerns about the feasibility of implementing balanced calendars within the existing infrastructures, particularly in schools with limited spatial capacities.

Costs for balanced calendar schools depend on what is looking to be accomplished. In the article "Year-round School: Difference-maker or Waste of Time? Is There Any Evidence That It Works?," the author admits that by having multi-tracks, districts can save a sizeable amount of money. For example, "a school that normally serves 750 students to serve 1,000 when going to a year-round, multiple-track schedule. This is because the schedule has different students taking breaks at different times" (Robinson, 2023). Additional challenges also include securing funding and managing children from one family who may have different calendars.

Financial obligations are a serious contention among proponents of calendar reform. As in any other challenge in education, redirecting resources, creating a need for additional funding, and relying on alternate ways of raising funds seem to be the answer not only for calendar reform but also for reform in general.

Facility Limitations

A significant challenge in extending the school year into the heat of summer is the insufficient availability of air conditioning in certain educational institutions. This deficit poses a substantial obstacle for schools aiming to prolong their academic calendar into the warmer seasons. However, a positive trend is emerging, as an increasing number of schools are now incorporating air conditioning into their renovation plans and new construction projects. This shift in infrastructure development indicates a proactive response to the evolving needs of educational environments, gradually overcoming the hindrance posed by the absence of adequate cooling systems.

With more schools embracing the integration of air conditioning, the once-prominent barrier to year-round schooling is expected to dwindle, facilitating a smoother transition to extended academic periods beyond the traditional boundaries of the academic year. This proactive approach not only tackles the immediate challenge of providing a comfortable learning environment during hotter months but also underscores a commitment to creating modern, adaptable educational spaces that cater to the changing needs of both students and faculty.

Some of these issues can fall back to long-term facilities plans. It is feasible that in the next 10–20 years all schools will be outfitted with adequate air-conditioning and heating. Most new buildings being constructed are equipped with such features. Schools, much like the rest of the infrastructure across our country, have to be routinely upgraded, making this issue less relevant.

Transportation

The implementation of calendar reform in schools can pose various transportation challenges in different scenarios. One such scenario involves a district aiming to add days to the existing calendar, which would necessitate paying bus drivers and aides additional compensation. This financial consideration adds a layer of complexity to the reform process, as budgetary constraints and negotiations may arise.

Conversely, if the reform involves spreading out the existing school days across the calendar without additional compensation for transportation staff, another set of challenges emerges. In this situation, bus drivers and aides may face the potential loss of opportunities for additional summer employment that typically supplements their incomes. This aspect highlights the multifaceted impact of calendar reform, extending beyond the academic realm and directly affecting the livelihoods of those essential to the transportation infrastructure.

Addressing these transportation challenges requires a nuanced approach that considers both the financial implications for the school district and the well-being of transportation staff. Striking a balance between educational objectives and the economic interests of those involved in school transportation is essential for successful and sustainable calendar reform. By fostering open communication and collaborative decision-making, school districts can navigate these challenges and ensure that the implementation of calendar reforms is equitable and beneficial for all stakeholders. This will also require schools to reexamine the contracts they have with employees who are their bus drivers but for third-party vendors as well.

Paying Teachers

Another significant financial challenge arises in the effort to secure funds for the additional contractual time required for teachers and other support staff during the implementation of calendar reform. It is crucial to emphasize that if the reform involves redistributing existing school days, the financial costs incurred are minimal. However, when contemplating the addition of days to the school calendar through intersessions or increased instructional time, additional resources become imperative.

The financial implications of extending teacher and support staff contracts demand careful consideration, as this directly affects the overall budget of the school district. Allocating funds for extended contractual periods necessitates strategic financial planning and resource management. Moreover, if the reform includes the introduction of intersessions or extra instructional days, additional expenses such as compensating teachers for their extended time commitment, organizing supplementary educational activities, and providing necessary resources must be factored into the budgetary considerations.

Addressing these financial challenges requires a comprehensive plan that involves collaboration among school administrators, financial planners, and educators. Exploring creative funding sources including grants and seeking community support may be integral to overcoming these hurdles, ensuring that the implementation of calendar reform is financially viable and sustainable in the long run. By navigating these financial considerations thoughtfully, school districts can enhance the educational experience without compromising the economic stability of the institution.

Sports

Managing athletic schedules becomes more complicated when neighboring school districts operate on different academic calendars. While disparities in school schedules have historically posed challenges, they can become particularly problematic when some schools are in session while others are not. Addressing scheduling conflicts due to varying school calendars has been an ongoing challenge for many districts. This issue is not limited to the academic year's start but extends to the overall structure of the school calendar, which can differ significantly from one district to another and even from region to region.

Despite the complexities arising from these differences, many schools have successfully navigated scheduling issues through collaborative efforts and effective communication. Schools recognize the importance of accommodating various academic calendars and have developed mechanisms to facilitate smooth coordination, especially in the realm of athletics.

The challenges posed by differing school schedules underscore the need for ongoing dialogue and coordination among neighboring districts. Finding common ground and establishing protocols for scheduling events, practices, and competitions can enhance the overall experience for student-athletes while fostering positive relationships between schools. As districts continue to grapple with these challenges, the emphasis on collaboration becomes paramount in ensuring the seamless integration of athletic programs across diverse academic calendars.

Disrupting the Status Quo

Resistance to change is a common theme among critics of school calendar reform who argue that the implementation of a balanced calendar disrupts the established status quo. Traditional academic calendars have deep-rooted cultural and historical significance, and opponents express concerns about the potential challenges and resistance that may arise when attempting to alter a system that has been in place for decades. Other parents, especially those with high school students, oppose the balanced calendar because their child may not be able to work as long in the summer to save for that car they always wanted or even college. Some parents argue against it because it may conflict with planned summer vacations.

Some individuals harbor concerns rooted in the disruption of established traditions, particularly when it comes to challenging the ingrained cultural norm of the summer vacation break. The extended hiatus from school during the summer has woven itself into the fabric of American culture. However, the landscape has evolved, and the era of lengthy vacations is becoming increasingly impractical in today's economic reality. The financial strain on parents, who find it challenging to afford a two-and-a-half-month break, is a significant factor. Disrupting a schedule that has endured for over four centuries presents a formidable undertaking that instills apprehension in many. Despite the enduring romanticized notion of a summer vacation, the practicality diminishes when faced with the contemporary demands of a fast-paced economy.

The economic reality is stark: few people can avail themselves for the entire months of June, July, and August. This reality is compounded by the financial burden of childcare during the summer months, a concern shared by many families. In this context, there is a growing desire for public schools to play a more active role in assisting and recognizing the challenges parents face in balancing work and childcare responsibilities during extended breaks.

Moreover, the evolving educational landscape has witnessed the implementation of diverse summer programs over the past few decades. These programs extend beyond the traditional model, incorporating year-round education for students with disabilities, language classes tailored for English language learners, and preparatory courses for higher-level academic pursuits. This transformative approach to summer education not only addresses the practical constraints faced by families but also aligns with the broader goals of inclusivity, language support, and academic preparation.

Essentially, while the idea of a cherished summer vacation persists in the hearts of many, the contemporary socioeconomic realities necessitate a reevaluation of entrenched norms. The shift toward more pragmatic and inclusive summer education programs not only accommodates the evolving needs of families but also reflects a forward-looking approach to education that prioritizes accessibility, support, and academic enrichment for all students. It is important to understand that the days of single-income families have all but disappeared. In addition, the halcyon days of anyone having two months of summer vacation are dwindling, forcing parents to provide for childcare during those summer months.

Educational Fads

Some other critics dismiss balanced calendar reform as a passing trend or fad without substantial evidence of long-term benefits. Skepticism about the sustainability and effectiveness of the revised calendar model may stem from a perception that it lacks a robust foundation or has not been thoroughly tested and proven over an extended period.

A prevailing perception among many is that educational reforms are often dismissed as fleeting trends or fads. This skepticism is rooted in recent history, where initiatives like the Common Core Standards faced criticism and scrutiny. Understandably, such experiences may contribute to an overall wariness toward educational reforms that emerge and, at times, fade away. However, the landscape of calendar reform stands out as a persistent and recurrent subject of examination. The ongoing reevaluation of academic calendars has become particularly pronounced in the aftermath of the COVID-19 pandemic, prompting individuals and institutions to reconsider how time is allocated and utilized.

Unlike certain educational initiatives that may come and go, calendar reform represents a continuous dialogue and exploration. The very nature of this ongoing reexamination suggests a recognition that the structure of time within the educational context requires periodic reflection and adjustment. The unprecedented disruptions caused by the pandemic have catalyzed people to critically reassess how they allocate and manage their time, with implications extending beyond the immediate crisis.

The recalibration of perspectives on calendar reform is emblematic of a broader societal shift, where the traditional norms and structures are being revisited in light of contemporary challenges and changing priorities. Rather than a transient trend, the reconsideration of educational calendars reflects a deeper commitment to optimizing educational experiences and adapting to the evolving needs of individuals and communities. As educational systems navigate the complexities of the post-pandemic era, the conversation around calendar reform emerges as a meaningful and enduring discourse, challenging the notion that all educational changes are merely fads.

It is quite difficult to argue that calendar reform is merely a passing trend, particularly because certain educational institutions have been actively implementing a balanced calendar system for an extensive period of 50 years. The enduring presence of such a system within schools lends credence to the idea that it transcends the realm of a mere fad.

Moreover, the repercussions of the pandemic have served as a catalyst, reigniting a profound interest in delving into the intricacies of time utilization. This renewed curiosity extends beyond the educational sphere, encompassing various facets of life within the United States. As society grapples with the aftermath of the pandemic, there is a growing recognition that examining how time is allocated and structured holds implications not only for educational institutions but also for broader aspects of our daily lives. This shift in focus reflects an evolving perspective on the significance of time management and the need for adaptable systems that can withstand unforeseen challenges.

Parents

Certainly, not every parent is convinced about the advantages of introducing a balanced calendar system in schools, and this sentiment is not limited to America but extends across international borders (Queensland, 2024). The opposition to such a reform is multifaceted, with concerns that merit consideration. One prominent objection revolves around the perception that summer vacation holds a special place in childhood and should not be deprived. They believe that kids deserve the same summer vacations that they had as children, Hornak said. Some parents argue against it because it may conflict with planned summer vacations (James, 2022).

This resistance to change often stems from a nostalgic view of summer vacation as a cherished and carefree period of a child's life. Critics argue that this break from academic routines plays a crucial role in fostering a sense of freedom, exploration, and personal growth. They contend that removing or altering this traditional break could potentially deprive students of valuable experiences and memories associated with the quintessential summer vacation.

Addressing these concerns requires a plan that acknowledges the importance of preserving aspects of childhood while also considering the evolving needs of education in a rapidly changing world. Striking a balance between tradition and progress becomes pivotal in navigating the complexities surrounding calendar reform, ensuring that educational innovations are met with understanding and acceptance from parents and stakeholders alike (Valle, 2023). Summers for future generations will indeed look different from previous generations, but the same could be said about a variety of ways children spend their time even today.

While arranging childcare during the summer can be difficult, it becomes even more challenging to plan for additional breaks when many full-day camps and recreation programs are not offered. This difficulty may even deter some parents from remaining in the workforce entirely. Von Hippel references a 2013 study, which discovered that mothers in districts following a year-round calendar were less inclined to join the workforce when their children entered kindergarten (Warner, 2023).

Negative Economic Impact

Detractors have leveled accusations, suggesting that balanced school calendars could yield adverse economic repercussions within their communities. These concerns range from practical considerations to more sweeping claims, such as asserting that the adoption of a four-day school week negatively impacts the local housing market. Evaluating the economic impact of educational reforms is inherently challenging, especially when the focus is on the holistic development of children, and the positive effects may not be immediately apparent.

Critics express reservations about the potential drawbacks associated with balanced calendars, highlighting practical concerns and raising questions about the economic viability of such changes. Some critics contend that the adoption of a four-day school week might have far-reaching consequences, influencing aspects as significant as the local housing market (Robles, 2023). While quantifying the immediate gains of educational reforms remains a complex task, proponents argue that the long-term benefits of investing in the education of students far outweigh any short-term costs.

As with any transformative change in education, there are inevitable costs and adjustments. However, proponents of balanced calendars emphasize that the investment in educating students to become productive members of society holds substantial and lasting value. Viewing the shift through the lens of long-term societal benefits encourages a broader perspective, acknowledging that the true impact of educational reforms may unfold gradually and extend beyond immediate economic considerations. While critics raise concerns about potential negative economic impacts, supporters underscore the enduring value of prioritizing a robust education system that nurtures the future contributions of students to society.

Employment

Detractors also often raise the issue of workforce reduction during the traditional summer break. Critics argue that the extended break provides seasonal employment opportunities for individuals, such as students and teachers, and altering this structure could potentially impact livelihoods and contribute to unemployment during certain periods.

Depending on the calendar being implemented, employment difficulties may arise. For example, one study found that "mothers who have children in districts that offer schools on the year-round academic calendar are less likely to take part in the labor market than mothers with no school-aged children." The study further goes on to add that "mothers with both pre-school- and school-aged children are most negatively impacted. The author asserts this is because the necessity to find childcare for children with different scheduling needs can be additionally challenging" (Anthony, 2016). But childcare issues are still a challenge today, even in traditional calendars. In balanced calendar schools that adopt summer intersessions, this could alleviate the need for additional childcare spending during the summer months.

Once again, the impact of extending the school year depends on whether a school chooses to adopt this change. Certain staff members, who rely on summer employment to supplement their incomes, may find themselves in a precarious situation. This concern underscores the broader issue of living wages rather than merely seasonal employment.

In terms of seasonal employment for teens, there may be opportunities to transform traditional summer jobs into more structured internships and alternative credit programs. This shift could benefit both employers and young workers. For instance, turning summer jobs into comprehensive projects that involve understanding areas such as marketing, accounting, investing, and management theory could provide students with credits for real-world experiences.

Concerns also arise about the impact of a modified school calendar on high school students, particularly regarding their reduced availability for summer jobs and participation in traditional summer activities like camps. While these concerns are valid, it is essential to highlight that the proposed changes do not necessarily exclude students from engaging in these activities. A flexible approach can be adopted to integrate summer work experiences into the academic structure, allowing students to earn academic credits for their vocational pursuits without being tied to traditional summer sessions.

By incorporating work experiences and summer activities into the academic framework, the system becomes more adaptable, offering a well-rounded educational experience that transcends the confines of the traditional school year.

Another critical consideration is the current state of teen employment in the United States, which is reportedly at an all-time low. Interestingly, prior to the pandemic, teen employment rates had been steadily decreasing. According to the U.S. Bureau of Labor Statistics, "teen participation rates in the labor market hovered around 34% between 2011 and 2019, down significantly from the 2000 peak of 52% of all U.S. teens" (Silverman, 2023). This reflects a broader societal shift in how young individuals engage with the workforce, aligning with the changing dynamics of the job market and the growing emphasis on acquiring diverse skill sets through various educational experiences.

While concerns about potential limitations on summer jobs and traditional activities are acknowledged, the adaptability of the proposed changes allows for creative solutions. Integrating work experiences into the academic structure not only addresses these concerns but also presents an opportunity to enhance student's educational experiences by bridging the gap between theoretical learning and practical application. The evolving nature of teen employment further emphasizes the need for educational systems to remain dynamic, ensuring that students are well-prepared for the multifaceted demands of the modern world.

Childcare Issues

Concerns regarding childcare emerge as a significant point of contention. Critics argue that the revised schedule may create challenges for parents in arranging suitable childcare during nontraditional breaks, leading to increased logistical complexities for families.

Transitioning to a year-round calendar presents a set of multifaceted challenges, and a significant aspect is the need to adapt childcare systems to align with the new academic schedule. Many parents currently incur premium rates for childcare services during the traditional summer months, as this period typically coincides with extended school breaks. Moreover, contemporary parents often grapple with the demand for increased flexibility due to disparate vacation schedules that may not align seamlessly with their children's school calendars. As a result, a noteworthy trend emerges wherein parents opt to withdraw their children from school during vacations to accommodate these scheduling discrepancies. With that, parents and guardians with children attending school on a balanced schedule have shared that they prefer to budget for a week or two of periodic breaks, rather than 12–13 weeks in the summer as this model is more in line with current lifestyles. Taking a week off in the fall to be home is often more acceptable by an employer rather than taking multiple weeks off each summer to care for children who are on summer vacation.

Efforts to address this issue include the proposition of providing more breaks throughout the academic year, thereby mitigating the need for extensive summer childcare. However, the nature of calendar reform introduces a potential paradox: depending on the specific type of reform adopted—it could either alleviate or exacerbate childcare challenges for parents. For instance, the implementation of a compressed four-day school week might necessitate additional childcare arrangements, given the condensed school week. On the contrary, an extension of the school year into the summer months has the potential to reduce the burden on parents for additional childcare during traditional breaks.

The balance among parental work schedules, school calendars, and childcare demands underscores the nuanced considerations required for implementing any calendar reform. A comprehensive approach that takes into account the diverse needs of parents, students, and educational institutions is crucial. By exploring calendar adjustments that align more harmoniously with contemporary family dynamics, educational systems can contribute to a more seamless integration of academic schedules with the practical realities of parental responsibilities and childcare requirements (Robinson, 2023).

Concerns extend beyond the education sector, as summer resorts and attractions also apprehend a potential loss in business if students are in session during the summer. As discussed earlier, even with traditional school calendars, the beginning and ending dates exhibit significant variations across the United States. There has been ongoing debate about when summer officially starts, with southern regions often initiating their summer vacation in early June, while other areas might start in mid or even late June. This diversity is also mirrored in the commencement dates, which can range from as early as August in some districts. Some parents have even gone so far as to "argue against it because it may conflict with planned summer vacations" (James, 2022).

Evidently, school schedules have always exhibited considerable variations, making it difficult for all states to uniformly adopt a calendar that could jeopardize summer attractions. Furthermore, over time, parents have opted to take their children on vacation irrespective of the school calendar, instead of organizing trips around their work schedules.

It is clear that the existing variability in school schedules, both in terms of starting and ending dates, makes it unlikely for a uniform statewide calendar to be universally adopted. This adaptability has allowed families to continue planning vacations, suggesting that while the academic calendar is a factor, it does not singularly dictate the timing of family outings. Acknowledging this dynamic, any proposed changes to the school calendar would need to consider the established patterns of family behavior, ensuring that educational reforms are implemented in a way that accommodates the diverse needs and preferences of both students and their families.

Data

A critical perspective often centers on the perceived inadequacy of supporting data when advocating for the implementation of balanced calendars. Skeptics contend that there is a lack of comprehensive and conclusive evidence demonstrating the unequivocal benefits of balanced calendars, thereby raising questions about the validity and reliability of the rationale behind reform efforts.

Articulating this argument proves challenging, however, and prompts a critical examination of the existing body of research. While skeptics question the efficacy of balanced calendars, it is essential to acknowledge the presence of numerous studies on the subject. The pertinent question revolves around the specificity of the desired data.

Dozens of studies exist, each potentially contributing to a certain understanding of the impact of balanced calendars on academic performance and various other factors. The key inquiry becomes: What types of data are stakeholders seeking? Are they focused on academic outcomes, comparing the achievements of students from balanced calendars with those from traditional calendars? If so, what specific grade levels or age groups are under consideration?

Moreover, stakeholders might be interested in addressing specific objectives, such as mitigating summer learning loss or saving financial resources. The multitude of studies available allows for a tailored approach to data interpretation and analysis, accommodating diverse perspectives and research objectives.

The argument challenging the implementation of balanced calendars gains depth when considering the multifaceted nature of the available research. It becomes apparent that the effectiveness of balanced calendars can be assessed through various lenses, making it crucial to define the specific metrics and goals guiding the evaluation process. This nuanced approach encourages a more comprehensive understanding of the potential benefits or drawbacks associated with balanced calendars, facilitating informed discussions and evidence-based decision-making in the realm of education reform.

For various reasons, numerous locations may be hesitant to adopt any form of calendar reform. The resistance to implementation is multifaceted, with instances of prior attempts being thwarted before execution and some places even retracting their plans for balanced calendars at the brink of implementation. This reluctance can be attributed to a combination of factors, including the lack of sustained momentum for change.

Implementing calendar reform is a complex process that involves navigating diverse challenges and considerations (Hackley, 2023). Instances, where previous attempts have been thwarted before execution, highlight the intricacies involved, ranging from logistical hurdles to resistance from stakeholders. These setbacks contribute to a cautious approach in many places, where the fear of repeating past failures may discourage proactive efforts toward calendar reform.

Additionally, the decision to retract balanced calendars right before execution highlights the delicate nature of this educational reform (Pringle, 2023). Factors such as community pushback, unforeseen logistical complications, or changing administrative priorities can lead to the abandonment of reform initiatives. The inherent complexity of aligning academic calendars with the diverse needs of students, educators, and communities underscores the need for careful planning and strategic implementation.

Furthermore, the lack of sustained momentum can play a pivotal role in hindering calendar reform efforts. Without a consistent drive and ongoing advocacy for change, educational institutions may find it challenging to overcome resistance or inertia within their communities. The absence of sustained momentum can create an environment where the status quo prevails, impeding the initiation of innovative approaches to the academic calendar.

The hesitancy of many places to implement calendar reform stems from a range of challenges, including past failures, logistical complexities, community dynamics, and a lack of sustained momentum (Livengood, 2023). Recognizing and addressing these multifaceted issues is essential for fostering a conducive environment for educational reforms that align with the evolving needs of students and the broader educational landscape.

Individuals who withdraw from involvement, either during the planning or execution stages, often cite the lack of consistent data on this subject as a primary reason. The available data can be broadly categorized into three groups: the first group, which will be explored in a subsequent chapter, encompasses current research highlighting positive outcomes associated with the topic. The second group encounters a substantial portion of students for whom the results are inconclusive (Finnie, 2019). The third group consists of individuals who focus on results that indicate negative effects. Indeed, the validity of these negative outcomes will be thoroughly examined in the following (Stark, 2018).

The group that focused on negative student achievement outcomes has encountered studies that fail to yield positive results. However, the challenge lies in the limited replication of many of these studies, which is compounded by the difficulty in replicating them due to a variety of variables. This complexity is evident, particularly when comparing the effectiveness of four-day and five-day school weeks. Additionally, another hurdle faced by this group is the scarcity of studies that have undergone successful replication (von Hipple, 2019).

Finally, there are studies asserting that there is no discernible academic benefit whatsoever, or at least not a statistically significant one. These findings contribute to the nuanced landscape surrounding the impact of certain educational reforms, adding a layer of complexity to the ongoing discourse on academic calendars. It underscores the importance of a thorough examination of diverse research outcomes and methodologies to form a comprehensive understanding of the potential effects of changes in the school calendar. The absence of a clear consensus in these studies highlights the need for continued exploration and critical evaluation to inform evidence-based decisions in education policy and practice (Sawyer, 2018).

Another goal of the year-round calendar is to raise academic achievement. These gains may or may not be expected when schools use a multi-track calendar for crowding, but gains are invariably promised when a district adopts a single-track year-round calendar as an educational reform (Annenburg Brown University, n.d.). Contrary to popular belief, certain studies suggest that summer might not be the primary culprit for academic disparities, as the achievement gap does not necessarily widen during the summer months (Johnson, 2017). Instead, when considering the economic status of school districts, it becomes apparent that Black students tend to experience fewer losses in academic skills over summer breaks compared to their White counterparts (Khufeld, 2019).

Moreover, numerous educators and policymakers have made assumptions concerning the causes and plausible remedies for summer learning loss. Commonly, it is assumed that transitioning to a year-round schedule or implementing school-based interventions for underprivileged students during the summer will effectively address the issue. However, while these explanations and potential solutions may be attractive, the research backing them is not as robust as commonly perceived. Based on recent studies, an underexplored explanation for summer loss is that the decline in test scores from spring to fall tends to be most pronounced for students who experienced substantial gains from fall to spring. Armed with this knowledge, schools that monitor students' fall-to-spring learning progress can identify those who made above-average gains in the current school year and may be particularly susceptible to losing ground during the summer (Kuhfeld, 2019).

In summary, the criticisms leveled against balanced calendar reform are diverse and multifaceted, encompassing financial, logistical, cultural, and employment-related concerns. As discussions around education reform continue, addressing these points of contention becomes essential to fostering a more inclusive and informed dialogue about the potential benefits and challenges associated with adopting a balanced calendar system. Quite possibly, it may not be the best approach for every single school, district, or state, but to unilaterally say that it does not work serves injustice. Like any reform, perhaps in all forms, consistency, monitoring, adjusting, and commitment are the main components. Any researcher saying that balanced calendar reform does not work is missing the bigger picture: This is not supposed to be a panacea but an attempt to restructure the traditional calendar. Of course, there will be variables that play into its execution but an entire denial that balanced calendars work is extremely limited.

Chapter 2

Reexamining Time in Our Schools

The academic year for most K–12 students in the United States spans approximately 180 days, featuring a lengthy summer break. However, our examination of 1,500 public school districts reveals notable regional variations in the academic calendar. For example, in New England, schools typically commence classes after August 28, whereas in Middle Atlantic states such as New Jersey and New York, roughly three-quarters of students start after Labor Day. State regulations play a significant role, with 16 states establishing parameters for school start dates (Pew Research Center, 2023).

Despite these regulations, there remains flexibility, often permitting schools to begin before or after a specified date. Additionally, districts can request waivers, further enhancing adaptability. The factors influencing start dates are multifaceted, influenced by local interpretations and needs. This complexity underscores the necessity for a nuanced approach to academic scheduling, one that balances regulatory standards with community demands. This prompts some educators, administrators, and policymakers to reevaluate established norms, advocating for a dynamic and adaptable educational system that can effectively meet the diverse needs of students, families, and communities in the 21st century (Walrath-Holdridge, 2023).

Despite this, the prevailing academic calendar in most American schools follows a 180-day structure, typically commencing around September and concluding in June. Variations in climate across the nation prompt states to further tailor their calendars to accommodate the unique needs of their communities.

A pervasive theme across various societies involves the conceptualization and naming of distinct periods, encompassing days, weeks, months, and ultimately, the overarching construct of a year. While numerous calendars are in use today, the Gregorian calendar, established by Pope Gregory in the 16th century, has evolved into the universally accepted international standard. Presently, a focal point in contemporary school calendar research revolves around discerning the merits and drawbacks of a full-year school model versus the perceived significance of the traditional summer vacation, as elucidated by scholars like Weiss and Brown (2003) and Gold (2002). The structural organization of the school day emerges as a pivotal consideration, notably underscored in *Prisoners of Time*, the seminal 1994 report from the National Education Commission on Time and Learning.

In addition to revisiting historical aspects of school calendar formation, this exploration extends to encompass both ongoing and forthcoming challenges in the realm of academic scheduling. In the current digital age, where virtual learning has become increasingly prevalent, the very essence of time takes on new dimensions, prompting profound questions about its significance in educational contexts. In navigating considerations of school time across past, present, and future landscapes, it is imperative to delve into the broader concept of the "calendar," recognizing its profound importance in shaping the dimensions of our lives. This discussion extends to an exploration of the "school clock" as a symbolic representation of temporal structures within the educational framework, ultimately serving as a gateway to understanding and addressing issues related to time and the effectiveness of school systems (Weiss, 2013).

Concerns about learning time in America have persisted for decades. In 2014, the report "Learning Time in America: Trends to Reform the American School Calendar" highlighted that over 35 districts, spanning more than 10 states, announced plans to implement or explore the possibility of a longer school day and/or year in certain schools. This proliferation of expanded-time schools is largely attributed to policies fostering the creation of new charter schools and providing autonomy to traditional district schools at the school level. The flexibility granted in governance empowers educators to restructure schedules, staffing, and budgeting, often resulting in significantly increased learning hours for all students.

In recent years, influential federal programs and state leaders have endorsed the expansion of time as a strategic approach to transforming chronically underperforming schools, offering additional resources to support the implementation of this strategy. The NCTL, dedicated to redesigning and expanding school time to enhance opportunities and outcomes for high-poverty students, collaborates with the ECS. This partnership aims to present a snapshot of public school time in America, building on previous reports in 2011 and 2013. By focusing on key actions at the federal, state, and local levels since 2013, the report aims to advance the national conversation on how schools can leverage time to achieve a vision of high-quality education for all.

The NCTL and the ECS have conducted a comprehensive review of legislative activity across all 50 states, identifying hundreds of filed bills seeking to establish rules around learning time or, more frequently, create pathways for schools and/or districts to extend school time. Out of these bills, over 40 have become law in the last two legislative sessions. This evolving landscape reflects a growing recognition of the significance of time in shaping the educational experience and underscores ongoing efforts to enhance learning opportunities for students nationwide (Faberman, 2011).

The traditional association of Labor Day with the impending commencement of the school year has evolved. Formerly symbolizing the final hurrah before schools swung open their doors for the new academic year, this connection has become less prevalent. In the current landscape, a mere handful of states are opting to kick off classes after the Labor Day holiday. The majority of districts, spanning most states, have shifted to an earlier start, commencing the school year in August. Surprisingly, in states like Arizona, Georgia, and Mississippi, a significant portion of public school students now return to their academic pursuits as early as the end of July.

The question arises: Why is there such a pronounced variation in school start dates?

The answers are diverse, and intriguingly, what might be in the best academic interests of students does not consistently hold the top position on the priority lists. From the week of July 4 to the week of September 4, the spectrum of school start dates is vast, reflecting the influence of multifaceted factors and considerations in the decision-making process. Understanding this complex web of influences is crucial to appreciating the intricacies of school calendar planning and its implications for students, educators, and communities alike (Heubeck, 2023).

The National Center for Education Statistics lists the number of school days by state around the country (2024). Although most are 180, there are a few exceptions with 160, Colorado, 170, Kentucky, and 175, Vermont and Wyoming. There are also a few with 185, such as Illinois and North Carolina.

A NATION AT RISK

A Nation at Risk, a seminal educational report, conducted a thorough examination of the declining state of the American educational system, specifically focusing on the performance of high school students in comparison to global standards (1983). The report meticulously identifies areas of concern and, importantly, proposes a set of recommendations designed to address these issues. The five key recommendations are thoughtfully organized under the categories of content, standards and expectations, time, teaching, and leadership with fiscal support.

In addressing content-related concerns, the report underscores the necessity of fortifying high school graduation requirements. These requirements encompass minimum standards for each student, mandating four years of English, three years of mathematics, three years of science, three years of social studies, and a half-year dedicated to computer science education. Concerning standards and expectations, the report advocates for the adoption of more rigorous and measurable benchmarks for academic performance and student conduct across educational institutions, from schools to colleges and universities. Significantly, it urges four-year institutions to raise admission criteria to ensure a higher standard for incoming students.

The report also delves into the dimension of time utilization, suggesting a potential extension of the school day or academic year to allocate more time for students to acquire the "New Basics." This initiative aims to provide a more comprehensive and enriched learning experience. To enhance the teaching profession, the report outlines seven strategies to improve teacher preparation, aspiring to elevate teaching as a more rewarding and respected career path.

Educational leadership and fiscal support are integral components of the report's recommendations. It offers six implementation guidelines to strengthen leadership within educational institutions and provides insights into enhancing fiscal support for the recommended reforms. This comprehensive approach, spanning multiple dimensions of the educational landscape, seeks to address the challenges outlined in the report and foster a more robust and effective American education system.

PRISONERS OF TIME

The Education Council Act of 1991 marked a pivotal moment in the history of school calendars by establishing the National Education Commission on Time and Learning as an independent advisory body. Its mandate was to conduct a comprehensive examination of the intricate relationship between time and learning in American schools. The subsequent report, released in May 1994, asserted that the success of school reform initiatives hinges on the provision of adequate time for learning *Prisoners of Time* (1994).

This review focuses on four substantive recommendations outlined by the commission, each identified as crucial for the enhancement of American education. The first recommendation emphasizes the need to reclaim the academic day, recognizing the pivotal role that dedicated instructional time plays in fostering student achievement. The second recommendation seeks to rectify the design flaw in educational programs, ensuring that the structure aligns seamlessly with learning objectives. Keeping schools open to meet the diverse needs of children and communities forms the third recommendation, acknowledging the multifaceted role educational institutions play beyond traditional instructional hours. Finally, the fourth recommendation underscores the importance of providing teachers with professional time and opportunities for continuous development.

The core concept conveyed in the 1994 report remains pertinent today. The fundamental idea is that, in schools, learning should serve as a constant, with time adapting to meet the individual needs of students striving for high standards. In this evolving perspective, it has become evident that meeting the learning needs of many students, particularly those from disadvantaged backgrounds, demands a significantly greater amount of time than the conventional 180-day, 6.5-hour daily calendar provides. This recognition underscores the ongoing imperative to reconsider and adapt educational structures to ensure they align with the evolving needs of students and the pursuit of academic excellence.

TOUGH CHOICES, TOUGH TIMES

In the field of educational reform, *Tough Choices or Tough Times*, the insightful report from the New Commission on the Skills of the American Workforce, serves as a guiding beacon (2008). This revealing document meticulously unravels the dynamics of the global economy, offering a prophetic glimpse into a future where the American standard of living faces a perilous decline. The crux of the report contends that without a groundbreaking overhaul of the education system—an endeavor unprecedented in a century—the nation risks succumbing to economic challenges on a scale not witnessed before.

This revised and expanded edition transcends a mere update; it delves into the core of the Commission's proposals, presenting a comprehensive summary that encapsulates the essence of transformative recommendations. The narrative unfolds further with insightful commentaries provided by thought leaders such as Denis Doyle, Lawrence Mishel, Michael Petrilli, Diane Ravitch, and Richard Rothstein. These commentaries engage in a thought-provoking dialogue, accompanied by responses from esteemed members of the Commission, creating a tapestry of perspectives that enriches the reader's understanding of the proposed educational metamorphosis.

SUMMER LEARNING LOSS

Both extended school days and year-round education share a common goal of increasing time on task, but year-round schooling sets itself apart by also aiming to mitigate academic losses experienced during the customary two-month summer vacation. Often referred to as *Summer Fade* or *Summer Loss*, this phenomenon entails a lack of student growth or, in some cases, academic regression upon their return from summer break (Pedersen, 2015).

Numerous studies highlight the negative impact of summer vacations on student achievement. Reading scores tend to decrease, and academic gains made during the regular school year are often lost during the extended break (Burkham, 2004). Moreover, a concerning gap emerges between students who can afford supplemental summer programs, such as day camps or academic enrichment, and those who cannot. Additional research suggests that students struggle to maintain their achievement levels over the summer (Stenvall, 2001). While these challenges affect all students, the repercussions tend to magnify when deficiencies occur in the early grades, potentially leaving students years behind their peers by the time they reach secondary levels.

Proponents of year-round education contend that a balanced calendar with shorter breaks serves as an effective intervention for students lagging while providing benefits for all students. Over a century of research underscores the reality of summer fade for many American children, prompting some to label it a national phenomenon that warrants serious attention (Bracey, 2002).

Curiously, despite the lack of significant evidence supporting the positive impact of summer vacations on student achievement, opponents of year-round education remain steadfast. Many educators acknowledge that the traditional two- to three-month summer break originated from the agrarian needs of students during the early days of America. This break was also influenced by the impracticality of using school facilities during the sweltering months of July and August, which posed challenges for both students and teachers.

While the historical context of summer vacations is rooted in an agrarian past, the ongoing debate surrounding its impact on student achievement lacks conclusive evidence in favor of the traditional break. The discussion between extended breaks and year-round education continues, fueled by the evolving needs and challenges faced by the education system in the United States.

One of the pivotal contributions to our understanding of the phenomenon known as *Summer Fade*, *Summer Slide*, *Brain Drain*, or *Summer Learning Loss* stems from the comprehensive research conducted by Cooper, Nye, Charlton, Lindsey, and Greenhouse, "The Effects of Summer Vacation on Achievement Test Scores: A Narrative and Meta-Analytic Review" (1996). Their seminal meta-analysis delved into the intricate dynamics of summer learning loss by scrutinizing 39 studies dedicated to this topic. The overarching findings of their investigation revealed a noteworthy decline in both math and language arts progress during the summer months.

The researchers found that the consequences of summer break were substantial, amounting to an approximate loss of nearly a full month of learning each summer. This revelation underscored the magnitude of the academic setback experienced by students during the extended break. Furthermore, the study shed light on the persistent nature of these negative effects, indicating that they not only endured but also intensified as students progressed from one grade to the next.

By meticulously synthesizing existing studies and revealing the cumulative impact of the summer break, their meta-analysis provided a nuanced understanding of how academic progress is susceptible to decline during the vacation period. This insight has since become instrumental in shaping educational policies and interventions aimed at mitigating the adverse effects of summer learning loss and fostering continuous academic growth for students across different grade levels.

COVID AND TIME

Although the pandemic was a time of great uncertainty, it did renew an interest in exploring how time was used in schools. Extensive discussions have taken place regarding the variety of temporary and enduring impacts of COVID-19 on education. Undoubtedly, it has accelerated the widespread adoption of online and hybrid learning, exacerbated issues related to equity and access, and laid bare the financial vulnerabilities of many educational institutions. Amid these changes, there is a significant and positive shift that has received limited attention, which may be the most substantial outcome prompted by COVID: the discussion of the conventional academic calendar.

Numerous universities have already undergone substantial modifications to their academic calendars this year in response to the challenges posed by COVID-19. Strategies such as commencing the semester earlier or later and concluding in-person classes before Thanksgiving have been seen in some schools. Similar to the rapid transition to online learning, universities efficiently implemented these calendar adjustments, albeit requiring substantial effort. Notably, some institutions, like Lynn University, embraced innovative new block schedules featuring four distinct four-week sessions in the fall. This model empowered students to seamlessly transition between online and in-person blocks, enabling an accelerated completion of the semester (Busteed, 2021).

After experiencing years of disrupted learning due to the pandemic, the most recent Nation's Report Card reveals a widespread decline in reading and math scores, with math scores decreasing in nearly every state (Wooley-Wilson, 2022). In light of the challenges posed by the COVID-19 pandemic in primary and secondary education, policymakers are contemplating modifications to the traditional school calendar. The paper "Views on Modifying the Traditional School Calendar for a Post-COVID World" explores the possibility of transitioning to a balanced calendar model as a response to the pandemic's aftermath. This approach, previously studied for decades with varied results on academic achievement, is now considered for its potential to counteract COVID-19-related learning loss. The discussion encompasses the broader goals of addressing achievement gaps, reducing viral transmission, and providing support to vulnerable student populations (Koning, 2022).

A special issue of *Psychology in the Schools* is dedicated to examining the multifaceted impact of the worldwide COVID-19 pandemic on children, families, and schools. The articles covered an array of topics, including

(1) an overview of the effects on children in both physical and psychological dimensions,
(2) the diverse challenges faced by professionals working with youth during the pandemic,
(3) the unique issues affecting college-age students, and
(4) the various factors influencing the extent of COVID-19's impact on children and their families. The collection aims to provide a comprehensive understanding of the repercussions of the pandemic across different aspects of the educational and psychological landscape (McIntosh, 2022).

LATER SCHOOL START TIMES

The discourse surrounding later school start times has experienced a resurgence, as highlighted in the article titled "Changing Times: Findings from the First Longitudinal Study of Later High School Start Times" (2022). The genesis of this conversation can be traced back to the early 1990s when medical research revealed that teenagers exhibit distinct sleep and wake patterns compared to pre-adolescents and adults. Capitalizing on this understanding, the Minneapolis Public School District underwent a significant shift in 1997, altering the start time of its seven comprehensive high schools from 7:15 a.m. to 8:40 a.m.

One article on this subject delves into the repercussions of this transformative change, presenting compelling findings that underscore its positive impact. The study identifies notable benefits, including enhanced attendance and enrollment rates, a reduction in instances of students dozing off in class, and a decrease in self-reported feelings of depression among students. The implications of these findings extend to policy considerations, acknowledging the contentious nature of this issue within school districts across the United States.

The exploration of such tangible improvements resulting from adjusted start times contributes to the ongoing dialogue on optimizing school schedules to better align with the biological rhythms of adolescents. In the early 1990s, medical research found that teenagers have biologically different sleep and wake patterns than the preadolescent or adult population. Based on that information, in 1997, the seven comprehensive high schools in the Minneapolis Public School District shifted the school start time from 7:15 a.m. to 8:40 a.m. (Walstrom, 2002).

This article also examined that change, finding significant benefits such as improved attendance and enrollment rates, less sleeping in class, and less student-reported depression. The researcher also goes on to recommend policy implications that are briefly discussed, acknowledging this to be a highly charged issue in school districts across the United States. This article presents findings from a 4-year study in a large, urban school district that altered high school start times significantly from 7:15 a.m. to 8:40 a.m. This change affected more than 12,000 secondary students within a total K–12 population of nearly 51,000 students.

This research information about the sleep needs of adolescents and the influence of sleep on learning and behavior has captured the attention of school districts across the United States. Physicians, parents, school board members, and others are asking school administrators and policymakers to acknowledge the medical evidence about the biological sleep patterns of teenagers and to adjust school schedules accordingly. The discussions and debates have been intense because this is a multifaceted issue. School administrators are being asked to weigh the factual information about the biology of adolescents' sleep patterns against the competing demands of teachers' work preferences, athletic and after-school activity schedules, and bus transportation schedules.

Furthermore, the integration of medical and educational research communities emphasizes the universal nature of the sleep–wake cycle shift in adolescents. It also acknowledges the challenges and politics involved in changing school start times, with concerns about community division and transportation costs. Despite the contentious nature of this decision, the study encourages districts to consider the positive long-term effects and evaluate the feasibility of adopting a later start time for high schools (Wahlstrom, 2002).

SCHOOL HOLIDAYS ARE INCREASING

School holidays are expanding across the United States, with many districts adopting more days off during the academic year. In "Changing Times: Findings from the First Longitudinal Study of Later High School Start Times," Stewart examines the challenges faced by families during school holidays and their impact on children's educational attainment and well-being (Stewart, 2018).

Some school districts are beginning to include more holidays in their academic calendars to recognize and accommodate religious diversity among students. For example, Howard County Public Schools in Maryland and schools in New York City have added holidays such as Eid, Lunar New Year, Yom Kippur, and Rosh Hashanah to their calendars. Recognizing these holidays not only acknowledges the diversity of the student population but also reduces absences for both students and teachers (Stewart, 2018).

Celebrating these major holidays often involves extensive and lengthy observances, making it difficult for students to attend school and observe the holiday. Many students, like those celebrating Eid, Yom Kippur, and Diwali, face the challenge of missing school for these holidays, potentially impacting their academic performance. Adding these holidays to the academic calendar would reduce absences and allow students to observe their holidays without missing important school activities. For example, in New Jersey, an increasing number of school districts in the state are closing their doors to observe new holidays, which include Diwali, Ramadan, Eid al-Fitr, and the Lunar New Year (Yellin, 2022).

While adding more holidays may extend the school year slightly, it would not significantly impact the overall length. For example, eight major holidays (Yom Kippur, Rosh Hashanah, Christmas, Easter, the two Eid holidays, the Eve of Lunar New Year, and Diwali) would still recognize the major religions in the American community. Moreover, the financial cost of adding holidays is often less than paying for substitutes to cover teachers who take personal days to observe holidays.

Promoting religious diversity in schools not only benefits the community but also contributes to a more tolerant society. Recognizing holidays from various religions demonstrates inclusivity and helps foster understanding among students. However, completely ignoring religion, as some districts have done by removing all religious references from the school calendar, may not be the best approach. A balanced approach that includes education about modern religious practices can promote tolerance and mutual respect.

Overall, incorporating more religious holidays into the academic calendar is a critical step toward promoting religious tolerance and understanding in

American schools. It can help bridge the gap between diverse religious communities and contribute to a more inclusive and accepting society (Garbarino, 2022). As schools become diverse, additional days are going to be expected from the parents (Sawchuk, 2020).

HOW MUCH VACATION IS REALLY NEEDED?

A 2012 study suggested that travelers' health and well-being peak on the eighth day of a holiday, indicating that a week-long vacation might provide the greatest benefits (de Bloom, 2013).

A 2024 study in the *Washington Post* suggests that travelers' health and well-being peak on the eighth day of a holiday, indicating that a week-long vacation might provide the greatest benefits (Sachs, 2024). However, there is no definitive formula for how long a vacation should be for optimal decompression, as it depends on individual preferences and the ability to switch from work to vacation mode. The study's lead researcher noted that it is challenging to investigate the optimal vacation duration due to the inability to assign people randomly to different vacation lengths and the influence of various factors like location and weather. The study found that vacation length and most activities, except "passive" ones, were only weakly associated with health improvements during and after trips.

The Harvard Business Review collaborated with the U.S. Travel Association to study the relationship between well-being and taking time off from work (Achor, 2016). They found that without adequate recovery periods, performance levels decline. Despite the common belief that working longer leads to more success, the study showed that regular time off is crucial. The study surveyed 5,641 American adults working over 35 hours per week with paid time off, using their responses to gauge the impact of time off on business and health measures. The analysis revealed a decline in vacation time taken by Americans, from nearly three weeks in 2000 to 16.2 days in 2015. Even during periods of high unemployment, such as in 2015, vacation time remained low, suggesting that unemployment rates do not directly influence time taken off.

Research, conducted on a nationally representative sample, confirms the positive impact of family trips on the academic achievements of young children (Park, 2016). Specifically, visits to museums, art galleries, and historical sites have been shown to improve reading scores. While the effects may not be immediate, the study indicates that these experiences contribute to children's academic attainment over the long term. Remarkably, family trip experiences occurring more than six months before the tests had a significantly positive impact on reading test scores. This underscores the importance for parents to prioritize family trips, even if they do not see immediate academic benefits, as these experiences play a crucial role in enhancing their children's educational outcomes.

This research also should prompt educators and policymakers that if adults benefit from more frequent breaks and peak on the eighth day of vacation, why would students benefit from 10 to 12 weeks of uninterrupted vacation?

Chapter 3

Exploring Diversity in School Calendars

A Comprehensive Analysis of Various Models

Researching the diverse landscape of school calendars while examining the different models implemented globally is critical in understanding the subject of calendar reform. The discussion encompasses traditional, year-round (balanced calendar), alternative, and extended-year calendars, providing insights into the advantages, challenges, and current trends associated with each. Drawing on research and educational practices assists educators, policymakers, parents and guardians, students, and researchers about the nuanced approaches to structuring the academic year.

Developing an agreed-upon academic school calendar can be complicated. Based on the lived experiences and the fact that nearly every adult has attended school, stakeholders often take the liberty to offer strong opinions to local educational leaders regarding how schools should function and when schools should be in session. Little credit is given to the educational leadership who have studied or researched best practices in education. This chapter will highlight the diverse landscape of school calendars being implemented globally.

Variations in the school calendar have existed since formal education was developed (Mattingly, 2007). In the 1800s, schools in large communities tended to operate for up to 12 months of the year; however, few students attended the whole year (Glines, 1995). In contrast, rural schools operated only three to six months of the year during the same period due to the agricultural lifestyle, weather, and transportation (Glines, 1995). Compulsory education and traditional school calendars were created for a manufacturing society on an agrarian calendar (Glines, 1995). These initiatives provided farming communities with a workforce to help work on the farm (Glines, 1995). With changes in family status, the need for parents to work required accountability reports such as Education Yes! and No Child Left Behind, as well as initiatives, Response to Intervention, which require schools to implement multitiered systems of support for all children, public opinion is now beginning to support a more extended school year (ESY; Rakoff, 1999). Proponents of the balanced school calendar often think that American children should be spending more time in school as the United States ranks near the bottom among industrial nations in the number of days children attend school each year (Barrett, 1990; NAYRE, 2009). Adding school days can be expensive and cost-prohibitive. As such, a pillar of the balanced school calendar is to reduce the length of summer intermission and use the allocated 180 school days more effectively across the calendar year (Hornak, 2015).

The balanced school calendar is not a new idea. Balanced calendar schools began in 1645 in Dorchester, England (Cammarota, 1961). By 1840, several major cities in the United States had school systems with calendars extending beyond the traditional calendar. In the 1800s, schools in New York City attended school for 49 weeks; in Chicago, 48 weeks; in Cleveland, 43 weeks; and in Brooklyn, Baltimore, and Cincinnati, which attended school for 11 months (Lane, 1932). Detroit and Philadelphia students attended the school over 250 days of the year (Lane, 1932).

Students attended school on the balanced school calendar for several reasons in the 1800s. Immigrants wanted their children to attend school for the entire year to help them acquire the English language and assimilate into the culture as soon as possible (Glines, 2009; Silva, 2007; Hermansen & Gove, 1971). Parents of immigrant children also desired to have their children supervised in schools while working in mills, factories, and professional shops (Hermansen & Gove, 1971). Hermansen and Gove stated that the length of the school year was directly related to the community's needs. In rural communities, schools were only open for three to six months as most of the learning was thought to occur by helping on the family farm.

In the last half of the 19th century, industrial society and life on the farm were becoming more mechanized, and community leaders became more concerned with providing all children, regardless of urban or rural, an equal opportunity to learn (Hermansen & Gove, 1971). During this period, state legislatures began to regulate education in state constitutions. As education became more controlled by each state, legislatures worked to balance urban and rural needs by establishing a minimum standard regarding the number of days and hours a child attended school (Hermansen & Gove, 1971). Gradually, by the beginning of the 20th century, the school day became standardized in law, with a minimum of 180 school days per year as established by state law (Hermansen & Gove, 1971).

Modern balanced calendar schools have ties back to 1904 (Fischel et al., 2003). The National Education Commission significantly increased attention to the alternative calendar idea in the *Prisoner of Time* report of 1994. The 2005 follow-up report describes:

> Learning in America is a prisoner of time. For the past 150 years, American public schools have held time constant and let learning vary. The rule, only rarely voiced, is simple: learn what you can in the time we make available. It should surprise no one that some bright, hard-working students do reasonably well. Everyone else—from the typical student to the dropout—runs into trouble. (NEC, 2005, p. 1)

The report continued to state:

> Our schools and the people involved with them . . . students, teachers, administrators, parents, and staff . . . are prisoners of time, captives of the school clock and calendar. The six-hour, 180-day school year should be relegated to museums, an exhibit from our educational past. Our usage of time virtually ensures the failure of many students. (NEC, 2005, p. 1)

The *Prisoners of Time* report was released when school accountability and resource reductions increased the interest in an alternative calendar and renewed the concept of year-round schooling. The traditional nine-month calendar became the norm despite social and economic changes in America (Fischel et al., 2003).

Schools have operated on the alternative calendar for many years. In the 1991–1992 school year, 23 states offered 1,646 schools that operated on the balanced school calendar (Stenvall, 2002). In the 2001–2002 school year, 44 states offered 3,011 balanced calendar schools in 559 school districts nationwide (Stenvall, 2002). The balanced school calendar provides flexibility to operate the school throughout the calendar year (Ballinger, 1995). Currently, approximately 4% of students across the nation attend school on a balanced calendar (Stark, 2018).

The traditional calendar was developed to assimilate immigrant children quickly into a local society (Heaberlin, 2002). The economy in America is no longer running on agriculture (Heaberlin, 2002). Schools are preparing children in the 21st century for jobs that have yet to be created. Therefore, there is little explanation for continuing to educate children on an agrarian calendar for a manufacturing society (Heaberlin, 2002).

School districts that choose to adopt the balanced school calendar typically make the move to solve a problem (Ballinger & Kneese, 2006). School districts frequently adopt a balanced school calendar to reduce the annual summer learning loss. By reducing the number of days and weeks a teacher is required to reteach each fall, supporters of the balanced school calendar agree there tends to be a positive impact on student achievement (Ballinger

& Kneese, 2006). When providing opportunities for students to continuously learn, school districts often adopt a single-track calendar in which all students and teachers follow the same schedule and learning periods (Ballinger & Kneese, 2006).

The most popular single-track balanced calendar schedule in the United States is the 45 days of instruction with a 15-day recess (Ballinger & Kneese, 2006). The modified school calendar has other benefits. Due to frequent breaks, there tends to be less student and teacher burnout, and both students and teachers have higher attendance levels, as dentist and medical appointments are often scheduled during breaks (Ballinger & Kneese, 2006). Also noted by Ballinger and Kneese is that attendance records tend to be better at schools that have adopted the single-track model. A second model is sometimes considered called the multi-track calendar. A multi-track balanced school calendar is sometimes used in schools where capacity is an issue. The multi-track model allows two groups of children to attend the same school at different times of the day or year (Pepper, 2009). The multi-track model is implemented with the same intent as the single-track model to minimize the impact of annual learning loss during summer recess (Ballinger & Kneese, 2006).

TRADITIONAL SCHOOL CALENDAR

Developed in the 1890s, the traditional school calendar, as the majority of us know in America, was established to allow students to work on local farms. It also provided opportunities for immigrant children to be taught the English language during the summer intermission, and another less often discussed reason is that the school calendar was modified in the 1890s to what the majority experience today. Doctors at the time believed that too much school was bad for adolescent brains. Traditional school calendars roughly operate from Labor Day to Memorial Day, with designated time off around national holidays and dedicated to giving students and staff a break each spring. In the United States, most schools function on the 180-day calendar.

In the United States, the traditional school calendar is about nine months long and operates between September and June, with a 12-week break for summer recess (Ballinger & Kneese, 2006). The traditional calendar has been called the agrarian calendar (Weiss & Brown, 2005). Weiss and Brown stated that the agrarian calendar is believed to have roots that date back two centuries when farming and ranching were the dominant way of life in the United States. With the boom of the industrial revolution and current urban technology-driven society, it is no longer necessary to hold firm to the 12-week summer vacation for children to help on the family farm or ranch.

According to Wilmore and Slate (2012), modern machines and farm equipment have reduced the need for many people to complete the tiresome tasks of planting and harvesting. Talbot (2000) related:

> It is true that summer vacation is a mere artifact of the days when farming played a role in our economy, now a precious artifact with an accretion of sweet associations and a sense of possibility all its own. (p. 6)

Summer recess remains intact due partly to the lifestyles developed over the 20th century by middle- and upper-class families who desire extended breaks from school for children to spend with their families (Talbot, 2000). Over the past 150 years, economic success has allowed families to budget for family trips during the long summer (Fischel, 2006). Three months off in the summer is no longer appropriate, considering that children enter the school year each fall already behind (Cramer, 2006). The typical home in America is no longer equipped to support children over the summer (Cramer, 2006). Hess (2006) stated that most children are in childcare or monitored by an older sibling while parents work. Hess also wrote that children are better off attending school in the summer rather than wasting time at home or in the community. Other advanced nations avoid providing an American-like summer recess (Hess, 2006).

In many cases, parents work to find a way to occupy their children while they are at work (Hess, 2006). Parents spend 30% of their time in the summer with their school-aged children, and according to Hess, families typically spend 8% of their summertime earnings on childcare. Simultaneously, expensive school facilities and resources sit idle (Hess, 2006).

Educational researchers have verified what teachers have been highlighting for years: students forget a considerable amount of knowledge annually each summer. Ballinger and Kneese (2006) stated that communities should be concerned with the amount of time teachers are taking each fall to reteach the knowledge that has been lost. Children who are not exposed to continuous learning opportunities throughout the year, especially in the summer, tend to lose ground academically (Lundstrom, 2005). Unless students are stimulated academically during the 12-week summer recess, they fall behind by roughly 12 weeks in their reading achievement (Lundstrom, 2005). Heaberlin (2002) also acknowledged that most children do not retain their academic knowledge after a 12-week summer break from school. Ballinger (1995) stated that the number one reason for changing the balanced school calendar from a traditional one is to eliminate the significant learning loss over summer break.

Summer learning loss impacts lower-income children who may already struggle more than their middle-class counterparts (Lundstrom, 2005).

According to Morse (1992), disadvantaged students forget more during summer break than any other child. If this pattern continues, in a few short years, a child could be several years behind, which accounts for 80–100% of the gap between low-income children and children from the middle class (Lundstrom, 2005).

Lundstrom (2005) stated that 61% of low-income families do not have books at home, and schools offer some of the only resources available to many children. Moving to a balanced school calendar will increase the performance of students who may not have readily available resources and may not be supported at home (Heaberlin, 2002). If a non-disadvantaged child either maintains an academic level or has the opportunities to gain exposure to literature, the gap between a non-disadvantaged child and a low-income child can become tremendous. The gap developed annually due to the length of the summer recess contributes to the dropout rate across the country (Ballinger & Kneese, 2006). The impact on math is more dramatic than the loss in language arts (Davis, 2006; Schulte, 2009). Heaberlin (2002) reported that summer intermission is most detrimental to math computation.

Traditional calendar schools tend to disadvantage at-risk children more significantly by holding to a long summer intermission between school years (Heaberlin, 2002). School officials need to be aware of the unintended consequences of continuing to operate on an outdated school calendar. Kneese and Knight (1995) reported that balanced calendar schools have a significant advantage over their counterparts on the traditional calendar when facing the summer slide. By shortening the 12-week summer recess, schools can minimize the regression caused by the summer recess (Heaberlin, 2002).

Traditional calendar schools disadvantage low-income children by holding firm to an outdated school calendar. The summer recess can amount to losing one week of knowledge retention each week a child is away from school. School officials must know the unintended consequences of operating schools on an outdated school calendar. Math computation tends to be the area of most significant loss (Heaberlin, 2002).

The faucet theory, developed by Entwisle, Alexander, and Olson (1997), underpins and illustrates the reason the traditional school calendar is so inequitable. When students are in school, resources flow at the same rate regardless of economic status; however, during the summer, the resources for the lower-income student are shut off while the middle- and upper-class student may still have opportunities to learn due to the fact that their families can afford to travel, send their children to summer camps, and visit the library.

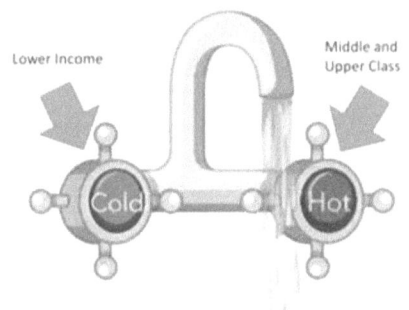

Figure 3.1

YEAR-ROUND SCHOOL CALENDAR/ BALANCED CALENDAR

A YRS calendar, or balanced calendar, is an alternative to the traditional academic calendar that typically features a long summer intermission. The primary characteristic of a balanced school calendar is the redistribution of vacation periods throughout the year, creating shorter breaks at regular intervals rather than on long extended summer vacations. Approximately 3 million students attend school on a balanced school calendar (Addison, 2023).

Key Features of a Balanced School Calendar

Shorter, Regular Breaks

Instead of a lengthy summer break, students on a balanced calendar have shorter breaks spread evenly throughout the year. This modification can help prevent the summer slide, a phenomenon where students may lose academic skills over an extended break.

Intersession

Balanced calendars include intersession periods, during which students can participate in additional learning opportunities, enrichment programs, or remediation sessions. These periods are designed to provide targeted academic support to enhance the educational experience and can come as preteaching, reteaching, or enrichment.

Continuous Learning

The balanced calendar promotes continuous learning by reducing the time between instructional periods. This can help maintain students' engagement and retention of information.

Flexibility

Balanced calendars offer flexibility in scheduling and can be customized to meet the needs of individual schools or districts and the community's needs. Some variations include a single-track calendar, where all students and staff follow the same schedule, or a multi-track calendar, where different groups of students and staff function on different schedules using the same school facility. This model is often used to address overcrowding or when a school is being renovated and must be temporarily closed. In the latter case, multi-track balanced calendars are adopted to address issues by staggering the schedules of different groups of students.

The balanced calendar models gaining popularity include the 45–15 or the 60–20 plans. In a 45–15 plan, students attend school for nine weeks and take a break for three weeks. In a 60–20 model, students attend school for 12 weeks and take four weeks off. While these two models are generally the most researched, the flexibility of the balanced calendar is one of the attractions. During an analysis of balanced calendar schools in Michigan, most are in session for six to seven weeks with a one- or two-week break scheduled around local events such as the county fair and state and federal holidays.

ALTERNATIVE CALENDARS—FOUR DAYS A WEEK SCHEDULE

Four-day school weeks are used in over 1,600 schools nationwide (Thompson et al., 2024; RAND, 2023). A four-day school week is an alternative to the typical traditional school calendar. A four-day school week eliminates one school day each week, adding additional instructional hours to the remaining 148 school days (Thompson et al., 2024). Four-day school weeks have been used in the United States since 1930 in some capacity or another (Donis-Keller & Silvernail, 2009). Despite the growing number of schools implementing a four-day school week, the data and effectiveness are still emerging.

Thompson et al. stated that a four-day school week may impact student achievement as the data collected and analyzed indicated that with the decrease in instructional time, there may be a reduction in performance on a standardized test. As such, school districts should conduct their research and study of the four-day school week to ensure it will produce the overall outcomes it was adopted to achieve.

EXTENDED-YEAR CALENDAR

While the dominant school calendar in America continues to be the traditional school calendar with 180 days scheduled from approximately Labor Day to Memorial Day annually, the extended-year calendar increases the number of school days annually. While this can be accomplished in several ways, Pedersen (2015) stated that school district leaders often use extended-year calendars to decrease the summer slide, increase the amount of instructional time, and create additional learning opportunities during the summer. The last idea is often used for special education students. The Individuals with Disabilities Education Act (IDEA) does not mandate that a specific procedure be followed to determine if a student is entitled to additional school days during the summer to help mitigate the summer slide (Burke & Decker, 2017). An analysis of a child's level regression and rate of recoupment often guides Individualized Education Program (IEP) teams in determining whether an extended year is required for some students (Burke & Decker, 2017).

GLOBAL PERSPECTIVES ON SCHOOL CALENDARS

Examining school calendars globally, this section highlights academic schedules in different countries. While it is expensive to extend a school year or add days to the existing school year, by adding 30 days of intersession, students who attend the balanced school calendar and intersession classes would advance to the top third of days attended by students worldwide.

It should be noted that cultural influences, economic factors, and societal expectations shape diverse approaches to structuring the school year around the globe.

For more perspective, in addition to family dynamics and expectations, the International Trends in Mathematics and Science Study (TIMSS) illustrates the type of calendar that may contribute to academic performance. It should be noted that the United States is not performing in sixth place internationally on the TIMSS test, but instead ranked 15th on the 2019 ranking.

Table 3.1 Number of Days in School by Country

Country	Days in School
Japan	243
South Korea	220
Israel	216
Luxembourg	216
The Netherlands	200
Scotland	200
Thailand	200
Hong Kong	195
England	192
Hungary	192
Swaziland	191
Finland	190
New Zealand	190
Nigeria	190
France	185
United States	180

(Smithing & Swain, 2011)

Country	Number of Instructional Days	Calendar Type	TIMSS 4th Grade Math 2011/2015/2019
Singapore	200	Balanced	606/618/625
Republic of Korea	220	Balanced	605/608/600
Hong Kong	195	Balanced	602/615/602
Chinese Taipei (Taiwan)	190	Balanced	591/597/599
Japan	243	Balanced	585/593/593
United States	180	Traditional	541/539/535

Figure 3.2 *Top Five Performing Countries on the TIMSS Test over the Last Three Testing Cycles. The United States Ranked 15th in 2019.*

Currently, no single balanced calendar model is used unilaterally across the United States. Balanced calendars, much like the traditional school calendars, allow for various local and state holidays in addition to federal ones to be scheduled off. Below are some of the most commonly used models found in schools today:

45–15 Calendar

Using this calendar, schools are open for 45 days, followed by a 15-day break. This could be used with the average 180 school days or include additional instructional days.

60–20 Calendar

In this model, schools are open for 60 days, followed by a 20-day break. This could be used with the average 180 school days or include additional instructional days.

90–30 Calendar

In the 90–30 calendar, students attend school for 90 days, followed by a 30-day break. This could be used with the average 180 school days or include additional instructional days.

Orchard Plan

Glines explains this model where "with a supplement in salary, teachers worked 225 days . . . with a 60–15 calendar." The students "went on vacation at the same time, with 20% of the class having a three-week vacation. This allowed students to rotate by groups of seven and reduced the maximum number of students in a classroom at a given time."

Dual-Track Calendar

This model uses a school-within-a-school approach where two calendars exist—a traditional 10-month calendar and a 12-month calendar. This model also allows personalized instruction, remote learning, and/or intersessions.

45-Day Four-Track Design Calendar

Adopting this format allows for 45 days of instruction and a 15-day break. This is similar to the 45–15 design, except that it uses rotating tracks of 25% of the student population on break, with the other 75% attending school.

60-Day Four-Track Design Calendar

This calendar follows the 45-day four-track design but has 60 days of instruction and a 10-day break. Once again, the students are placed on a rotating schedule, with 25% of the student population always on break and the other 75% attending school.

Build Your Own Balanced Calendar

This model allows local leaders and members of the learning community to co-construct a calendar that meets the school district's needs. By looking back at five years of student and staff attendance to identify patterns and community events that often conflict with the school calendar, such as the county fair, school leaders can often construct a school calendar that better meets the needs of the local learning community. For example, below, you will find a crosswalk between a balanced and traditional school calendar in the same state. In this case, there is a scheduled school break roughly every five to seven weeks, often tied to a federal, state, or local holiday or tradition.

Table 3.2 Sample School Calendar Comparison

	Balanced Calendar	Traditional Calendar
First Day of School	August 3	August 18
No School	August 13	
No School	August 16	
No School	September 3	September 3
No School: Labor Day	September 6	September 6
No School: Fall Break	October 11–15	October 11–15
No School: Fall Break	October 18–22	
No School: Thanksgiving Break	November 22–26	November 24–26
No School: Winter Break	December 20–31	December 20–31
No School: MLK, Jr. Day	January 17	January 17
No School: Mid-Winter Break	February 18–25	February 21–25
No School: Spring Break	March 25–April 1	March 25–April 1
No School: Spring Break	April 4–8	
No School: Memorial Day	May 30	May 30
No School: Memorial Break	May 30–June 3	
Last Day of School	June 22	June 10

CHALLENGES AND CONSIDERATIONS

Developing an agreed-upon academic school calendar can be a complex process. Stakeholders often have strong opinions based on their lived experiences, and the history of school calendars reflects this complexity. From the early days of education, variations in the school calendar have existed to accommodate different needs and contexts. The traditional school calendar, developed for an agrarian and manufacturing society, is still dominant today and is challenged by the balanced school calendar offering a more continuous approach to learning.

The balanced school calendar is not new, with examples dating back to the 1800s in England and the United States. In the modern era, interest in alternative calendars has grown, driven by concerns about summer learning loss and the need for continuous learning opportunities. Research suggests that a balanced school calendar can positively affect student achievement, attendance, and engagement.

Despite these benefits, the traditional school calendar remains dominant in many parts of the United States. However, there is growing recognition of the need for change, particularly as educational goals and societal needs continue to evolve. The balanced school calendar offers a flexible and adaptable alternative to meet the needs of diverse communities.

As we look to the future of education, it is essential to consider the impact of school calendars on student learning and well-being. By exploring different approaches and learning from global perspectives, we can work toward developing school calendars that support the success of all students and the staff supporting them each day.

Chapter 4

Redefining Time

The Future of School Calendar Reform

In a more flexible school system, students would have the opportunity to attend school when they need additional support or instruction rather than being bound to a fixed schedule. This system would allow for personalized learning experiences tailored to each student's needs, ensuring they have the necessary resources and support to succeed.

One aspect of flexibility could involve a mastery-based approach, where students advance through the material at their own pace, mastering concepts before moving on to new ones. This approach would allow students to spend more time on challenging topics while moving more quickly through material they grasp easily.

Additionally, a flexible school system might include alternative schedules, such as year-round schooling or extended school days, to provide more time for learning and support. This would give students more opportunities to receive individualized instruction and teacher support.

School calendar reform refers to efforts to change schools' traditional academic calendars. The traditional calendar typically includes a long summer break, with shorter breaks during the school year for holidays and vacations. School calendar reform and efficient use of time are essential for several reasons, including reducing learning loss, improving academic performance, and addressing equity issues, current lifestyles, and educator retention. While many of the topics discussed in this chapter have been fully implemented in some cases across the nation, in other cases, these ideas may be new. Each of these topics deserves more research and investigation.

REDUCING LEARNING LOSS

Long summer breaks can lead to learning loss, especially for students from disadvantaged backgrounds. A more balanced calendar can reduce this loss by providing consistent learning opportunities throughout the year.

IMPROVING ACADEMIC PERFORMANCE

By spreading out the school breaks and providing more instructional days through intersessions and summer school, students have more time to master concepts and engage in deeper learning, leading to improved academic performance. A balanced school calendar can improve student outcomes, including higher academic achievement and graduation rates. This can have long-term benefits for students and society (Hornak, 2015).

ADDRESSING EQUITY ISSUES

Students from low-income families often lack access to educational resources and opportunities outside of school. A balanced calendar can help level the playing field by providing more consistent access to learning and other resources such as breakfast and lunch for all students.

ALIGNS BETTER WITH CURRENT LIFESTYLES

The traditional school calendar was developed to accommodate an agrarian society, where children were needed to work on farms during the summer. Today, most families no longer rely on agriculture, so a more flexible calendar can better align with modern lifestyles and needs. A more balanced calendar can make it easier for working parents to manage childcare during school breaks, as they are more evenly distributed throughout the year allowing families to better budget for childcare during the periodic breaks rather than 12 consecutive weeks on a traditional calendar.

EDUCATOR RETENTION

A balanced calendar can reduce burnout among teachers by providing more frequent breaks and opportunities for professional development, leading to increased morale and retention rates.

PERSONALIZED LEARNING

A more flexible school calendar can allow personalized learning experiences tailored to each student's needs. This can help students achieve their full potential and develop the skills necessary for success in the future.

PREPARATION FOR THE FUTURE

The future job market will likely require different skills than in the past. A flexible school calendar can help schools adapt their curriculum to better prepare students for the future workforce.

ADDRESSING LEARNING GAPS

Long summer breaks can contribute to learning loss, particularly for students from disadvantaged backgrounds. A balanced calendar can help reduce these gaps by providing consistent learning opportunities throughout the year.

PROMOTING INNOVATION

Flexible school calendars can promote innovation in education by allowing schools to experiment with different approaches to teaching and learning. This can lead to new and more effective methods of education.

MEETING THE NEEDS OF A CHANGING SOCIETY

The school calendar is one of the few things that has been held steadfast over the past 135 years in education. As society changes, so too must our educational system. A flexible school calendar can help schools adapt to the changing needs of society, students, families, and communities.

Overall, school calendar reform is vital in shaping the future of education by promoting personalized learning, addressing learning gaps, preparing students for the future, and promoting innovation in education.

Several innovative approaches to school scheduling have been developed to meet the evolving needs of students, families, and their communities. As noted throughout this book, these approaches include a balanced school calendar, flexible scheduling, extended school days, intersessions, compressed school weeks, community-based learning, and customized learning plans.

The previous chapter discussed intersessions and a compressed school week. Therefore, this chapter will focus on school calendar reform, which has not yet been discussed.

FLEXIBLE SCHEDULING

Some schools are adopting flexible scheduling options, such as allowing students to start and end the school day at different times or offering online classes that can be completed at any time. This can help accommodate the diverse needs of students and families.

EXTENDED SCHOOL DAY

Extending the school day allows for more instructional time, which can lead to improved academic outcomes. This approach can also help working parents by providing their children with a safe and structured environment after regular school hours.

COMMUNITY-BASED LEARNING

Community-based learning programs involve students in real-world projects and activities that benefit the local community. This approach helps students develop essential skills and connections while meeting community needs.

CUSTOMIZED LEARNING PLANS

Some schools are adopting customized learning plans for students, where students have more control over their learning pace and path. This can help meet students' individual needs and promote a more personalized learning experience.

Regardless of the type of calendar reform, there is no substitute for excellent instruction, solid class management, and proficiency-based grading, also known as competency-based education, where teaching, learning, and assessments focus on students demonstrating mastery of specific skills and competencies. Unlike traditional grading systems that are often based on seat time and may rely heavily on standardized tests, proficiency-based grading emphasizes students' ability to demonstrate what they know and can do. Key features include the following:

Clear Learning Targets

Proficiency-based grading begins with clearly defined learning targets or competencies students must master. These targets are often aligned with academic standards and are communicated to students at the outset of a course or unit.

Flexible Pace

In proficiency-based grading systems, students can progress through material at their own pace. Students who master material quickly can move on to more challenging material, while those who need more time can receive additional support and practice.

Multiple Assessment Opportunities

Proficiency-based grading allows students multiple opportunities to demonstrate mastery of a competency. This might include quizzes, tests, projects, presentations, or other assessments enabling students to show their understanding differently.

Focus on Growth

Proficiency-based grading emphasizes student growth and improvement over time. Instead of focusing solely on grades, the emphasis is on students developing the knowledge, skills, and attitudes necessary for success.

Feedback and Reflection

Proficiency-based grading often includes regular teacher feedback and opportunities for students to reflect on their learning. This feedback helps students understand their strengths and areas for improvement and encourages them to take ownership of their learning.

Competency-Based Progression

In some proficiency-based grading systems, students advance to the next level of learning once they have demonstrated mastery of all required competencies. This allows students to move through the material at their own pace and help ensure that they are well-prepared for future learning.

CURRENT CHALLENGES AND LIMITATIONS

The dominant school calendar used nationwide continues to be the traditional school calendar. This particular calendar has approximately 180 school days and is operated from approximately September to June annually. While the history of the traditional calendar has been discussed in previous chapters, the current challenges and limitations of the traditional calendar still need to be addressed.

Seen as one of the most inequitable things in education, the traditional school calendar plans for remediation annually. In fact, according to Ready Nation, in 2015, schools across the nation spent 21 billion dollars remediating the learning losses that the traditional calendar contributed to each year. In other words, school districts are operating a school calendar that plans for remediation (Clifford, Christenson, & O'Connor, 2015). Due in part to the fact that most Americans went to school and likely attended school on a traditional school calendar, parents and guardians often think that the current model is best. They have not studied school calendars or educational systems; instead, because they attended school a certain way, it should stand. The long summer intermission limits a school district from providing academic support and multiple daily meals. The current calendar contributes to the learning gaps educators nationwide are working hard to close. It is time for a systemic change. What other profession schedules 12–13 weeks off consecutively? The traditional calendar is outdated and no longer in alignment with current lifestyles.

RETHINKING THE USE OF TIME

Extending the school day, balancing the calendar, and a myriad of other ideas have been previously discussed in this book. However, some districts rethink the time available to instruct students. Acceleration and extended days are additional ideas considered in schools nationwide (Woulfin & Spitzer, 2022).

ACCELERATED LEARNING

Accelerated learning programs aim to increase learning (Woulfin & Spitzer, 2022). As a result, accelerated learning programs often speed up the teaching and learning that occurs to meet designated outcomes. Frequently, according to Woulfin and Spitzer (2022), accelerated learning requires blocks of time to provide intensive instruction to impact test scores. As with any educational initiative, careful planning, hiring, and implementation can impact the outcomes. Offering educational leaders the flexibility to create accelerated programming can yield benefits if supported accordingly (Woulfin & Spitzer, 2022).

EXTENDING THE SCHOOL DAY

As indicated, accelerated learning often speeds up teaching and learning. This section will focus on extending the school day. Many schools, especially secondary schools, will implement a zero hour or a seventh hour to the school day. By doing so, students can attempt to recover credits while taking a full schedule of other classes. This model often works with summer school to help students remain on pace to graduate on time. The notion of extending the school day can also be framed as an intersession of sorts.

In some cases, school districts operating on a balanced school calendar have opted away from offering an intersession during a scheduled school break to extend the school day for select students to be pre-taught concepts, remediated, or enriched at the elementary and middle levels. This model takes advantage of the intersession principles and allows staff to rejuvenate during a scheduled school break rather than teaching intersession. Sullivan (2022) and Dill (2022) both question the feasibility of implementing an extended school day, as finding the staff to teach an extended day is often challenging.

VIRTUAL LEARNING

Teachers are turning to digital online tools at a record pace to enhance instruction delivery (Caprara, 2021). Online learning tools have become widespread post-pandemic because of the potential for providing more flexible access to content and instruction regardless of the time of day or night (Means et al. 2009). While there are numerous ethical components to virtual learning, such as access, trust, and more, persisting in the status quo of the traditional school calendar may continue to leave students vulnerable to practices that may underserve students and leave a lasting impact.

EQUITY AND ACCESS CONSIDERATIONS, INCLUDING INVOLVING YOUR LEARNING COMMUNITY

As with any reform initiative, it is essential to consider equity and access and involve your learning community regarding the why. One of the most inequitable things in education is the traditional school calendar. The summer learning loss may have an even more significant effect on lower-income children who may already be struggling (Lundstrom, 2005). If this pattern continues, in a few short years, a child could be several years behind, accounting for 80–100% of the gap between low-income children and children from the middle class (Lundstrom, 2005). The impact on math is typically significant (Schulte, 2009). Lundstrom (2005) stated that 61% of low-income families do not have books at home, and schools are some of the only resources available to many children. Haeberlin (2002) acknowledged that most children do not retain their academic knowledge over a 12-week summer break from school. Ballinger (1995) stated that the primary reason for changing the balanced school calendar from a traditional one is to eliminate the significant learning loss over summer break.

According to Morse (1992), disadvantaged students forget more during summer break than any other child. Moving to a balanced school calendar will increase the performance of students who may not have readily available resources and may not be supported at home (Haeberlin, 2002). Suppose the average child maintains an academic level or has the opportunity to gain exposure to math concepts. The gap between an average middle-class child and a low-income child can become tremendous. Traditional calendar schools disadvantage disadvantaged children more significantly by holding to a long summer intermission between school years (Haeberlin, 2002). School officials need to be aware of the unintended consequence of continuing to operate on an outdated school calendar. Because summer recess is most detrimental to math, Kneese and Knight (1995) reported that balanced calendar schools have a significant advantage over their counterparts on the traditional calendar when facing summer learning loss. By shortening the 12-week summer break, schools can minimize the regression caused by the summer recess (Haeberlin, 2002). The newest research indicates that the balanced school calendar positively impacts all students (Hornak, 2015).

In addition, schools are now access points for students to receive two meals each day and often a weekend food pack that supplies food for a student to eat over the weekend. During the long summer intermission, school districts, usually well-intended, attempt to provide food by delivering food to specific neighborhoods or establishing various pickup locations. However, in the end, nothing replaces the day-to-day access the school year offers.

Finally, with any reform initiative, it is essential to ensure that stakeholders understand the need for change. School districts often use one or more of the following as a compelling reason when considering a shift in the balanced school calendar.

ADDRESSING UNFINISHED LEARNING

On the heels of a pandemic, school districts are grappling with ways to address the learning gaps that online instruction and time away from the classroom may have caused. Adding school days to the school year is costly for school leaders. Rather than adding days, the balanced school calendar provides additional instructional days when targeted students are selected to return to school for real-time remediation, pre-teaching of concepts, or enrichment during a scheduled school break. Balanced calendar school districts can add 30–45 days of additional instruction when implementing intersession during scheduled school breaks and the summer.

IMPROVING ACCESS TO STUDENTS

As noted, the traditional calendar is one of the most inequitable things in education. While in school, providing students multiple meals daily, access to educational instruction and materials, care, and so much more has become second nature for schools. However, many students lose access to food and educational materials during a scheduled break or a 12–13-week summer.

IMPROVING ATTENDANCE AND HEALTH

Balanced calendar schools can be deep cleaned more frequently. As such, the attendance levels of the students and staff tend to be better than the attendance rates on the traditional school calendar. In addition, reducing the length of summer tends to keep students and families more in touch with their schools (Baber et al., 2021).

IMPACTING TEACHER BURNOUT/MORALE

Educators with experience working on the balanced calendar credit the year-round calendar and believe that it substantially enhances the professional environment due to the frequency of breaks. Teachers also share improved morale and motivation and less burnout and stress while working on a balanced calendar.

IMPACTING THE NATIONWIDE SUBSTITUTE TEACHER SHORTAGE

Employees on the balanced calendar have better overall attendance levels than their counterparts on the traditional calendar. This is because balanced calendar schools are deep cleaned more frequently, and employees on the balanced calendar often schedule annual dentist and doctor appointments during a scheduled school break rather than taking a sick day during the week.

While many of these ideas need additional research, several are being implemented in schools nationwide today. Each, in coordination with a balanced school calendar, may benefit students and staff substantially. School is the conduit for acquiring knowledge, skills, and social and emotional development (Radinger & Boeskens, 2021). Educational reform initiatives and their successful implementation can significantly impact the future of education. It is time for continued innovation and collaboration in reimagining the school calendar to serve better the needs of students, families, and communities. This chapter has explored the concept of school calendar reform and the potential benefits of a more flexible school system. By rethinking how school time is structured, educators can create more personalized learning experiences for students and provide additional support to those who need it most. Whether through mastery-based approaches, alternative schedules, or other innovative strategies, the future of school calendar reform holds promise for improving student outcomes and ensuring that all students can succeed.

Implementing a more flexible school system will require careful planning and consideration. Educators will need to develop new strategies for scheduling and instruction and may need additional training and support to implement these changes effectively. It will also be essential to involve stakeholders, including students, parents, and community members, in the decision-making process to ensure that the new system meets the needs of all involved. Additionally, ongoing evaluation and adjustment will be necessary to assess the impact of the changes and make improvements as needed. Overall, while school calendar reform presents challenges, it also offers exciting opportunities to improve education and better meet the needs of students in the 21st century (Johnson, 2023).

Chapter 5

Modified School Calendars Today

In response to the challenges posed by traditional academic calendars, schools are increasingly turning to modified schedules to mitigate learning loss and enhance educational outcomes. These modifications include adopting four-day school weeks, extending the school year by adding days to the calendar, implementing intersession breaks for targeted learning opportunities, and incorporating hybrid learning models. These approaches reflect a growing recognition of the need for flexibility and innovation in education to meet the diverse needs of students and address the complexities of modern society.

LEARNING LOSS

The widespread learning loss resulting from pandemic-related school closures has prompted administrators to reassess the conventional school calendar. Recognizing the urgent need for timely remediation among the country's most vulnerable students, some propose substantial changes, including an earlier start date, a later end date, and extended breaks throughout the year. This reimagined calendar aims to facilitate swift interventions for children in need while providing enriching opportunities for those who are not facing academic challenges.

David Banks, school chancellor of New York City, has advocated for his district to attend classes not only during the regular school week but also on Saturdays and throughout the summer. This proposal is geared toward addressing the learning gaps exacerbated by the disruptions caused by the pandemic. In a similar vein, Hartford Public Schools in Connecticut have already taken steps to open several buildings on Saturdays, offering around 800 students who have fallen behind a chance to accelerate their learning.

ADDITIONAL DAYS

The focus on extended school time as a strategy to enhance academic achievement has gained attention, particularly in response to the significant learning loss experienced by vulnerable students during pandemic-related school closures. The idea revolves around modifying the traditional school calendar and incorporating an earlier start date, a later end date, and extended breaks throughout the year. Proponents argue that this approach can bring both learning and nonacademic benefits, providing timely remediation for struggling students and enrichment for those performing well.

U.S. education secretary Miguel Cardona has even expressed support for this shift in mindset. Questioning the conventional system that leaves kids disengaged for two months during the summer, he urged a reevaluation of the existing educational structure in November. The call to rethink traditional academic calendars reflects a growing awareness of the need for innovative approaches to education that can better accommodate the diverse learning needs of students and mitigate the impact of unforeseen disruptions like pandemics (Napalitano, 2022).

Patall, Cooper, and Allen's work in 2010 examined 15 empirical studies conducted since 1985. The literature suggests that while research designs for causal inferences are generally weak, extending school time can effectively support student learning. The findings emphasize the importance of considering how time is utilized, with the most consistent positive results observed in studies employing strong research designs.

In conclusion, while the research on extended school time presents promising insights, it acknowledges the need for stronger research designs, consideration of nonacademic outcomes, and a comprehensive understanding of the optimal amount of additional time. The ongoing discourse calls for continued research to determine the conditions under which extending school time proves most beneficial for student learning and development.

FOUR-DAY SCHOOL WEEKS

A growing trend across the United States has seen hundreds of schools opting for a four-day week (Cohen, 2023). Between 1999 and 2019, the popularity of four-day school weeks surged, a trend further accelerated by the pandemic. Districts adopted shortened weeks as a strategy to retain teachers and reduce costs. Some districts managed to maintain instructional hours by extending the school day, but this adjustment still led to a reduction in learning time by three to four hours per week. While qualitative data indicated positive feedback from families and educators regarding the four-day schedules, challenges such as teacher retention and budget constraints persisted largely unchanged (Luna, 2022). The motivations behind this shift vary among districts, yet the adoption of this model is becoming more widespread. While the evidence supporting the benefits is still in its early stages, there is a noticeable embrace of this approach by parents, teachers, administrators, and students alike. School districts nationwide are increasingly considering and implementing four-day school weeks as a strategic move to achieve multiple objectives, including cost savings, improved student attendance, and enhanced teacher recruitment. Each month, it seems that the popularity of this calendar increases (Peetz, 2024).

The decision for schools to transition to a four-day school week is fueled by diverse factors unique to each district. Whether motivated by financial considerations, the desire to boost student engagement, or the need to attract and retain quality educators, schools are recognizing the potential advantages of this condensed schedule. As this educational paradigm gains momentum, stakeholders are navigating the uncharted waters of this evolving model, exploring its impact on educational outcomes, student well-being, and the overall school dynamics.

As parents find themselves adjusting to a modified academic calendar, teachers are adapting instructional strategies to maximize the shortened week's effectiveness. Administrators are evaluating the financial implications and potential savings, which can be redirected to other critical areas. Concurrently, students are experiencing an altered school routine, raising questions about the impact on their learning experience and academic performance.

The conversation around four-day school weeks extends beyond the immediate benefits of cost reduction and increased attendance. It delves into broader considerations, such as the potential for enhanced teacher recruitment and retention, as educators seek a work–life balance that aligns with this innovative schedule (Lipson, 2023). Districts navigate the intricacies of implementing this model while addressing concerns related to childcare, extracurricular activities, and the overall educational landscape.

While the evidence supporting the widespread adoption of four-day school weeks is still emerging, the current momentum suggests that stakeholders are open to exploring alternative educational structures. As more districts join this trend, ongoing research and comprehensive evaluations will provide valuable insights into the long-term effects and implications for the future of education in the United States. The shift toward a four-day school week reflects a response to the evolving needs of educational institutions and their communities.

WHY ARE PEOPLE SWITCHING?

The paradigm of the four-day school week is making waves across the educational landscape, with a notable shift observed in just over 2,100 schools spanning 26 states. This transformative approach, as indicated by the latest estimate from the Four-Day School Week Policy Research Team at Oregon State University, reflects a strategic move by educational institutions. Motivated by multifaceted objectives, this shift is not merely a change in scheduling but a calculated response to the evolving needs of schools nationwide.

One of the primary drivers behind the adoption of the four-day school week is the compelling quest for teacher recruitment. In an era where the demand for skilled educators surpasses the available supply, schools are leveraging this innovative scheduling model to attract and retain quality teaching professionals. The condensed schedule offers educators a flexible work arrangement, aligning with the changing dynamics of the modern workforce seeking a harmonious balance between professional and personal commitments.

Financial considerations play a pivotal role in this educational reform. The shift to a four-day school week is seen as a strategic avenue for cost savings, with school districts eyeing potential financial benefits that can be redirected to address various pressing needs. This financial reconfiguration extends beyond operational costs, influencing resource allocation, infrastructure management, and the overall fiscal health of educational institutions.

Another driving force behind this educational shift is the aspiration to boost student attendance. Schools anticipate that the condensed schedule will infuse a renewed sense of engagement and dynamism into the learning environment, ultimately enticing students to actively participate in their educational journey. However, the alteration in routine prompts critical questions about the potential consequences on academic performance, social dynamics, and the overall learning experience.

As the number of schools embracing the four-day week continues to rise, it becomes increasingly imperative to delve into the nuanced landscape of benefits and consequences associated with this innovative model. The research team at Oregon State University stands at the forefront of this exploration, conducting comprehensive studies to shed light on the multifaceted impact of the four-day school week.

Beyond the immediate benefits, educators, parents, administrators, and policymakers grapple with the complexities of adjusting to this modified academic calendar. The implications extend into areas such as childcare arrangements, extracurricular activities, and the broader educational landscape. In this era of educational innovation, the four-day school week emerges as a compelling experiment, demanding a thoughtful understanding of its effects on various stakeholders and the overall educational ecosystem.

The ongoing research initiatives led by the Four-Day School Week policy research team are poised to contribute valuable insights that extend beyond mere scheduling adjustments. These insights will shape the ongoing dialogue around the future trajectory of education in the United States, providing a foundation for informed decision-making and the continued evolution of educational practices (News Staff, 2023).

SAVING MONEY

The adoption of four-day school weeks is gaining popularity across the United States, and this phenomenon is rooted in various strategic considerations that extend beyond mere scheduling adjustments. One of the prominent drivers behind this trend is the potential for significant cost reductions, especially in the realm of building expenses and *power consumption.* As detailed in "Why Four-Day Weeks Are Becoming Popular among US Schools?," the economic benefits associated with the four-day week model ripple through different facets of school operations, presenting a compelling case for educational institutions seeking financial optimization (2022).

One notable avenue through which four-day weeks contribute to expenditure reduction is in the realm of transportation costs. By operating on a condensed schedule, schools can curtail bus transportation services by one day each week, leading to a tangible decrease in fuel consumption. This not only aligns with environmentally conscious practices but also translates into substantial financial savings for school districts. The ripple effect extends to reduced wear and tear on transportation assets, contributing to long-term cost-effectiveness.

Beyond transportation, the shift to a four-day school week introduces opportunities for minimizing lighting and other facility-related expenses. With one fewer day of active facility use, schools can implement energy-saving measures, such as optimizing lighting systems and regulating heating, ventilation, and air conditioning (HVAC) units. These adjustments not only contribute to lower operational costs but also align with sustainability initiatives, fostering a more environmentally friendly educational ecosystem.

Additionally, the consolidation of school activities into a four-day week allows for more efficient utilization of school facilities. With fewer operational days, schools can implement strategic scheduling to optimize maintenance and cleaning activities, reducing the need for continuous facility upkeep. This streamlining of maintenance efforts contributes to extended equipment life cycles and lower maintenance expenditures, ensuring that financial resources are allocated judiciously.

The financial advantages of four-day school weeks extend beyond immediate operational considerations to encompass broader financial planning and resource allocation. School districts, grappling with budget constraints, view this innovative scheduling model as a viable strategy for optimizing financial resources. The potential for reduced transportation, facility-related costs, and enhanced operational efficiency positions the four-day week as a strategic tool in addressing fiscal challenges faced by educational institutions nationwide.

As the adoption of four-day school weeks continues to grow, it prompts a nuanced examination of the multifaceted implications associated with this scheduling model. While the economic benefits are apparent, educators, parents, administrators, and policymakers must navigate the complexities of adjusting to a modified academic calendar. This necessitates a comprehensive understanding of the potential consequences on student learning, extracurricular activities, and the overall educational experience.

In conclusion, the surge in popularity of four-day school weeks in the United States is intricately linked to the pursuit of financial sustainability and operational efficiency. The economic advantages, ranging from reduced transportation costs to streamlined facility management, position this scheduling model as a noteworthy innovation in the ever-evolving landscape of American education. Ongoing research and thoughtful evaluation will be crucial in shaping the future trajectory of this transformative approach to schooling.

TEACHER RETENTION AND RECRUITMENT

A noteworthy trend is emerging in small, rural schools grappling with teacher shortages—the adoption of a four-day school week, strategically choosing to have either Mondays or Fridays off, thereby providing teachers and students with a coveted three-day weekend every week. This innovative approach aims to address staffing challenges while introducing a novel scheduling paradigm that has garnered attention from education stakeholders (News Staff, 2023).

The essence of this trend lies in its adaptability to the unique needs of small, rural schools, where teacher shortages can have pronounced effects on educational continuity. By opting for a four-day school week, these institutions seek to attract and retain educators by offering an appealing work-life balance, a factor increasingly recognized as crucial in the competitive landscape of education recruitment.

To compensate for the reduced instructional time resulting from the shortened week, school officials implement strategic measures, such as extending the daily schedule on the remaining four days. This thoughtful adjustment aims to ensure that the overall instructional hours align with educational standards, maintaining the quality of education despite the condensed schedule.

Interestingly, in places where schools have embraced this scheduling innovation, school district leaders are reporting notable increases in applications from teachers and other job seekers. The allure of a consistent three-day weekend appears to resonate with educators, addressing their desire for a more flexible and balanced work schedule. This shift not only serves as a solution to teacher shortages but also contributes to a positive work environment, potentially enhancing teacher satisfaction and retention rates.

One compelling example of this trend can be observed in Montana, where schools have successfully made the switch to a four-day week. The impact of this change is not only evident in the altered schedule but also in the broader context of its effectiveness in attracting qualified staff. Montana's experience serves as a case study for understanding the implications, both positive and potentially challenging, associated with the implementation of a four-day school week.

As education leaders in Montana assess the outcomes of this innovative approach, they contribute valuable insights to the ongoing dialogue surrounding the adaptation of school schedules to meet the evolving needs of educators and students (Amestoy, 2023). The Montana case study prompts discussions on the potential replicability of this model in other regions facing similar challenges, encouraging a collaborative exploration of solutions to teacher shortages in rural areas.

The adoption of four-day school weeks by small, rural schools navigating teacher shortages represents a dynamic response to the evolving landscape of education. Beyond being a scheduling adjustment, this trend serves as a testament to the willingness of educational institutions to innovate and tailor their approaches to address specific challenges. As the impact of this scheduling model continues to unfold, it sparks conversations about the future of school schedules, teacher recruitment, and the pursuit of a resilient and adaptable education system. Not only does this strategy seem to be attracting teachers, but it is retaining them as well (Gonzalez, 2023).

The advantages of transitioning to a four-day school week extend beyond teacher retention, encompassing a spectrum of benefits for both educators and students. Noteworthy outcomes include heightened attendance rates among students, providing them with an additional day to explore diverse opportunities such as job shadowing, engagement in dual credit programs, and participation in volunteer activities. This expanded scope for student involvement aligns with the evolving expectations of modern education, fostering a dynamic learning environment.

Furthermore, the condensed schedule offers teachers valuable time for planning, collaboration, and professional development, addressing critical aspects of their roles that often face time constraints in traditional five-day weeks. The emphasis on a balanced "work/life" equilibrium emerges as a defining feature of the four-day school week, acknowledging the importance of holistic well-being for both educators and students.

In the end, it appears that the rise of the four-day school week emerges as a response to the pressing challenges faced in the teaching profession. Not only is the profession in crisis with remuneration, but some districts have even begun offering housing for their teachers (Powel, 2024). By strategically leveraging innovative scheduling, schools seek not only to attract and retain teachers but also to cultivate an environment conducive to enhanced morale, academic quality, and overall well-being. As this educational paradigm continues to evolve, it prompts reflection on the broader implications for educational systems nationwide, encouraging a reevaluation of traditional structures in favor of adaptable and teacher-centric approaches (Strategic Communication, 2022).

TEACHER MORALE

In the evolving landscape of education, the adoption of four-day school schedules has gained momentum, with 17 states embracing this innovative approach as early as 2008. This paradigm shift involves extending the hours of each school day to meet instructional time requirements, culminating in a welcome break every Friday. The driving force behind the widespread adoption of the four-day schedule lies in its potential to address pressing challenges faced by school districts, ranging from transportation and operating costs to attendance-related concerns.

The primary impetus for school districts opting for the four-day schedule is the tangible reduction in transportation and operating costs. By condensing the school week into four days, districts experience cost savings in various facets, including fuel consumption for buses and a reduction in facility-related expenses. This strategic maneuver allows schools to reallocate resources more efficiently, fostering financial sustainability in an era marked by budgetary constraints.

Beyond the economic advantages, school districts have reported noteworthy positive outcomes associated with the four-day school week. A significant reduction in absenteeism and dropout rates has been observed, suggesting that the condensed schedule contributes to a more engaged and committed student body. This positive trend aligns with the broader goal of enhancing overall educational outcomes and student success, with some districts even using this reform as a recruitment strategy (Peetz, 2024).

A pivotal study conducted by the Colorado Department of Education nearly 20 years ago in 2006 shed light on the widespread acceptance of the four-day schedule within school communities. Analyzing the experiences of 62 out of 178 school districts in Colorado, the report revealed that a staggering 80–90% of teachers, parents, and students favored the four-day schedule over the conventional five-day counterpart. This overwhelming support underscores the effectiveness of the new paradigm in meeting the needs and preferences of key stakeholders in the education system.

Surveys conducted as part of the study further illuminated the transformative impact of the switch to a four-day schedule. Notably, school morale experienced a marked improvement, indicating that the innovative scheduling approach positively influenced the overall atmosphere within educational institutions. The findings suggest that the four-day school week goes beyond merely addressing logistical and financial considerations; it also fosters a more positive and vibrant learning environment.

As the adoption of four-day school schedules continues to expand across states, this innovative approach prompts reflection on the potential for reshaping the traditional education model. The balance between economic efficiency, student engagement, and stakeholder satisfaction positions the four-day school week as a dynamic and adaptable solution for contemporary educational challenges (Facts, 2022).

MODELING FOUR-DAY WORK WEEKS

The discourse around four-day models is gaining prominence not only in the realm of education but rather has followed some of the trends in various other professions across the nation, marking a transformative shift in traditional work paradigms (Valley, 2023).

The momentum behind the transition to four-day work weeks has received a compelling endorsement through a six-month trial initiated in February 2022. Thirty-three companies, spanning six countries, courageously embraced a reduction in their employees' workload to four days or 32 hours a week. This groundbreaking experiment, orchestrated by 4 Day Week Global, aimed to evaluate whether employees could maintain or even enhance productivity within an 80% timeframe while receiving the same compensation. The outcomes were resoundingly positive, with participating companies reporting increased revenue, heightened employee health and well-being, and a notable positive impact on the environment. Encouraged by this success, a hundred more companies, collectively employing thousands, are contemplating or have already initiated the adoption of this progressive four-day workweek approach (Lipson, 2023).

Similar to this paradigm shift in the professional landscape, four-day school weeks are experiencing a surge in popularity among American adults. What was once perceived as a niche concept, primarily embraced by remote rural districts seeking cost-saving measures, has now captured the imagination of a broader demographic. A remarkable 53% of U.S. adults express support for the implementation of a four-day school week in their local communities (Prothero, 2023).

The convergence of these trends reflects a broader societal reassessment of conventional work and educational structures. The success of the four-day workweek trial demonstrates that innovative scheduling models can yield positive outcomes not only for businesses but also for the well-being of employees. Simultaneously, the growing endorsement of four-day school weeks among American adults suggests a willingness to explore alternative educational frameworks that align with evolving societal needs and preferences (Prothero, 2023).

As conversations around these transformative models continue to gain traction, the collective shift toward more flexible and efficient work and educational arrangements appears to be an integral part of adapting to the dynamic demands of the contemporary world. The intersections between professional and educational realms present opportunities for holistic changes that prioritize productivity, employee satisfaction, and a healthier work–life balance.

WHAT HAPPENS ON THE FIFTH DAY?

In certain communities, the transition to a four-day school week is proving to be a boon for families. The Turner district in north-central Montana, for instance, where the decision to observe a four-day week, with Fridays off, is strategically designed to address challenges arising from extracurricular events. Superintendent Tony Warren highlights a common scenario where basketball games, often located three or more hours away, result in a significantly reduced students' presence at school on Fridays. The implementation of a four-day week mitigates such disruptions and contributes to a more family-friendly schedule (*The Sacramento*, 2023).

A case in point is the public schools in Havre, Montana, which adopted a four-day school week in the academic year 2022–2023. This transition prompted proactive measures from the local Boys and Girls Club, anticipating an increased demand for childcare services. Tim Brurud, the program's executive director, adeptly adjusted operating hours to align with the extended school days from Monday through Thursday. The club extended its services from noon to 6 p.m. on Fridays, demonstrating flexibility to meet the evolving needs of families within the community (Rispens, 2023).

The trend toward a four-day school week also gained traction in Montana, with 222 schools, more than one-quarter of the total, operating on this schedule by the end of the 2022–2023 academic year. This marks a significant increase of 47 schools from the previous year, signaling a growing acceptance of this alternative educational model.

Under the new schedule, Mondays witnessed a shift in traditional lessons, making room for optional programming catering to diverse student needs. This includes academic support programs for students lagging behind grade level, engaging field trips, internships, and specialized support for special education. Sports activities, games, and practices will continue as usual on Mondays. Additionally, the district plans to offer childcare services on these *fifth days* at a cost to parents, creating a convenient solution for families seeking extended care. The district emphasizes its commitment to providing enrichment opportunities on Mondays, aligning with staff professional development days scheduled once or twice a month. This comprehensive approach not only redefines the weekly academic schedule but also showcases a dedication to the holistic development and support of students and their families (Wallington, 2022).

CONCERNS

Despite the reluctance of many Americans to embrace a four-day school week, challenges in recruiting and retaining educators persist across districts. One survey indicated that 48% of those polled believe that increasing teachers' salaries represent the most effective solution to address the shortage, while 13% favor providing stipends or granting teachers more autonomy over the curriculum (Dorn, 2023).

For example, although two remote California school districts, Leggett Valley Unified in Mendocino County and Big Sur Unified in Monterey County, have successfully implemented a shortened school week, such a model faces feasibility issues for most other schools in the state. California's Education Code mandates schools to conduct classes five days a week or risk reduced funding. Despite exemptions granted to select districts in remote areas, the majority must adhere to the five-day schedule, with some districts abandoning or never implementing the truncated week.

Leggett Valley Unified was granted permission to operate on a four-day schedule nearly 14 years ago, which serves as a notable success story. Superintendent Jeff Ritchley emphasizes that the four-day week meets the needs of families, offering additional time for errands and doctor's visits, especially important in areas requiring extensive travel. The community strongly supported the model, with any attempt to revert to a five-day week met with resistance (Lampert, 2023).

Nationally, approximately 90% of four-day school weeks cater to rural, predominantly White populations. Notably, Colorado's 27J School District, the largest district utilizing a four-day model with nearly 23,000 students, faces challenges as a preliminary study reports a decline in home prices and student achievement. Similarly, Independence School District in Missouri, serving over 14,000 students, adopted the four-day week but encountered negative consequences.

Insights from an MIT study reveal that districts employing the four-day model have smaller portions of Black and Asian students and a higher proportion of free or reduced-price lunch-eligible students compared to five-day districts. To address potential drawbacks, policy recommendations include maintaining instructional time by either lengthening the school day or offering remedial or experiential learning opportunities on the off day when transitioning to a four-day week (Black, 2023).

Dr. Paul Thompson, an associate professor of economics at Oregon State University, noted that while the four-day week may benefit high school students, negative impacts are observed for younger grades. The findings underscore the importance of considering the age group when implementing such scheduling changes, with a focus on minimizing the potential negative effects on achievement. The experience of School District 27J outside Denver serves as a notable example, showcasing academic and community downsides associated with the adoption of the four-day school week (Sparks, 2023).

RESULTS

There are now compounding studies that are showing four-day school weeks are neutral at best. The four-day week did not appear to affect student-absenteeism rates or result in more food insecurity for students. The focus group interviews, in the meantime, fleshed out just why district leaders were willing to make the shift. They also provided context for other research showing that districts usually save below 3% of their costs, mainly in transportation, operations, and support-staff salaries, when moving to a shorter week (Kingson, 2023).

A recent study conducted by the Missouri Department of Elementary and Secondary Education has revealed that the switch to a four-day school week resulted in little to no learning loss. The findings add to the growing body of evidence suggesting positive outcomes associated with this alternative scheduling model (Hanshaw, 2023).

In Texas, several school districts in the central part of the state, including China Spring ISD, have transitioned to a four-day school week. The move was driven, in part, by the need to address a shortage of teachers. The revised schedule has proven effective in managing teacher workloads, allowing educators to utilize the additional day for essential tasks such as planning, grading, and communication with parents. Superintendent Dr. Mark Faulkner emphasized the positive impact on both students and staff, as reflected in a

September feedback survey. The balanced schedule throughout the week has contributed to improved outcomes and enhanced efficiency in various aspects of school operations (CNN, 2023).

Beyond addressing workforce challenges, the four-day school week has demonstrated potential benefits in reducing operational costs. Schools have reported savings on electricity and other building-related expenses. This financial advantage further adds to the appeal of adopting a condensed weekly schedule.

As more school districts explore alternative models to enhance educational delivery and adapt to changing circumstances, the success stories emerging from Missouri and Texas contribute valuable insights into the potential advantages of the four-day school week. The positive outcomes observed in terms of learning outcomes, teacher workload management, and cost savings provide a compelling narrative for considering innovative scheduling approaches in the realm of education (Wong, 2023). At the very least, discussions are being had now, arguing for more breaks and even longer weekends (Chipman, 2024).

WHAT DOES A TYPICAL FOUR-DAY SCHOOL LOOK LIKE

Transitioning to a shorter school week presents a range of advantages for students and educators, though it is not without its challenges. Positive outcomes have been observed in districts that have adopted the shorter week. Rice notes marked improvements in absenteeism and discipline referrals at Gayville-Volin, and similar successes have been reported by Superintendent Amy Britt in Bakersfield R-IV School District in Gainesville, Missouri. In Brighton, Colorado's School District 27J, Superintendent Chris Fiedler highlights increased graduation rates, especially among Latino students, since the implementation of a four-day school week in 2018 (Ferrarin, 2022).

On average, districts with four-day weeks extend daily hours by about an hour, resulting in students spending 85 hours less in the classroom over the school year compared to those on traditional five-day schedules. High school students often utilize the fifth day for internships, community service, or employment opportunities. Some districts go beyond and offer additional instruction for those who need it on the fifth day. Others require students struggling in reading and math to receive in-school tutoring on the fifth day, while the rest of the student body engages in at least two hours of virtual instruction (Ferrarin, 2022).

The fifth day also serves as an opportunity to provide extra mental health services to students. One middle school offers Friday group therapy for middle-school girls dealing with trauma, highlighting the holistic approach that can be integrated into the four-day school week model (Ferrarin, 2022).

"You're going to earn that extra day off. That's pretty much the vow that we all took; we're not going to show up here and have any slack," expressed one principal. Elaborating on the commitment, he stated, "We have learned how to take advantage of every opportunity and how not to waste any time so that you can optimize your educational experience and turn it up a notch." Reflecting on the impact of implementing the four-day week at the high school, he reported observing the highest attendance and lowest behavioral problems in his four years as principal (Wrigley, 2023).

In Queensland, Australia, a groundbreaking initiative is underway, allowing students the flexibility to engage in remote learning for one day each week or opt for a condensed school schedule with fewer school days. According to one of the officials there, students at Chevalier College would need to undergo an "extensive" qualification process to be eligible for a day dedicated to learning from home. This forward-thinking model aims to provide students with enhanced educational options while ensuring a rigorous and thorough evaluation process for those seeking the benefits of a learn-from-home day at Chevalier College (Comini, 2023).

Despite students being physically present in the building for four days, the schoolhouse remains operational five days a week, with teachers actively engaged on the fifth day. While this concept appears highly advantageous, it is crucial to acknowledge an unforeseen drawback—school lunches and buses are only available for four out of the five days.

In North Dakota, for example, their state reports that many teachers and administrators utilize the fifth day for teacher preparation. However, the question arises: how do test scores compare between a five-day school week and a four-day one? Baesler asserts that "consistency in this aspect must be maintained" (Oglesby, 2023).

"If students need most of the models of the four-day school week," one superintendent stated,

> they can still be in the building if there's a necessity for extra instruction and catching up. Even if you're not behind, if you want acceleration, if families want their child to attend on that fifth day, there are programs and learning opportunities available for that student. But the required school week is Monday through Thursday . . . Although students are only physically present in the building for four days, the schoolhouse operates five days a week, with teachers remaining employed and active on the fifth day.

While this concept appears entirely advantageous, it is crucial to note an unexpected harmful aspect—school lunches and buses will only be available for four out of the five days.

In the state of Missouri, every school district is required to do 1,044 hours. You can structure your calendar however you like. There is a required start date from the state, but after that, it is really up to the local school districts and communities to determine how they want to get those. Under their schedule,

> students will no longer attend school on Mondays, shortening the week to Tuesday through Friday. Passing time and other school hours will be scaled up to match the longer school day. This includes a longer recess time at elementary schools, and no more early release days at the high schools. (Wallington, 2022)

With more states and schools adopting the four-day school week, it is only a matter of time before this model may become something that fits into the needs of today's parents (Rahman, 2024).

BALANCED CALENDARS

The adoption of YRS calendars is gaining momentum across the United States, with certain states actively incentivizing districts to make the transition. According to the ECS, 25 states currently permit year-round schooling, and among them, 11 states actively endorse and promote this educational approach. This shift is fueled, in part, by the aftermath of the COVID-19 pandemic, which exacerbated learning gaps among students who struggled with virtual education.

Recognizing the challenges posed by summer learning loss, exacerbated by the disruptions caused by the pandemic, states are offering incentives to school districts willing to embrace year-round schooling. The motivation behind this trend is a collective effort to address the educational setbacks students faced during the pandemic. The impact of COVID-19 on traditional school calendars prompted educators to seek innovative solutions to mitigate learning gaps.

Statistics indicate a noteworthy increase in the adoption of year-round calendars, with the percentage of schools making this transition rising from 2.5% in 2018 to 4% in 2020. This shift in educational calendars has directly influenced over 3 million students, reflecting a growing interest and acceptance of alternative scheduling models to enhance educational outcomes. As the educational landscape continues to evolve, the move toward year-round schooling is not only a response to pandemic-related challenges but also an exploration of innovative approaches to address broader issues of learning continuity and academic achievement (Addison, 2023).

A balanced academic calendar, often referred to as a modified academic calendar or year-round school, presents a significant departure from the traditional 180-day school year structure. Unlike the conventional academic calendar, characterized by an extended summer break with intermittent short breaks during the rest of the year, the balanced academic calendar seeks to redistribute the temporal structure of the school year. This reorganization involves a reduction in the length of the summer break while concurrently elongating other breaks distributed across the school year.

In practical terms, a school district opting for a balanced calendar might implement a system with 45-day quarters, interspersed with 15-day breaks between them. Alternatively, the district may choose to adopt a 60-day trimester model, incorporating 20-day breaks to create a more evenly distributed academic schedule.

The rationale behind this approach is to foster a more continuous and evenly paced learning experience for students throughout the year. By reducing the extended hiatus of a traditional summer break, educators aim to minimize the learning loss that often occurs during extended periods away from academic activities. The modified calendar also serves to address issues associated with the summer slide, ensuring that students remain engaged and actively learning at more consistent intervals.

This innovative approach to structuring the academic year reflects a commitment to optimizing educational outcomes by embracing alternative scheduling models that prioritize learning continuity and adapt to the evolving needs of students and the education system. As school districts explore diverse academic calendar configurations, the balanced calendar emerges as a compelling option for fostering a more consistent and sustainable approach to education (Breazeale, 2023).

The most common form is the *single-track* modified calendar, also known as a *balanced calendar*. The second is the *multi-track calendar*. Neither one is typically an extended year. Instead, both calendars involve moving the 180 school days around so that there are multiple short breaks as opposed to the typical long summer break.

Single-track calendars have all students following the same schedule. This type of calendar often includes intersessions that provide additional opportunities for learning rather than "summer school." While a multiple-track calendar is usually created to alleviate school overcrowding, some students are on campus while others are on break.

Balanced calendars often take the form of 45 school days followed by 15 days of break, or 60 school days followed by 20 days of break. Other kinds of modified calendars with shorter intersessions exist in states like Mississippi and South Carolina (Robinson, 2023).

INTERSESSIONS

Reimagining the traditional nine-month agrarian calendar, the modified calendar offers a transformative approach to education. By minimizing the lengthy summer break and introducing more frequent breaks throughout the year, this calendar allows for a continuous and dynamic learning experience. These shorter breaks are not merely periods of rest but are strategically designated as *intersessions*, providing valuable opportunities for both remediation and enrichment. This innovative model seeks to address learning loss, enhance educational outcomes, and optimize the 180 mandated instructional days in most states.

As schools reassessed their educational strategies in the 2020–2021 academic year, there was a growing openness to reconsider options that were previously deemed too disruptive, unpopular, or challenging to implement. One such option that gained renewed attention was the concept of year-round schooling, more accurately referred to as a balanced calendar schedule. This alternative extends the conventional academic calendar, reducing the length of the traditional summer break while incorporating regular intersessions throughout the academic year.

Unlike the conventional calendar, the modified calendar acknowledges that learning is a continuous process that benefits from ongoing engagement. The strategic placement of intersessions provides educators with opportunities to address specific student needs, whether through remediation for those requiring additional support or enrichment for those seeking advanced challenges. By adopting this approach, schools aim to create a more fluid and responsive learning environment, better suited to the diverse needs of students.

In the current landscape of education, characterized by evolving challenges and uncertainties, the modified calendar stands out as a forward-thinking solution. Its emphasis on continuous learning not only aligns with the changing needs of students but also positions educators to extract maximum value from the mandated instructional days. As schools navigate the complexities of the 2020–2021 academic year, the adoption of a balanced calendar schedule emerges as a pragmatic and adaptable strategy, offering potential benefits for both students and educators alike (Superville, 2022).

In Dallas, Texas, a significant educational shift has taken place, with 41 schools embracing an innovative intersession calendar. This groundbreaking approach extends the traditional school year, commencing in early August and concluding in late June.

The intersession calendar introduces an additional five weeks spread strategically throughout the academic year. During these intersession weeks, a selected group of students are provided with tailored and more personalized attention in smaller groups. Simultaneously, educators benefit from extended planning time at the commencement of each intersession week. It is important to note that not all students are required to attend these extra intersession weeks, ensuring flexibility and consideration for individual needs.

The decision to adopt this alternative calendar was informed by comprehensive survey results, revealing overwhelming support from families, teachers, and staff alike. The majority of stakeholders expressed a favorable stance on the intersession calendar, recognizing its potential to enhance the overall educational experience. This widespread support underscores the collaborative nature of the decision-making process, aligning the educational system more closely with the needs and preferences of the community it serves (Time to Learn, 2024).

By extending the school year and incorporating intersession weeks, Dallas schools aim to create a more dynamic and responsive learning environment. The emphasis on personalized attention during intersession weeks reflects a commitment to addressing individual student needs and providing educators with valuable planning time. As Dallas pioneers this alternative calendar, it serves as a notable example of how educational institutions can adapt to the changing needs and preferences of their communities (Time to Learn, 2024).

A Maryland school uses another form of an intersession. This four-day period, strategically placed in the early second semester, provides seventh- and eighth-grade students with a respite from their regular academic routine, allowing them to engage in an array of one- and two-day activities. Remarkably, intersession consistently emerges as a highlight of the Norwood middle school experience, shaping the educational journey for students year after year (Norwood, 2024).

While intersessions may span just one short week annually, its impact is profound. This innovative program serves as a powerful means to strengthen bonds between students and teachers, fostering a sense of camaraderie among peers. Beyond the classroom, intersession plays a pivotal role in advancing Norwood's mission and educational philosophy, which places joyful learning at its core.

The intersession experience can create exciting new experiential learning opportunities. These activities, both on- and off-campus, cater to a range of interests and are designed to open minds and hearts to new possibilities. From witnessing open-heart surgery to delving into the intricacies of cake decorating (and everything in between), the intersession program embodies a commitment to exploration and discovery (Norwood, 2024).

HYBRID LEARNING

The landscape of education has been significantly reshaped by technological advancements, ushering in transformative changes in the delivery of educational content. Technologies have become integral to various pedagogical activities, giving rise to innovative modes of education. Among these, hybrid learning and teaching have emerged as particularly noteworthy, harnessing the power of information and communications technologies to redefine instructional approaches.

Hybrid learning and teaching represent a dynamic educational model that seamlessly integrates both face-to-face and online instruction. In one review conducted, a discernible upward trajectory in research and exploration of hybrid learning and teaching methodologies has been observed over the past decade. This surge in interest is further accentuated by the unprecedented global events of the COVID-19 pandemic, which has spanned the last few years (Kazu, 2022).

As governments worldwide imposed lockdowns and social distancing measures in response to the pandemic, traditional face-to-face classes were abruptly halted in educational institutions globally. Faced with these challenges, hybrid learning and teaching emerged as a strategic response and alternative to the conventional in-person approach. The swift adoption of this mode of education was necessitated by the need for continuity in education during times of crisis.

The significant paradigm shift in educational delivery triggered by the pandemic has, in turn, accelerated the development of hybrid learning and teaching. This sudden and widespread adoption has propelled the evolution of this educational model, prompting educators, institutions, and students alike to adapt rapidly to a new and dynamic learning environment.

In essence, the convergence of technological advancements and the global health crisis has propelled hybrid learning and teaching to the forefront of educational methodologies. The adaptability and resilience demonstrated during this period of transformation underscore the potential of hybrid learning to provide a robust and flexible educational framework that can thrive in both conventional and challenging circumstances.

Hybrid learning and teaching involve the integration of technology to create diverse learning environments, catering to students' preferences and enhancing their educational experiences. Gao emphasizes the characteristic combination of "online + offline" and "in-class + extra-curricular" activities in this approach. Linder identifies key features, such as customized learning activities for different student groups, increased active learning through the flipped model, and the development of self-regulated learning skills. Marchisio et al. highlight the simplicity, flexibility, and value added to face-to-face attendance in higher education hybrid learning. Miller et al. further describe hybrid learning as offering students choices in attendance, equivalent activities across delivery modes, and fostering technological skills. Reported benefits include catering to learner diversity; increasing engagement, persistence, and retention; fostering autonomy; improving learning performance; enhancing access to resources; providing flexibility; and maximizing social presence (Linder, 2017).

Hybrid learning and teaching over the years have been implemented in different disciplines such as nursing education, business education, science education, second language learning, and medicine education. The existing body of work on hybrid instruction has focused on several major areas.

Evaluating hybrid learning and teaching is crucial for aiding education practitioners in making informed decisions about planning and implementation, including considerations for student types, course components, material design, and assessments. Existing literature has predominantly focused on factors influencing effectiveness, such as course objectives, student motivation, pedagogies, and technological resources. However, there is a recognized gap in empirical investigations into diverse participant groups, particularly academic staff. The study emphasizes the need for more evaluation studies based on the results of hybrid learning implementation, addressing the necessity for professional development and support for academic staff. Contextual factors, such as technological development in a region and educational institution, significantly impact implementation effectiveness. In the Hong Kong context, where there is a well-developed technological infrastructure, the study aims to bridge the gap by examining how academic staff evaluate their hybrid teaching practices. This research intends to provide valuable insights into the challenges faced by academics in hybrid learning and teaching and explore potential solutions (Li, 2023).

The rapid spread of the highly contagious COVID-19 virus in 2019 prompted the suspension of educational institutions worldwide, leading to a significant impact on traditional learning methods. As a response to the pandemic, central exams were postponed, face-to-face education activities were halted, and distance education became the norm. In the post-pandemic period, hybrid learning, which combines traditional and distance education, gained prominence. Hybrid learning is characterized by a blend of face-to-face lessons and technology-supported teaching, aiming to optimize student learning through effective and efficient use of educational environments. Various web tools, such as Moodle, Blackboard, and Google Docs, are utilized to manage distance education components.

The literature reveals divergent findings on the impact of hybrid learning on academic success, with some studies suggesting a positive effect while others report no significant influence. To address this discrepancy, the study aims to conduct a comprehensive meta-analysis, analyzing studies conducted between 2010 and 2020 to interpret and synthesize existing findings. Despite previous meta-analyses in the literature, there is a perceived need for an international meta-analysis specifically focusing on the 2010–2020 period. The study is considered crucial in the context of the increased popularity of hybrid learning, especially following the onset of the coronavirus pandemic, to provide a quantitative assessment of its effect on academic achievement. The overarching goal is to synthesize existing research findings and establish the overall magnitude of the impact of hybrid learning on academic achievement.

The creation of hybrid learning environments involves more than just technological setups; it is integral to understanding the broader user experience within a given setting. The learning space is viewed as an ecosystem encompassing learners, teachers, pedagogical practices, digital and material resources, buildings, and furniture. This perspective emphasizes investigating the interrelations within this educational ecosystem, particularly exploring how individuals perceive and experience hybrid models of teaching and learning.

AROUND THE NATION

Across the nation, educational institutions have embarked on diverse experiments and embraced various types of calendar reforms in their pursuit of enhancing the overall learning environment. These reforms range from the incorporation of intersessions to the addition of extra days in the academic calendar, and some schools have even transitioned to a 40-day school week. However, the outcomes of these reforms exhibit considerable variation among districts, revealing distinct patterns in their approaches to restructuring the academic calendar.

One noticeable trend emerges when considering the geographical distribution of these reforms. Rural districts, faced with unique challenges, frequently opt for the adoption of four-day school weeks. This scheduling strategy not only addresses logistical and budgetary concerns but also allows for longer weekends, potentially contributing to improved teacher and student well-being. On the other hand, districts from suburban and urban areas tend to lean toward more comprehensive approaches, embracing intersessions, summer programs, and even additional days to the traditional academic calendar.

As of the latest developments in calendar reform across the United States, several noteworthy initiatives have gained prominence. One prevalent trend is the incorporation of intersessions and summer programs into academic calendars, particularly in suburban and urban districts. These additional sessions provide students with opportunities for remediation, enrichment, and skill development beyond the confines of the traditional school year. Another emerging approach involves extending the regular school day, allowing for more focused and intensive learning experiences without necessarily extending the overall number of days in the academic year.

In the realm of rural education, the adoption of fourday school weeks continues to be a prevalent strategy, offering a unique perspective on calendar reform. This approach reflects the necessity for flexibility in calendar design to address the specific needs and preferences of diverse communities. Moreover, the ongoing dialogue surrounding calendar reform emphasizes the importance of community engagement. School districts are increasingly recognizing the value of involving parents, teachers, and other stakeholders in decision-making processes, ensuring that the chosen calendar model aligns with the values and preferences of the local community.

As these calendar reforms unfold, the education landscape in the United States remains dynamic, with institutions actively exploring innovative approaches to optimize learning opportunities for students across various settings. The evolving nature of these initiatives underscores the ongoing commitment to refining and tailoring the academic calendar to better serve the diverse needs of students and communities nationwide.

The following information provides some highlights from each state as of the time of this publication.

Alabama

- The state has guidance on how to implement a new calendar in Balanced School Calendar: Key Considerations for Implementation (Louisiana Department of Education, 2021).
- House Bill 333 introduced in Alabama proposes the Alabama Modified School Calendar Grant Program, offering additional funding for schools opting to extend their instructional days. The bill aims to address concerns about summer learning loss by promoting a more consistent year-round school schedule with breaks (Burke, 2023).
- In 2021, Red River Parish Public Schools in Louisiana adopted a balanced calendar, reducing the traditional long summer break and incorporating two-week breaks every nine weeks. The goal is to address summer learning loss and provide consistent academic support to at-risk students. The new schedule also helps ensure regular access to school meals for low-income students (Juhasz, 2021).

Alaska

- Each school has its calendar posted, which has varying start and ending times (Alaska School Database, 2024).
- They incorporate year-round nutrition programs with some charter schools that will serve students year-round (Alaska Public Media, 2022).
- Alaska has All Year Montessori schools. After careful consideration and months researching year-round academic calendars used throughout the lower 48, we paved a new way for Alaska educational experiences in the fall of 2014 when we implemented a year-round academic calendar for all ages (All Year Montesorri, 2024).

Arizona

- The Arizona Education Department website includes year-round calendars (School Finance Manual).
- Liberty Elementary School District in the United States has officially adopted a four-day school week, starting from August 7. The decision was made after extensive committee work, research, and community engagement. Originally explored as a cost-saving measure in 2021, the idea gained strong support from staff and families. The district aims to address various issues, including teacher recruitment in a nationwide shortage, reducing absenteeism, and improving student behavior. The extended day program will continue to offer before- and after-school care, with an option for full-day childcare on Fridays. Ongoing input will be sought to adjust the four-day week dynamics for the success of students, families, and teachers (Liberty, 2023).
- Several school districts in Arizona, including Tempe Elementary School District, Kyrene Elementary School District, and Tempe Union High School District, are transitioning to a year-round calendar model. The three Tempe districts are following the lead of other East Valley districts that have already adopted this schedule. Gilbert Public Schools, for instance, shifted to the year-round model recently and is surveying parents and staff to assess its impact on students' academic performance (Dao, 2023).
- The Cartwright School District in Phoenix transitioned to a four-day workweek for teachers, cafeteria workers, bus drivers, and other staff members, mirroring the existing schedule for students. This shift aims to attract and retain qualified employees. Preliminary efforts have shown success, with increased interest from prospective employees and low turnover rates among current staff. The district previously implemented a four-day school week for students during the COVID-19 pandemic, citing surveys that indicated that longer weekends benefited scholars (Shappell, 2023).

- The Tempe Union High School District, Kyrene, and Tempe Elementary, three public-school districts serving South Tempe and West Chandler, have unanimously approved unified calendars and a modified year-round schedule, known as 2-2-2, starting in the 2023–2024 school year. The 2-2-2 schedule includes two weeks off for fall, winter, and spring breaks, aiming to shorten the summer break for better information retention (Shappell, 2023).

Arkansas

- The state of Arkansas has provided some Guidance for Adopting School Calendars (ADE).
- The number of Arkansas school systems adopting nontraditional school year schedules, particularly four days a week, has increased from one district in 2018 to 40 in 1921. Some districts operate on a four-day schedule, while others follow a year-round calendar with shorter summer breaks and longer breaks during the year (Howell, 2023).
- The Lincoln School District in Arkansas has considered a four-day school week to attract and retain teachers, enhance staff and student attendance, reduce the dropout rate, and achieve financial savings. The proposed schedule includes school from Tuesday to Friday, with an additional hour and 20 minutes added to each day. Mondays, designated as a day off, would be used for professional development and teacher–parent conferences (Associated Press, 2023).
- The Cutter Morning Star School District in Arkansas has stated that their four-day school week was successful, reporting positive effects on attendance and mental health. Superintendent Nancy Anderson notes improved preparedness and well-being for both students and staff. The high school has seen a 43% decrease in unexcused absences, a 25% decrease in all absences, and an enhanced focus on academics. Lower grade levels also experience increased attendance, with a 2.65% rise at the elementary level. Mental health has been a significant focus, contributing to a positive school culture. Students express happiness with the four-day week, and surveys indicate a overall positive feedback from the community (Smith, 2022).

California

- The California Department of Education offers a comprehensive online resource detailing various permissible year-round and balanced calendar options in the state. One widely utilized model is the Multi-track Year-round calendar, which addresses issues of overcrowding in district schools.

This approach involves students attending shorter academic sessions (45, 60, or 90 days) followed by vacations (15, 20, or 30 days) (Year-Round Education Calendars, 2024).
- The Manteca Unified School District is exploring YRS options The district is considering various scheduling options, such as three or four tracks, to address capacity issues, with a potential 33% increase in seating capacity using a four-track system. Year-round education aims to maximize existing facilities without resorting to double sessions, and research suggests it may positively impact student achievement by minimizing information loss during shorter, more frequent vacations (Wyatt, 2023).
- The Los Angeles school board's decision to shorten winter break from three weeks to two has sparked controversy and legal action. Superintendent Alberto Carvalho supports the change, emphasizing its benefits for students, employees, and family needs (Blume, 2023).

Colorado

- Colorado has several extended year programs that help service special needs students (ESY).
- Colorado was once a pioneer in adopting four-day school weeks, leading the United States in the number of school districts with this schedule. The state legislature permitted alternative schedules in 1980, with 12 districts making the switch by 1981. This number nearly tripled by the early 1990s. As of August, approximately 128 Colorado school districts, along with others with charter or alternative operations, followed a reduced academic calendar, but not all adhered to the four-day school week, as per the Colorado Department of Education (Cook, 2023).
- The Morgan County RE-3 School District has adopted a four-day school week in 2023. Superintendent Rob Sanders mentioned that the choice to take Mondays off was influenced by the majority of vacation days falling on Mondays (Reyes, 2023).

Connecticut

- New London Public Schools offers programs for those interested in the nontraditional 10-month school calendar (McGirl, 2021).
- Hartford Public Schools have initiated Saturday openings for several buildings, providing approximately 800 struggling students with an opportunity to catch up on their education. This effort aims to address learning gaps and enhance educational outcomes by offering additional learning opportunities outside regular school hours. The extended access to facilities on Saturdays

reflects the district's commitment to supporting students who require extra assistance in their academic progress (Napolitano, 2022).

Delaware

- The Delaware Department of Education offers initiatives like the Governor's Summer Fellowship, offering hands-on, paid work opportunities, mentoring, and networking for high school students. The Governor's Summer Learning Resources website provides families with information about diverse programs across the state, promoting academics and offering opportunities such as taekwondo and art camp (Governor's Summer Fellowship, 2024).
- Milford School District has expanded its summer programs to provide additional support and opportunities for students. These include the Beginning Buccaneer program for kindergarten readiness, limited opportunities for the Voyagers program, a language acquisition program called Hola targeting Spanish Immersion students, a STEAM-based Voyager camp at Banneker Elementary, and academic skill reinforcement at Milford Central Academy (Rogers, 2022).

Florida

- Chiles Academy in Volusia County, Florida, is experimenting with a four-day school week, aiming to reduce absences and provide more flexibility for teen moms completing their high school degrees. Principal Abby Ferguson notes a 40% decrease in daily absences and positive feedback from both students and parents. Some research suggests that shorter school weeks can reduce burnout and increase student engagement. Meanwhile, the Brevard County School District in Florida is considering a year-round approach, or a balanced school year, to address chronic absenteeism (Prieur, 2024).
- In 2023, Florida Governor Ron DeSantis signed HB 891 into law, initiating a four-year pilot program for year-round schooling in the state. The program aims to assess whether learning losses over the summer decrease with year-round education (Zizo, 2023).
- A House panel in Florida approved a bill (HB 891) proposing a four-year pilot program for YRSs to study the potential benefits, particularly in helping students recover from learning losses during the COVID-19 pandemic. The program aims to assist school districts in establishing YRS programs in at least one elementary school, with five districts selected

by the state education commissioner to represent various demographics. Districts applying for the program must provide information on enrolled students, academic performance, absenteeism rates, and the commitment of instructional personnel and students to the year-round program (Andrews, 2023).
- Hillsborough County Public Schools is considering creative ideas, including a potential move to a four-day school week, to attract teachers after a failed millage property tax increase intended to raise salaries (Mesmer, 2022).

Georgia

- The Richmond County School System in Augusta, Georgia, is considering a "modified year-round calendar," extending from July 24, 2025, to May 29, 2026, with a 7½-week summer break. The proposal includes a week-long "intersession" each semester for intervention and enrichment, providing extra help for struggling students while others enjoy a break. Two options are presented, with Option 1 following a more traditional school calendar but incorporating four digital learning days. Option 2, the modified year-round schedule, starts on July 24, 2025, and features intersession days throughout the year, with a 7½-week summer break (Staff, 2024).
- A six-year-old boy named Brodie Kenyon from Georgia gained attention after making a video protest requesting a four-day school week instead of the usual five (Mackey, 2023).

Hawaii

- Year-Round Education has been implemented in Hawaii's public schools since the early 1970s (Implications of Year-Round Education, 1972).
- The Hawaii State Teachers Association has provisions in its contract for Multi-Track YRS (Agreement, 2023).
- Lanai High & Elementary operates on a modified year-round schedule and provides an open and welcoming learning environment. The elementary section follows a self-contained class model for Grades K–2 and a two-teacher model for Grades 3–4. The program for Grades 6–8 includes exploratory and advisory activities along with core and elective classes. High school students attend three 85-minute classes per day, allowing for an extended period of instruction with various teaching methods and activities, including direct instruction, hands-on application, individualized help,

independent research, cooperative learning, group work, and enrichment opportunities (Lanai, n.d.).
- In Hawaii, specific schools implement a multi-track year-round schedule to maximize facility utilization. Students are organized into groups with staggered schedules and diverse vacation periods, ensuring a steady attendance throughout the year. While the school functions year-round, students experience extended vacations and summer breaks, with a redistribution of the total number of school days. Moreover, numerous public schools provide 4–6-week summer sessions, catering to needs like remedial courses, credit recovery, grade advancement, and enrichment activities. The nature of these programs varies, and some schools collaborate with colleges to offer early college credits (Smith, 2023).

Idaho

- Idaho Department of Education allows for four-day schools and balanced calendars (Instructional, 2022).
- The Teton County (Idaho) School District has approved a transition to a four-day school week (Boner, 2023).
- The Post Falls School District transitioned to a four-day school week. This move aligns the district with over 82 other Idaho districts and charters that have already adopted the four-day schedule. Superintendent Dena Naccarato anticipates that this change will help improve attendance and reduce staff turnover, which has been a significant issue in the district. Given the proximity to the Washington–Idaho border, where teachers can secure higher-paying out-of-state positions, the district hopes to enhance retention and attract more staff. In the past two years, Post Falls has experienced a loss of over a third of its certificated staff. Naccarato acknowledges the challenge of competing with the higher wages offered in Washington.
- YRS is seen as a solution to alleviate overcrowding and address educational requirements. Although not universally favored, three schools in Idaho, including Preston with an 11-year history, have embraced this schedule. Both Preston and Blackfoot implemented year-round schooling to manage overcrowding, with Blackfoot introducing it for sixth, seventh, and eighth graders last year (Associated Press, 1993).
- Facing a $6 million deficit, the Coeur d'Alene School District weighed options for next school year that include implementing a four-day school week (Hyun, 2024).

- The Mountain View School District 244, approved another year of four-day weeks for the 2024–2025 school year (Palmer, 2024).

Indiana

- Some Indianapolis school districts, like Perry Township, use fall break for educational purposes, focusing on areas like early literacy for students needing extra help. Approximately 200 third graders spent four hours a day during fall break to enhance their reading skills. While some districts adopted a two-week fall break for remediation, others, like Indianapolis Public Schools, returned to longer summer breaks. Wayne Township values the mental health benefits of extended breaks, providing students and teachers with a reset, and Perry Township adapts its fall intercession program to address the highest needs, such as reading (Star, 2023).
- The Indiana Department of Education reports that more than 300 schools classify themselves as year-round or balanced calendar. Some Southern Indiana school districts, initially adopting year-round calendars for increased learning benefits, are now considering a return to traditional school years. The year-round schedule, with shorter summer breaks and two-week breaks at the end of each quarter, was intended to enhance student learning, attendance, and morale (Clarke, 2017).

Illinois

- Illinois legislation has made allowances for modified school calendars (Public Act).
- The Seamless Summer Option integrates elements from the National School Lunch Program, School Breakfast Program, and Summer Food Service Program (SFSP), streamlining administrative processes. This approach simplifies the task for schools, enabling them to feed children from low-income areas not only during traditional summer breaks but also for YRSs and extended vacation periods. By participating in the Seamless Summer Option, schools contribute not only to their students but also to the broader community. According to Public Act 096–0734, Illinois school districts with over 50% of students eligible for free or reduced-price meals must operate a summer feeding program if conducting an academic summer school or enrichment program (Seamless Summer Option).

Iowa

- The board of directors of a school district and the overseeing authorities of an accredited nonpublic school have the option to seek approval from the Department of Education to implement a YRS calendar for an attendance center or a school catering to prekindergarten through Grade 8 students. It is essential, however, that the board conducts a public hearing before submitting any proposal related to the authorization of a YRS calendar. The first application for such a calendar requires careful consideration and adherence to the outlined procedures (Iowa, 2024).
- In 2023, Cardinal Community Schools introduced a four-day school week, citing the benefits of built-in time for professional development, a competitive edge in teacher recruitment and retention, improved morale, reduced absences, and increased time for teacher planning and collaboration (Leone, 2023).
- Moravia Community School District has transitioned from a five-day to a four-day school week, aligned with the trend observed in other districts like Cardinal and Moulton-Udell. Superintendent Sam Swenson mentioned addressing attendance issues in the high school as a motivation for the change, with hopes that the condensed week will enhance attendance by prioritizing quality teaching. The district is also exploring additional daycare options for working parents and ensuring meal provisions for students on the shortened Friday. Despite the shift, there will be no salary cuts for teachers, and Swenson anticipates that this change will attract more students and educators to the district (Redfield, 2023).
- WACO Community School District adopted a four-day school week a decade ago, with students attending Monday through Thursday and extending daily hours to meet state instructional requirements. Since then, three more districts have embraced the four-day week, finding it beneficial for recruiting and retaining educators, especially in rural areas. Despite concerns, research indicates no negative impact on students' test scores. The academic calendar remains similar to other Iowa districts, with a late August start and an end to summer break in late May, along with two-week winter and spring breaks. In the Iowa City Community School District, officials are considering the four-day school week, with ongoing discussions and studies (King, 2023).
- Iowa City school leaders are exploring the possibility of transitioning to a four-day-a-week, YRS calendar to combat the "summer slide" and improve teacher retention. Superintendent Matt Degner presented preliminary calendars featuring Monday-to-Thursday school days with extended breaks, including weeks off in the summer. While there is board support, concerns

about childcare for families on Fridays were raised during the 30-minute discussion. The proposal is in its early stages, and no official decisions have been made. Iowa law outlines restrictions on year-round schooling, including a maximum six-week break between classes and limitations up to eighth grade (Krejci, 2023).

Kansas

- Independence School District in Missouri, with nearly 14,000 students, is the largest in the state to adopt a four-day school week, a change aimed at addressing staff recruitment and retention amid statewide shortages. Superintendent Dale Herl noted a significant increase in teaching applications since the transition. The move has received mixed responses from families, ranging from positive reactions to concerns about childcare. The shift follows a trend observed in 25% of Missouri school districts by the start of the previous school year. The change was approved with a 6–1 vote by the district's board of education.
- An increasing number of schools and districts are adopting balanced calendars. "Seventy-seven school buildings in approximately 29 districts across the state have implemented a four-day week this year, up from 60 in 2023" (Fortino).

Kentucky

- The Kentucky Department of Education has provisions for amending days to the school calendar (Amending the Calendar, 2024).
- Kentucky has had YRSs since 1971 (Big School System, 1971).
- The Independence school board initiated an exploration into the possibility of implementing a four-day school week, as a response to the widespread teacher and worker shortages faced by schools nationwide. Superintendent Dale Herl explained that while the potential schedule change would affect students, it might not necessarily impact district employees. This move also aligns with a trend observed in rural schools in the region (KY SB50, 2016).

Louisiana

- The Louisiana Department of Education provides guidance and guidelines on how to implement a balanced calendar (Balanced School Calendar, 2021).
- The St. Helena Parish School District, anticipating 11,000 students, is gearing up for the upcoming school year with new safety measures, a reinforced

focus on literacy, and the introduction of a four-day school week. Students have Mondays off, and in the spring, Fridays off, with school hours from 7:50 a.m. to 3:30 p.m. (Conejo, 2023).
- Grant Parish residents adopted a four-day school week. A local gym has introduced the "Out of School Camp" for students in Grades 2–5. This program offers more than typical camp activities, including sports, life skills programming, and free literacy tutoring. The gym's owner, Bonita Armour, emphasizes the various opportunities the campus provides for children, such as batting cages and outdoor fields (Roland, 2023).
- The Rapides Parish School Board has approved the Mid-August Start Calendar for the 2023–2024 school year. This option brings slight changes, mainly affecting the first and last days of school. Students are scheduled to begin on August 14 and conclude on May 23. Notably, the first semester will extend beyond Christmas break. Additionally, a few teacher workdays will be adjusted. Superintendent Jeff Powell emphasized the board's commitment to seeking input and presenting various options, including innovative ideas like the balanced calendar, to accommodate community preferences and event planning (Roland, 2023).

Maine

- The state department of education states that a school administrative unit must ensure that all its schools are operational for at least 180 days per year, with a minimum of 175 days designated for instruction. Within the 180-day requirement, up to 5 days may be allocated for teacher in-service education, administrative meetings, parent–teacher conferences, records days, and similar activities. The commissioner has the authority to reduce or waive the mandated minimum days upon application from a school board. The commissioner retains the authority to make necessary adjustments, ensuring fair distribution of state aid without exceeding the allowable subsidy (Title 20-A, 2023).
- Portland Public Schools in Maine is shifting to a four-day school week specifically for special education students due to difficulties in filling teaching positions. The district is currently facing a shortage of approximately 30 education technician positions, along with a need for teachers and therapists, to adequately support around 1,000 special education students, as reported by the *Portland Press Herald* (Thies, 2024).

Maryland

- Several school systems currently implement extended time options and intersessions for students to accelerate or recover credits during the

evening, weekend, or summer. Through the use of grants, state funds, and/or federal funds, school system leaders have provided options for students to receive additional instruction beyond the traditional school schedule (Innovative School Schedules, 2017).
- Some school leaders within the state want the freedom to explore all different types of modified schedules and calendars (Hutzell, 2023).

Massachusetts

- Massachusetts Expanded Learning Time (ELT) is a program that empowers schools to significantly extend their school schedules, enhancing learning experiences for all students in alignment with state and federal laws. The extended hours aim to improve student achievement and engagement by: (1) providing additional instructional time in core subjects like math, literacy, and science to meet state standards; (2) incorporating enrichment and applied learning opportunities into the school day that align with both state standards and 21st-century skills; and (3) allocating more time for teacher planning, analysis, lesson design, and professional development, which may involve professionals from partnering community-based organizations in some cases (Massachusetts Department of Elementary and Secondary Education).

Michigan

- The Michigan Department of Education has an initiative known as ELT, funded through line item 7061-9412, which empowers schools to significantly extend their hours and days, fostering integrated learning experiences for all students that address their needs and aligning with the heightened expectations established by state and federal laws. These extended schedules aim to enhance student achievement and engagement by: (1) providing additional instructional time in core subjects like math, literacy, and science to meet state standards; (2) incorporating enrichment and applied learning opportunities into the school day that complement both state standards and 21st-century skills; and (3) allocating more time for teacher planning, analysis, lesson design, and professional development, which may involve professionals from partnering community-based organizations in certain cases (Balanced Calendar).
- Michigan public schools typically operate for 180 days per school year, running from September through June with a 10-week summer vacation. The Michigan Department of Education defines a YRS as having a summer break lasting no longer than six weeks. Some YRS schools achieve this by

extending the school calendar to operate for as many as 200 days a year, while others maintain 180 days but shorten the summer break to six weeks, incorporating weeklong breaks throughout the rest of the school year—a model referred to as a "balanced calendar" YRS. The primary aim of YRS is to increase educational opportunities, addressing the "summer slide" phenomenon, where students may experience learning losses during long summer breaks. In southeast Michigan, some dedicated YRS schools operate for 200 days a year, exceeding the traditional academic calendar and often implementing a more rigorous academic program. The Cornerstone School in Detroit is an example, serving approximately 500 students from preschool through eighth grade with a school year extending from late August to early July (MacDonnell, 2019).

Minnesota

- According to Minnesota Statutes, section 120A.41, the school board's annual calendar must encompass a minimum of 165 days of instruction for students in Grades 1–11, unless approval for a four-day week schedule has been granted by the commissioner under Minnesota Statutes, sections 124D.12 through 124D.127. This regulation applies to various school district types, including independent school districts, education districts (such as cooperatives and intermediate districts), and charter schools are exempted. Education districts, formed by school districts, must adhere to the same requirements for programs operated on behalf of member districts, as outlined in Minnesota Statutes, section 123A.17, subdivision (Sec. 120A).
- In the fall of 2023, Harnett County Schools will introduce its inaugural YRS at LaFayette Elementary, located at 108 LaFayette School Road, Fuquay-Varina. The lottery enrollment opportunity for students will commence on January 3. Dr. Aaron Fleming, superintendent of HCS, conveyed in a recent letter to parents that while this may not align with everyone's preference, the district is pleased to provide this option to families seeking a more flexible schedule throughout the year. Under the year-round calendar, students will still complete the same number of school days but experience multiple breaks distributed across the year instead of a traditional three-month summer break (Weaver, 2022).

Mississippi

- The School Calendar Grant Program allows school districts to seek funds for the initial expenses associated with adopting a modified ("year-round")

school calendar. This calendar involves reducing the traditional summer break and introducing shorter, more frequent intersessions evenly distributed throughout the year, while maintaining the standard 180-day school year. Schools could utilize intersessions for student remediation or enrichment activities. The bill aims to encourage districts to adopt or maintain the modified calendar, with several districts, including Corinth, Laurel, Simpson County, Lamar County, Starkville, and Gulfport, having already transitioned. SB 2361, currently with the Senate Education Committee, awaits further action. Eligible districts, planning to implement the modified calendar in the 2023–2024 school year, can apply for funds, covering staffing, remediation/enrichment programs during intersessions, and additional utilities/transportation costs. The funds cannot be used for land purchase, construction, or debt repayment. Eligible districts may receive up to $200,000 annually for a maximum of three years, with the award size based on proposed budgets, calendars, student numbers, and related factors (Ballard, 2024).
- Both the Columbus Municipal and Lowndes County school districts have transitioned from the traditional school calendar to a modified school year. The new schedule involves an earlier start and a later end to classes, with breaks interspersed throughout the year. Intersessions, occurring roughly halfway through each traditional semester, provide voluntary opportunities for students (881 participated in Columbus) to engage in remediation, enrichment, athletics, field trips, and other activities. Participation is optional for both teachers and students, offering flexibility in attending sessions tailored to individual needs (Jones, 2023).
- Perry County will commence the school year under a new modified schedule, featuring extended breaks throughout the academic calendar. Superintendent Dr. Titus M. Hines emphasizes that these breaks aim to provide both teachers and students with intervals to refresh, regroup, and return with increased vigor between each grading period. The expectation is that this modified schedule will contribute to enhanced attendance and reduced burnout (Raines, 2023).
- In recent times, numerous Mississippi schools have shifted to a modified school calendar, commencing classes in July instead of the typical early August start. The Mississippi Department of Education reported that while only 12 school districts followed this calendar in 2022, the number has increased to 29 this year. Senate Bill 2361 proposes the establishment of the Mississippi Modified School Calendar Grant Program, allowing school districts to seek funds to cover the initial expenses associated with implementing a modified calendar year. This alternative calendar involves reducing the traditional summer break and incorporating shorter, more frequent intersessions evenly throughout the year (*Clarion Ledger*, 2023).

- The Laurel School District has implemented a new modified school calendar this year, incorporating an additional two weeks to the school year for certain students. The revised calendar commences on July 22, which is two weeks earlier than the usual start for some students. Superintendent Dr. Toy L. Watts clarified that participation in intersession during those two weeks is by invitation only, not mandatory for all students. While some students attend school during intersession, others have a break for the entire two weeks. The primary objective behind the schedule change is to enhance student achievement. Dr. Watts emphasized that the focus is on boosting proficiency numbers, and the effectiveness of the implemented changes will be gauged based on this criterion. Despite the added days, students will receive a break as an alternative arrangement later in the year (Laurel School District, 2022).
- During his speech at the Neshoba County Fair in 2022, Lieutenant Governor Delbert Hosemann expressed his desire to incentivize Mississippi school districts to transition to an academic calendar that evenly distributes student class time throughout the year. Hosemann, a Republican, advocates for the adoption of a "modified calendar" or "year-round calendar" to enhance competitiveness and maximize educational opportunities. He emphasized the need to make better use of the 180-day education requirement, including testing and other educational activities, to ensure that students receive a more comprehensive year of learning (Vance, 2022).

Missouri

- The Missouri Department of Education website details that summer school programs in their state must be approved by local school boards and can take place between the end of the regular school term and the start of the next term. Districts with a "year-round" schedule can conduct summer school during breaks. These programs, for Missouri-domiciled students at the elementary or high school level, must have a minimum of 120 clock hours for students without disabilities. Programs for students with disabilities should align with IEP.
- The State School Board can authorize summer school programs at elementary or high school levels, with minimum clock hour requirements. An elementary program can include Grades K–8, and a high school program can include Grades 7–12. Districts or charter schools may operate one or more summer school programs at any level, with a "stacking" method to meet the 120 clock hour requirement. Regular summer school hours can be combined with special education ESY programs. Individual courses or segments have a minimum of 30 hours, excluding break and lunch times. "Year-round" school districts may include instructional

hours from a structured summer school during breaks in the regular term (Mo. Code, 2024).
- The Boys and Girls Clubs of Springfield have introduced a new initiative for Marshfield in response to the upcoming shift to a four-day school week in the 2022–2023 academic year. The program aims to accommodate approximately 200 students from kindergarten to eighth grade, offering breakfast, lunch, and an afternoon snack. The scheduled programming will run on Mondays, from 8:00 a.m. to 4:00 p.m., starting on August 29. Registration for the program opens on July 25 (Replogle, 2022).
- Over 120 districts in Missouri have transitioned to a four-day school week, prompting a statewide report to examine the impact on education. According to the Department of Elementary and Secondary Education, there is no significant advantage or disadvantage associated with either schedule. However, Twin Rivers Superintendent Rob Brown highlighted how the four-day week has allowed his district to attract and retain teachers, offering a competitive edge in rural areas. The streamlined schedule provides teachers and students with predictable routines and flexibility for appointments or personal needs. Feedback from parents and educators suggests that the extra day off fosters a more relaxed atmosphere and does not negatively affect academic performance. Superintendent Brown also noted improvements in student attendance since adopting the new schedule. While the report calls for further investigation into academic outcomes and classroom efficiency, the consensus so far indicates positive results from the transition to a four-day school week (Clark, 2024).

Montana

- To counteract the teacher shortage, Montana schools have implemented four-day weeks, aiming to enhance the recruitment and retention of educators. This innovative approach not only provides a solution to staffing challenges but also introduces a more attractive work schedule for teachers, fostering a positive impact on the education system. The condensed week structure is anticipated to contribute to a more sustainable and fulfilling teaching environment, ultimately benefiting both educators and students alike (Rispens, 2024).
- In response to the teacher shortage, the rural school district recognized the need to enhance its competitiveness urgently. Superintendent Rob Pedersen explained that they lost teachers to neighboring schools due to lower pay and the prevalence of four-day school weeks in the area. To address this, the district decided to implement a four-day school week for the upcoming academic year and increased the base pay by 16% (West, 2023).

- The Cut Bank School Board unanimously approved a transition to a four-day school week for the 2023 school year, aligning with 157 other school districts in Montana. The new schedule will consist of 150 school days with classes held from Monday to Thursday, each day running approximately half an hour longer than the current schedule. To accommodate the longer days, 15 minutes will be reallocated from the lunch period to dedicated educational class time. The change applies to all District 15 public schools in Cut Bank (Karle, 2022).

Nebraska

- The Nebraska Board of Education Legislature aims to enhance the efficiency of public school facilities by implementing a year-round operation program for the state's public schools. Recognizing that the cost of education significantly rises when schoolhouses remain unused for three months each year, the Legislature acknowledges that the historical reasons for the summer closure of public schools in rural and pioneer areas are no longer applicable to many school districts in the state.
- Goshen County Schools prepare to begin four-day school weeks. Goshen County School District is gearing up for the upcoming school year with significant modifications. The district is shifting from a traditional five-day school week to a four-day week, featuring slightly extended daily schedules and occasional Fridays-only attendance. Superintendent Ryan Kramer notes that 21 Fridays in the school year will be dedicated to intervention and extension activities. Aligning with other Wyoming schools that have adopted the four-day week influenced this decision. While some finer aspects of the transition are still being worked out, the essential details have been finalized (White, 2023).

Nevada

- The start and end times for the upcoming four-day school week in Elko and Spring Creek have been established, commencing as early as 7:15 a.m. and varying across different schools. The schedules of all schools within the Elko County School District adhere to the state's education requirements, measured in minutes. School days conclude at different times, such as 3:50 p.m. for Sage Elementary School in Spring Creek, primarily influenced by bus schedules. According to the school district's documents submitted to the Nevada Department of Education, Elko High School students will receive 66,390 minutes of education, while Adobe Middle School children will have 64,307 minutes, meeting the state's

stipulated requirements for instructional minutes per school year across various grade levels (Harding, 2023).
- The Nevada State Board of Education is initiating the development of a regulation to establish guidelines for high school start times in school districts. This initiative aims to strike a balance between addressing the physical and academic needs of students and ensuring smooth school operations (Garcia, 2023).

New Hampshire

- Nodaway-Holt and West Nodaway share their perspectives on the adoption of a four-day school week for the upcoming 2023–2024 school year. Both schools have undergone the initial review of the proposed school calendar, which features a four-day school week from Tuesday through Friday. The transition to this schedule was implemented at the start of the 2022–2023 school year, and with over 16 weeks completed, parents, staff, and other stakeholders have experienced and adapted to the lifestyle changes brought about by this alteration (WN, NH, 2022).

New Jersey

- Some members of the public in New Jersey seek year-round calendars in school to address pandemic losses (Letters to the Editor, 2021).
- One charter school has implemented a Year-Round Calendar that exemplifies our dedication to student success. "By maintaining continuous engagement in learning throughout the entire year, we prioritize the ultimate goal of high school graduation. Our perspective on the learning process is akin to a marathon, emphasizing endurance rather than a sprint" (The Academy, 2024).
- The "summer slide" phenomenon, causing students to lose knowledge during summer break, motivated the East Orange School District to combat this trend. Initiatives like the "Top Readers with Frequency" program and the "Summer Reading Launch Party" aim to promote reading, celebrate students, and reduce the achievement gap, with recent efforts bringing together over 350 attendees for the "2nd Summer Reading Launch Party" themed "One World, Many Stories" (East Orange, 2022).

New Mexico

- Rio Rancho Public Schools have explored implementing a balanced calendar (Fjeld, 2023).
- The Albuquerque Public Schools board has approved a proposed academic calendar for the 2023–2024 school year. The updated calendar

starts on August 3, 2023, one week earlier than the previous schedule, and concludes on May 31, 2024, following Memorial Day. The extension of the school year results in a shorter summer vacation period (Egbuonu, 2023).
- The 2022–2023 school year at Las Cruces Public Schools started the implementation of a YRS calendar. This new calendar includes 10 additional days of instruction, shortens the summer break, and introduces a two-week fall intercession. Kindergarten, sixth-, and ninth-grade students will commence classes on July 20, while all other students will return on July 21 (Cook, 2022).

New York

- The New York Department of Education has information on its website for guidance on ESY (Division of School Business, 2020).
- The Schools Chancellor of New York City (NYC), David Banks, has proposed an overhaul of the education system, including longer school days, Saturday classes, and summer sessions. As part of his plan, Banks aims to retrain early childhood teachers, shifting the focus from the "balanced literacy" method to emphasize phonics and sounding out words. Banks contends that the current approach, used in NYC schools for the past 25 years, has not been effective, particularly for Black and brown children (Russo, 2021).

North Carolina

- A school employing a single or multi-track instructional calendar, established before March 1, 2020, operates with instructional days spanning the entire school calendar year, from July 1 to June 30. The school follows either of the following plans: dividing students into four groups, with each group attending school during assigned and staggered quarters throughout the school calendar year, or implementing a plan where students are scheduled to attend an average of 44–46 instructional days, followed by an average of 15–20 days of vacation, with this cycle repeating throughout the school calendar year.[1]
- A total of 16 school districts in North Carolina are challenging state law by commencing the school year earlier than the legally mandated period. According to North Carolina law, the majority of traditional public schools are prohibited from starting the school year until the last week of August, with this year's official date set for August 28. Despite this, an increasing number of districts across the state are choosing to

start earlier, highlighting a disagreement among Republican lawmakers. The school calendar law, established in 2004, aimed to restrict school officials from initiating the school year before the last week of August, prompted by concerns about the impact on family vacation time and coastal vacation rentals, as advocated by a group called Save our Summers in collaboration with the state's tourism industry (Bergin, 2023).

North Dakota

- In Bismarck, North Dakota, students attend the school building for four days, but the school remains open five days a week, and teachers are active on the fifth day. However, a potential drawback is that school lunches and buses are only available for four out of the five days (Oglesby, 2023).
- North Dakota provides guidelines on operating schools with four-day school weeks (North Dakota).
- In 2024, as per the Department of Public Instruction, 13 schools in North Dakota, including Dunseith, Belcourt, Mandaree, White Shield, Alexander, and Horse Creek School in the Cartwright area, currently have a waiver for a four-day school week. The four-day week maintains the state's mandated 1,050 hours in a school year by extending the minutes in the average school day while reducing the traditional five-day calendar to four days (Crane, 2024).

Ohio

- The Ohio Department of Education and Workforce provides guidance on how to modify a school calendar (Changing the Schedule).
- North College Hill City School District has implemented a four-day school week, which, according to Superintendent Eugene Blalock Jr., is designed to enhance students' academic success and has also significantly benefited the mental well-being and preparedness of the staff. In a district survey, teachers expressed gratitude for the change, noting that the additional day off from regular classes (Mondays) allows them to focus on lesson preparation, collaborative team meetings, student data review, and professional development opportunities. The shift to a four-day week was prompted by challenges in teacher recruitment amid the national teacher shortage, as well as concerns about teacher absenteeism and burnout following the impact of COVID-19 on educators (Enquirer, 2023).
- Canton Harbor High School is one of the first in Stark County to implement a four-day school week (Belay, 2023).

Oklahoma

- The Oklahoma State Department of Education (OSDE) has information on YRSs and four-day week schools calendars (School Calendar Information, 2017).
- Following approval from the OSDE, two rural school districts are set to transition to four-day school weeks. Roff Public Schools will enter its eighth year with this schedule, while Stonewall Public Schools' request for 156 school days was also approved, marking their eighth year of implementing a four-day week (Chasanov, 2023).
- In Oklahoma, the adoption of four-day school weeks initially aimed to enhance financial conditions. The practice has gained widespread popularity, with nearly 100 districts implementing it over the past decade. Despite efforts by Oklahoma lawmakers to restrict this practice, educators, students, and parents in rural communities are actively advocating to maintain it (Korth, 2022).

Oregon

- After implementing the four-day school week, Superintendent Don Kordosky of Oakridge School District in Oregon noted an improvement in test scores (Wells, 2022).
- Portland school district considers four-day school weeks (Lee, 2022).

Pennsylvania

- The Pennsylvania Department of Education classifies a YRS calendar with regularly scheduled school days on a year-round basis (Pennsylvania Department of Education).
- In 2023, Philadelphia School Superintendent Tony Watlington unveiled his five-year strategic plan to the school board, offering the public insight into his vision to transform Philadelphia into the "fastest-improving urban school district in the country." Alongside initiatives like a year-round schooling pilot in up to 10 schools, the plan encompasses pilots for evidence-based intensive in-school tutoring, swim lessons, and teacher retention programs (Shepelavy, 2023).
- The Lancaster County School Board has endorsed a modified year-round calendar for the 2024–2025 school year, commencing and concluding a week ahead of the usual schedule. The academic year will commence on August 12, 2024, and conclude on May 30, 2025 (Jones, 2023).
- In a memorandum addressed to lawmakers, State Representatives Dave Madsen (D-Dauphin), Chris Pielli (D-Chester), and Josh Siegel (D-Lehigh)

highlighted significant shifts in the labor market since the establishment of the traditional five-day workweek over a century ago. They outlined proposed legislation aimed at incentivizing companies to adopt a four-day, 32-hour workweek. Under the proposed Department of Labor and Industry pilot program, participating employers may qualify for a state income tax credit (Stockburger, 2023b).

Rhode Island

- Governor McKee introduced a new program aimed at enhancing out-of-school learning. Dubbed Learn365RI, the initiative provides students with an extra 1 million hours of educational opportunities beyond the standard 180-day school year (Andrade, 2023).

South Carolina

- The Williamsburg County School District (WCSD) has decided to implement a modified year-round calendar starting from the 2024–2025 academic year. Following the footsteps of over 60 school districts in the state and neighboring Georgetown County, WCSD aims to maintain the standard 180-day school year. However, the modified calendar reorganizes these days to ensure that each grading period and semester comprises 45 and 90 days, respectively. Instead of extending the traditional school year, this adjustment distributes the 180 days more evenly and introduces additional breaks, such as in October and February (Renaud, 2024).
- The Aiken County Public School District implemented its modified academic calendar for the 2023–2024 school year, commencing in July. A notable alteration in this new calendar was the introduction of two-week long fall, winter, and spring break periods. While the summer break was reduced, more breaks were interspersed throughout the academic year. This transition toward a "year-round school" approach aimed to enhance learning retention and afford more substantial mental rejuvenation periods for both students and teachers, as stated by school officials (Weeks, 2023).
- Georgetown County School District implemented a new modified year-round calendar. Under this calendar, summer break starts at the end of May instead of the beginning of June, but it will be shorter, with students returning to school in early August. In return for the reduced summer break, students will have two additional breaks in October and February, in addition to the usual Thanksgiving and Christmas holidays. Superintendent Keith Price mentioned that the decision was made based on feedback

from surveys conducted with parents, students, and employees (Evans, 2023).

South Dakota

- South Dakota Codified Law 13-26-1 permits schools to operate on a year-round basis (South Dakota Legislature, 2024).
- In 2019, nearly 25% of South Dakota school districts adopted a four-day school week.
- The four-day school week was originally used in South Dakota in the 1930s (Donis-Keller, 2009).

Tennessee

- The Knox City School District provides guidance on Balanced Calendars (South Dakota Legislature, 2024).
- In 2023, the West Memphis Schools District adopted a year-round calendar. The calendar has been described as a "balanced" hybrid schedule that runs July 26 through June 3 (West Memphis School District, 2023).
- According to Tennessee state law, school districts must begin the academic year no earlier than August 1, unless they opt for a year-round or alternative calendar for their schools. All school district calendars for the 2022–2023 academic year must be submitted through student management systems by May 13, 2022. These calendars should include specific dates for five in-service days, one parent–teacher conference day, and four other days designated by the local board of education. Any calendars not complying with state law will be addressed with instructions to rectify the discrepancies (Tennessee Department of Education, 2022).

Texas

- The Texas Education Agency offers a list of all Texas Public School Campuses on Year-Round Education Calendars, 2020–21 (Alagoz, 2021).
- Some Central Texas school districts tout positive results with a four-day school calendar (Stroudmire, 2024).
- The rural Chico ISD is in Year 2 of implementing a four-day school week (Nachtigal, 2023).
- In 2023, the San Elizario Independent School District of 3,200 students moved to a four-day school week Tuesday through Friday (Sanchez, 2023).

- In Bandera, Texas, the school district will move to a four-day school week, where "the school day will be extended by 10 minutes in the morning and 25 minutes in the afternoon" (reports, 2024).

Utah

- The Utah State Board of Education granted approval to the Piute County School District's proposal to adopt a four-day school week beginning in the 2023–2024 academic year. Superintendent Koby Willis emphasized that the decision is driven by a desire to provide students with additional opportunities for learning experiences beyond the traditional classroom setting, rather than financial considerations (Harris, 2023).
- The Logan City District is mandated to offer educational services for at least 180 school days annually, with the following exception: The Board has the authority to allocate up to 32 instructional hours or four school days for teacher preparation or professional development through a two-thirds majority vote in a duly notified and conducted public meeting.
- Canyons Online, previously known as Canyons Virtual High School, is an extensive online learning initiative catering to numerous students statewide in Utah. Specifically designed for students in Grades 9–12, Canyons Online operates year-round and welcomes enrollment from both the Canyons School District and other districts across (Franchi, 2023).

Vermont

- The Seamless Summer Option (SSO) is a federally funded program managed by the Vermont Agency of Education Child Nutrition Programs, supported by the United States Department of Agriculture. It operates as part of the School Meals Programs, combining elements from both the School Meals Program and SFSP. This initiative allows School Food Authorities to offer meals to children aged 18 and under at various sites during summer breaks, as well as during extended school vacation periods exceeding 10 days in YRSs (SSO).
- The Vermont Agency of Education provides clarification on YRSs in a 2020 memo (Agency, 2020).

Virginia

- The Virginia Department of Education provides guidance in educational institutions adopting year-round schedules; instructional days are spread out over 10, 11, or 12 months instead of the conventional nine-month calendar. While the summer break may be abbreviated, additional breaks,

referred to as intersessions, could be inserted during customary transition periods like the end of a semester. These intersessions might offer chances for remedial support or academic enrichment. Extended year calendars supplement the required annual instructional days and may incorporate other elements typical of a year-round calendar.
- The Virginia Assembly enacted legislation to allow for a year-round calendar utilizing a waiver (Bill Tracking, 2020).

Washington

- The Washington Office of Public Instruction provided Balanced Calendar Grant Funding through the Balanced Calendar Initiative and "supported school districts to explore pathways for increasing student learning opportunities and shrinking summer learning loss by balancing or modifying their school year calendars" (Year Round and ESYs).
- In 2023, it was reported that 45 Washington school districts received grants in the 2021–2022 and 2022–2023 school years for balanced calendar implementation (Hornak, 2023).
- In the 2022–2023 academic year, Winlock introduced a revised calendar featuring three weeklong "intersessions" dispersed throughout the year and reducing the summer break from 11 weeks to 8 weeks. Initial data indicate positive trends in assessment scores among elementary school students in the district due to these additional learning opportunities. Michelle Jeffries, Special Programs Director at Winlock School District, noted, "Students who participated in all three Intersessions showed notably higher test scores than the average." She added, "For instance, one student progressed from below grade level in early second grade to at grade level by late third grade. Witnessing such advancements has been truly rewarding" (OSPI, 2023).

Washington, D.C.

- On March 10, 2011, the Division of Special Education within the Office of the State Superintendent of Education issued the "Extended School Year (ESY) Services Policy." This policy mandates that every local education agency (LEA) is tasked with determining ESY eligibility and providing appropriate services for all students with IEPs. The aim of this guidance document is to offer further clarification to aid LEAs in aligning their implementation of the policy with the mandates outlined in the IDEA, 20 U.S.C. §§1400 et seq (Nonregulatory Guidance, 2012).

West Virginia

- The Piedmont School in Charleston provides year-round education for its students (Piedmont Year-Round Education).
- In 2023, a potential solution to address staffing challenges in West Virginia schools is on the horizon with a new bill proposed by the Senate Education Committee. Senate Bill 736, if enacted into law, mandates the state superintendent to initiate a three-year pilot project in up to five county school districts. Under this proposal, students would attend school four days a week, with alternative methods providing instruction on the fifth day (Schultz, 2023).
- The West Virginia Department of Education stipulates that all pre-k classes must have at least four days of instruction per week in order to meet calendar requirements (West Virginia Department of Education, 2018).

Wisconsin

- The Wisconsin Department of Public Instruction provided guidance on year-round calendars as well as *interim session classes*. They also stipulate that "year-round school calendars may have no more than 45 calendar days between consecutive regular school year sessions" (Commencement of School Term).
- In 2014, a state law eliminated the requirement for districts to adhere to a 180-day school year and instead established minimum instructional hours as the sole standard. Schools must ensure a minimum of 1,137 hours of instruction for Grades 7–12, 1,050 hours for Grades 1–6, and 437 hours for kindergarten students not in full-day programs. This change grants school leaders flexibility in crafting and adjusting calendars to suit local needs, potentially allowing for fewer total school days while meeting hourly requirements. Additionally, schools have the liberty to extend remaining school days to make up for lost instructional time due to weather disruptions, without needing to add extra days (Anderson, 2014).
- Milwaukee Public Schools provides guidance on traditional and year-round calendars (school calendars).

Wyoming

- Little Powder School, the sole remaining rural school operating on a five-day schedule, has taken the initial step toward transitioning to a four-day school week, aligning with other rural schools in the area. Previously, Recluse, 4-J, as well as both schools in Wright including Cottonwood and Wright Junior-Senior High, shifted to a four-day schedule back in 2019. During a recent board meeting, Campbell County School District

trustees unanimously endorsed alternative calendars for Little Powder for the upcoming 2023–2024 and 2024–2025 school years. The next stage involves seeking approval from the Wyoming State Board of Education (Catteral, 2023).
- As early as 2013, the state of Wyoming had incentives for schools to adopt year-round calendars (Nicholas, 2013).
- Sweetwater County School District No. 1 adopted a four-day schedule in the 2021–2022 school year (Sweetwater County Board, 2020).

AROUND THE WORLD

The adoption of modified calendars extends beyond America's borders, with many countries around the world operating under unique educational systems. Unlike the traditional 180-day academic year commonly seen in the United States, some Asian countries have historically implemented longer instructional periods. However, in the wake of the pandemic, numerous nations have intensified their efforts to refine modified calendars as a response to the exacerbated learning loss.

In contrast to the American model, which typically encompasses a fixed number of instructional days, these international approaches often emphasize flexibility and innovation to accommodate diverse educational needs. For instance, some Asian countries have extended their academic calendars beyond the standard 180 days, recognizing the importance of prolonged learning opportunities in fostering academic excellence.

Moreover, the global shift toward modified calendars has gained momentum in the post-pandemic era, as countries seek to mitigate the adverse effects of disrupted learning. In this evolving landscape, educational policymakers worldwide are exploring novel strategies to optimize instructional time, enhance student engagement, and address the challenges posed by prolonged periods of remote learning.

By embracing modified calendars tailored to their specific contexts, countries are not only adapting to the evolving educational landscape but also reaffirming their commitment to providing quality education for all students. As nations continue to navigate the complexities of the post-pandemic era, the development and implementation of innovative educational practices will remain paramount in fostering resilience and ensuring academic success.

Below are some of the highlights from places outside of the United States:

- In New Zealand, thousands of students rallied behind a petition advocating for a shift to a four-day school week, raising questions about the feasibility of such a change within the existing educational framework. In its plea for reform, the petition highlights concerns about the current schooling system being overly demanding, describing it as "draining" for students (Newshub, 2023).
- In Australia, students attend school for a total of 200 days per year, spanning from late January to mid-December. Given Australia's location in the Southern Hemisphere, its school year aligns with summer during the Northern Hemisphere's winter. Summer break for Australian students occurs from mid-December to late January. The school year is structured into four terms, each lasting between 9 and 11 weeks, with two-week breaks in between. School days typically run from 9 a.m. to 3:30 p.m., with lunch provided on campus. Compulsory schooling lasts for 11 years, although most students complete 12 years of education. On average, classes consist of 24 students.
- As China is situated in the Northern Hemisphere, its summer season aligns with that of Asia, Europe, and North America. The academic year in China usually commences in early September and concludes in mid-July. During the summer break, students often engage in additional classes or prepare for entrance exams. A typical school day spans from 7:30 a.m. to 5 p.m., including a two-hour break for lunch.
- The majority of Japanese schools operate on a trimester system, starting in April and concluding in March of the subsequent year. The academic year is divided into three terms, interspersed with breaks for summer, winter, and spring. Students are mandated to wear uniforms, and there are comprehensive regulations regarding various aspects such as hair styles, footwear, socks, skirt length, makeup, accessories, and more (Infoplease, 2023).
- The Calgary Board of Education has made provisions of up to 200 school days in Canada (Unique Setting).
- Spain is reconsidering its school calendar, aiming to introduce more breaks throughout the academic year and reduce the length of summer holidays. Researcher and professor Daniel Gabaldon suggests this approach to align Spain's school calendar with the European trend of distributing holidays more evenly across the year, aiming for fewer idle days (Spain Considering Limited School, 2023).
- Many countries globally have adopted year-round schooling or similar educational programs. These include China, Japan, Nigeria, Australia, South

Korea, and North Korea. In these countries, school terms usually span 11 months and follow a trimester or quarter system, with short breaks between each term (What Countries Have Year-Round Schooling?, 2023).

NOTE

1. Division of School Business. (2020). Guidance of calendar requirement. In NC Department of Public Instruction. https://files.nc.gov/dpi/documents/fbs/accounting/calendar/sb704-calendar-requirements-052020.pdf

Chapter 6

Current Research on Schools with Modified Calendars

The timing of the return to school for most public school students varies significantly between states, reflecting historical regional needs and a strong emphasis on states' rights in America. Broadly, schools in the South and Southwest typically start earlier, while those in the Northwest and along the East Coast tend to start later, as per Pew Research Center's 2019 analysis of over 13,000 public school districts.

Some of the key findings of the study include the following:

- By mid-August, nearly all public school students in Alabama, Kentucky, Mississippi, and Tennessee were back in school.
- Conversely, not a single district in New England and the Middle Atlantic states returned until late August.
- Some districts following modified year-round calendars commenced in late July.
- In New Jersey, some students did not return until the second week of September.

These variations underscore the wide range of approaches to school scheduling, a landscape that has seen further changes due to the COVID-19 pandemic (Walrath-Holdridge, 2023).

The exploration of balanced calendars' effectiveness traces back to the 1980s, with a landmark study emerging in 1996 by Cooper, Nye, Charlton, Lindsey, and Greenhouse. Their meta-analysis highlighted improvements in student performance. However, subsequent research on year-round education and balanced calendars has yielded disparate and sometimes conflicting findings. The complexity of this subject stems from the multitude of variables involved.

For instance, certain studies have delved into multi-track calendars, wherein students attend school for specified durations while their peers are on break. Although primarily addressing overcrowding concerns, this approach is not solely focused on academics. Comparing such calendars to those with extended or redistributed school days is not equitable.

Hence, arriving at definitive conclusions to appease all critics poses a formidable challenge. Some individual school districts have undertaken their own evaluations to determine the efficacy of their respective models. Furthermore, considering the variety of calendars implemented since 2008, as documented by the National Center for Education Statistics, pinpointing the most effective calendar model becomes increasingly intricate (National Center for Education Statistics).

EducationWeek shed light on a trend emerging in several states, including Arkansas, Iowa, and Texas, where four-day school weeks are being implemented (Heubeck, 2022). According to their findings, teachers perceive that the extended learning activities associated with this model positively impact student achievement in various ways. Teachers emphasize the value of these activities as enrichment opportunities, emphasizing the importance of planning engaging and hands-on activities. The increasing popularity of this model, attributed to its positive impact on teacher retention and morale, suggests that neighboring states may also consider adopting similar approaches in the future.

For instance, the academic studies delve into various grades and subjects, with math and language arts being typical indicators. However, spelling, science, and social studies have also been explored. While the following section on teacher morale may not directly impact student achievement, it is pertinent to acknowledge the nationwide teacher shortage, which could eventually affect student success without a consistent instructional staff.

Economic studies within this chapter cover diverse subjects such as budget savings and travel expenditures, although their direct impact on student achievement may be minimal. Nevertheless, it is crucial to examine how calendar reform can influence broader aspects beyond the school system. Additionally, social and emotional learning (SEL) has gained prominence, particularly in the post-pandemic educational landscape, with research highlighting its connection to students' ability to learn effectively.

Dissertations encompassing all these topics utilize various research methodologies, including quantitative, qualitative, mixed-methods, and phenomenological studies. While it is challenging to draw a comprehensive conclusion on calendar reform, the consensus among studies tends to indicate either major gains, minor gains, or limited gains. Importantly, no study has identified negative effects associated with calendar reform.

What follows is some of the most recent research of note that encompasses all of the single-track calendar reform models. As noted before, the multi-track, primarily utilized for rapid population growth, will not be included. For classification purposes, the studies have been organized into Academic, Teacher Morale/Retention, Economic, Health/Medical, and Social/Emotional Factors. Finally, the last section is dedicated to Dissertations. The purpose of this chapter is to provide an expansive view of all of the research being conducted on this topic, but it does have some limitations.

RESEARCH STUDIES

2022

Types of School Choice

Many families opt for their neighborhood public schools by relocating to an address within the district boundaries of their preferred school. While this is a common choice, there exists a myriad of other avenues through which families can select the most suitable educational environment for their children. Beyond residential locations, families can explore various options such as charter schools, magnet programs, homeschooling, online education platforms, private schools, and specialized programs catering to specific interests or learning styles. Additionally, considerations such as extracurricular activities, school culture, academic rigor, and support services also play pivotal roles in the decision-making process. By exploring diverse educational pathways, families can ensure that their children receive an education that aligns with their unique needs and aspirations (EdCoice, 2023).

2023

National Council of State Legislatures—
Four-Day School Week Overview

Twenty-four states have at least one school district using a four-day school week schedule, an increase of over 600% since 1999. Approximately 850 of the nation's school districts use a four-day schedule, up from 650 in 2020. Most four-day-a-week schools operate Monday through Thursday, with a few opting for Tuesday through Friday. School days are lengthened to deliver the same amount of instructional time over fewer days, as required by state law. Some schools may offer optional enrichment activities, tutoring, or time for teacher development during the fifth day (Four-Day School Week, 2024).

Effects of Summer Numeracy Interventions among French-Language Students in Ontario

This article examines summer numeracy programs in Ontario French-language schools. Studies indicate that students often experience a decline in numeracy skills over the summer break, but these programs have shown potential in mitigating these losses. The research suggests that these programs can serve as effective short-term solutions to boost achievement and reduce disparities among Ontario French-language students. The article also suggests avenues for future research to explore the long-term effects of these programs and their relevance in the post-COVID-19 educational landscape (Davies, 2023).

A Longitudinal Randomized Trial of a Sustained Content Literacy Intervention from First to Second Grade: Transfer Effects on Students' Reading Comprehension

A sustained content literacy intervention was used from Grade 1 to Grade 2 and evaluated transfer effects on students' reading comprehension outcomes. A total of 30 elementary schools were randomly assigned to a treatment or control group. Over 12 months, the treatment group students participated in literacy lessons in science and social studies followed by wide reading of thematically related informational texts during summer. This study highlights the benefit of sustaining learning of related topics and aligning science content across grades so that children can read with greater comprehension (Kim, 2023).

Effects of Changes to the School Year and Alternative School Calendars: Qualitative Research and an Updated Review of the Evidence

A study in Wales discovered that the current school calendar could negatively affect student attendance and lead to short-term learning setbacks. Feedback indicated that extending the autumn half-term and reducing the length of the summer break helped mitigate these issues to some extent. There are indications that the lengthy summer break might widen the disadvantage gap, as some families face challenges with childcare. Extending the October half-term was viewed positively for both staff and student well-being. Changes to the school calendar in England and Scotland often mirrored those of neighboring authorities. While some evidence suggests that providing educational activities during breaks could help reduce learning loss, further investigation is needed in this area (Cummings, 2023).

Could the Four-Day Week Work? A Scoping Review[1]

Although the purpose of this study did not focus on education, it still highlighted the growing interest in the concept, implementation, and acceptance of the four-day workweek. The study reports that research on this subject dates all the way back to the 1970s. The conclusion states, "the fact that so many companies are now trialing the 4DWW, in response to increased demand for FWAs and rising burnout amongst employees, highlights the demand and need for more contemporary research into this topic" (Jahal, 2023).

2024

Study of the Impact of the Four-Day School Week on Academic Achievement and Building Growth

The Missouri Department of Elementary and Secondary Education commissioned a study examining the impact of transitioning to a four-day school week. According to the findings presented by SAS, there was no statistically significant effect on academic achievement or building growth observed statewide (Study of the impact of the Four-Day School Week, 2024).

As you have read, the research continues to be conflicted regarding the impact of the four-day school week in relation to academic achievement. As such, school districts considering this transition should conduct a comprehensive study prior to making any recommendations or changes as some reports have found that the four-day school week has a negative impact on student achievement (Thompson, et al., 2021).

Enhancing Summer Learning: The Power of Data-Driven Educational Activities at Camp

The American Camp Association created this piece that explores the importance of summer activities to ameliorate summer learning loss. They also highlight the positive effects on children from low socioeconiomic areas (Enhancing Summer Learning: The Power of Data-Driven Educational Activities at Camp, 2024).

DISSERTATIONS

In the past 10 years, doctoral dissertations on the subject of calendar reform have not been as prevalent as other topics. Three recurring themes that have been found are teacher morale/retention, student achievement, and comparing calendar models.

2013

Teacher Perceptions Regarding the Relationship of Modified Year-Round School Calendars with Student Achievement, Student Behavior, and Teacher Efficacy

In this dissertation, a questionnaire was distributed to 106 teachers from public schools in North Carolina with both traditional and balanced calendar schedules. The author discovered that "a strong positive correlation was found between teacher perceptions of year-round school calendars and improved student achievement. Similarly, the study revealed a significant relationship between teacher perceptions of year-round school calendars and positive student behavior" (Huffman, 2013).

2014

The Effects of Experiential, Service-Learning Summer Learning Programs on Youth Outcomes

This study sought to determine if a summer intervention program could mitigate summer learning loss. Utilizing a "hands-on, experiential service learning curriculum" based on the work of Alexander, Entwisle, and Olson's (2001) faucet theory, this study explored the implementation of two summer programs in Rhode Island schools. One of the programs was implemented in a low-socioeconomic school setting while the other was in a mixed-income neighborhood. The findings indicate that experiential summer programs, "had significant positive effects on a variety of student outcomes." The researchers also recommended further quantitative research to find remediations for, "reducing summer learning loss and helping to stem the growth of achievement gaps during the summer months" (Greenman, 2014).

2015

Identification of Summer School Effects by Comparing the In- and Out-of-School Growth Rates of Struggling Early Readers

This study used a repeated-treatment design "to examine the academic year and summer oral reading fluency outcomes for students attending a district-sponsored summer literacy program." The data for this research was collected for students in their first and second grades over the summer break. The results showed gains in reading fluency among students who attended the summer program in comparison to their counterparts who did not attend. The authors observed that continuous and uninterrupted education has a positive effect on schooling and academics (Zvoch, 2015).

Good Continuous Calendar and Academic Growth: A Study of the Impact of Continuous Calendar Schools on Academic Growth of Low-Socioeconomic-Status Students

The author used a quantitative research design approach to, "compare academic growth in the areas of reading and math of low-socioeconomic-status (SES) students in a continuous calendar school versus a traditional calendar school in the state of Nebraska." Data were collected from the 2011–2014 school years from low-SES third, fourth, and fifth graders. The test results from the continuous calendar school students were compared to scores from the traditional calendar school students in the subject areas of reading and math. The study found "that there was not a significant difference in the areas of reading, math, and guided reading levels among students at the continuous calendar school versus the traditional calendar school" (Schumacher, 2015).

Impact of Summer Recess on Mathematics Learning Retention

This quantitative research study was designed to investigate the impact of summer recess also known as summer vacation on mathematical computation skills. Assessing children in second and third grades from two different school calendars accomplished this on two separate occasions. First, children from a traditional calendar school and a balanced calendar school were assessed the last week of school respectively using a standardized benchmark assessment called the M-COMP. The same children were then post-tested using the same test following the summer recess. For the traditional calendar children, the length of time between each assessment was 12 weeks. Participants from the balanced school calendar were post-tested following a six-week summer recess. A paired-samples t-test was used to determine the significance of the mean values while comparing the results from each school. In addition, a multiple regression was conducted to determine if there was a significant relationship between independent variables: economic status, gender, type of school attended, and whether or not a student received math enrichment or remediation and the dependent variable, post-test results. The results of the statistical analyses indicated that the type of school a student attends makes a difference on the retention of mathematical computation skills. In addition, children who received either remediation or enrichment retained more of these skills. There were no significant findings in regard to the economic status or gender of a student. As a result of this empirical study, students who attend the balanced school calendar retain more mathematical computation skills than their counterparts on the traditional school calendar. Administrators seeking ways to increase student achievement in mathematics may consider moving to the balanced school calendar (Hornak, 2015).

2016

Missouri School Superintendent Perceptions of Year-Round School Calendars

The study aimed to analyze Missouri superintendents' perceptions of year-round school calendars across four themes: Time, Student Learning and Achievement, District Cost, and Family Cost and Support. Year-round calendars aim to combat summer learning loss by providing shorter, more frequent breaks. Despite a low response rate, findings suggest positive perceptions regarding Time and Student Learning, with a more neutral stance on Family Cost and Support, and negative views on District Cost. Gender did not impact responses, but urban superintendents tended to rate more positively than rural or suburban counterparts. There were no significant differences based on the percentage of free/reduced lunches (Cook, 2016).

Knowledge Decay between Semesters

This study focused on summer learning loss with postsecondary students who took sequential courses from the fall and spring semesters. The fall semester students had a shorter break, while the spring students experienced a much longer break during the summer and then resumed their studies the following fall. Their results showed that a long gap from the spring semester students was more prevalent with lower grades (Dills, 2015).

Views of Teachers on the Benefits of After-School Programs and Summer Programs in Terms of Social-Emotional Learning

This study examined the benefits of after-school and summer programs in relationship to SEL. A qualitative research experiment was conducted and a method was used to evaluate and compare the views of teachers on After-school Programs. The research was conducted with the participation of 14 Primary and Secondary School teachers in Erzincan City. The views of the teachers obtained through interviews show that after-school programs, youth centers, and youth clubs as well as Summer Programs play a significant role for the students to develop SEL skills. This paper draws attention to the views of teachers in classroom management as a means of increasing both the parents' and the student's awareness of SEL (Kaylar, 2016).

2017

Investigation of Summer Learning Loss in the UK— Implications for Holiday Club Provision (Shinwell, 2017)

This study examined how spelling and reading are impacted by summer learning loss. Based on a population of 77 students, the authors studied male and female primary school students between the ages of 5 and 10 years from three schools in Scotland and England. A spelling test was given before the summer break, after the summer break, and then once again seven weeks later. The results showed that scores were lowest at the end of the summer break and suggested, "Summer learning loss occurred, or at least stagnation in learning, in a population of primary school aged children attending schools in areas of low SES in relation to spelling" (Kaylar, 2017).

Effects of a Summer Mathematics Intervention for Low-Income Children

The authors of this study examined "a randomized experiment of a summer mathematics program conducted in a large, high-poverty urban public school district." They found that students from third to ninth grades "scored higher on the measure of a summer home and family mathematics engagement." They further added that the summer intervention reported, "significantly higher levels of summer home and family mathematics engagement compared with children in the randomly chosen control group." Lastly, this intervention yielded results that suggest that students, especially from low-income households, can increase math engagement with summer intervention (Lynch, 2017).

A Summer of Distinction: Exploring the Construction of Educational Advantage Outside the Academic Year

The researchers for this study sought to merge the disciplines of sociology and education to spotlight the implementation of summer programs of "class- or race-based gaps in academic achievement." In studying what activities students do during their summer vacations, the authors looked specifically at which students were participating in supplemental academic enrichment between the end and beginning of school. Their findings showed that participating in summer programs afforded students, "advantageous results" (Scarbrough, 2017).

Goodbye to Summer Vacation? The Effects of Summer Enrollment on College and Employment Outcomes

The researchers based the work of this study on the model of Academic Momentum Theory, which looked into the effect of continuity in instruction (Attewell, 2012). They found that students enrolling in summer classes can have positive "college outcomes." The enrollment in these classes also saw that students had "higher bachelor's degree completion rates than summer non-enrollees." The article goes on to add that colleges may be interested in this data to encourage additional summer intersessions to assist students in staying focused on their coursework (Liu, 2016).

Can Schools Enable Parents to Prevent Summer Learning Loss? A Text-Messaging Field Experiment to Promote Literacy Skills

The authors in this piece sought to examine how summer learning activities can benefit student achievement. This study "explores the potential of enabling parents to [summer] provide literacy development opportunities at home as a low-cost alternative." The results suggest that "the text-messaging programs for parents have potential but that design details and implementation strategies matter" (Kraft, 2017).

A Case Study of Elementary School Parents as Agents for Summer Reading Gain: Fostering a Summer Leap and Holding Steady

This case examined the role that parents play in student achievement using a summer reading intervention. The goal of this research was to determine the effectiveness of using parents as a means of intervention during a summer enrichment program. What they found was that "parents [acted] as school agents fostered a summer leap by which students gained in reading levels or at the very least maintained their learning from the prior school year" (Parker, 2017).

Summer Learning Loss: What Is It, and What Can We Do About It?

This article examined a home-based summer reading program for elementary school students. In this instance, students received a book and instructional materials to be utilized during their summer break. The data found a positive impact on the reading comprehension of low-income students who used either of those resources. These parents were actively engaged in the intervention process and were found to be an integral part of the overall intervention. The authors found that "home-based programs such as these can be more cost-effective than school-based interventions" (Quinn, 2017).

2018

A Comparative Study of the Academic Performance of Schools on Year-Round and Traditional Calendars

This study was designed in response to the lack of literature concerning the impact of school calendar type on student achievement scores. The results of this study indicated no statistically significant difference in the academic performance on Reading and Mathematics STAAR between schools on year-round calendars and schools on traditional calendars. Additionally, studies are recommended to fill the gap in the literature, as studies including the relations between the performance on STAAR and school calendar type were limited. It is also recommended that this study be replicated as a statewide study (DeLeon, 2021).

Year-Round Education and Student Learning: A Case Study of Stakeholders' Perceptions

This qualitative study examined one Michigan public school that has worked under a single-track year-round calendar since 1983. Teacher and administrator participants shared their lived experiences, perceptions, and details of how student learning is supported by a year-round calendar approach. This study identified themes that the participants perceived to be relevant to student learning within a year-round education calendar. Additionally, study data were applied to the theoretical framework of Carroll and Spearitt's (1967) Model of School Learning and Dempster's (1988) Spacing effect. The researcher concluded that participants have an overall positive perception of student learning within a year-round education calendar (Sciullo, 2018).

Preventing Summer Learning Loss: Results of a Summer Literacy Program for Students from Low-SES Homes

The researchers in this article studied the challenges that students from low socioeconomic backgrounds face as they impact their levels of summer achievement. The selected subjects for this study were elementary students who "participated in a summer program designed to improve oral and written narrative skills." The results showed that the students in the treatment group, "revealed a significant improvement in oral narrative skills and written composition." Lastly, the authors believed that "a well-designed summer program at a local community center can improve narrative outcomes for students from low-SES homes" (Bowers, 2018).

Effects of a Summer Reading Intervention on Reading Skills for Low-Income Black and Hispanic Students in Elementary School

The authors studied "the effects of a summer reading intervention with a sample of low-income Black and Hispanic students who were struggling readers." Their results for these second and third graders found "significant growth on most reading measures for rising 3rd graders. The school district also provided reading fluency and composite measures of reading for the intervention students and for a comparison sample of students who did not receive the intervention" (Beach, 2018).

Meta-Analytic Evidence for Year-Round Education's Effect on Science and Social Studies Achievement

In this meta-analysis, the authors examined "single-track, year-round education's effect on science and social studies achievement." Their results found that the students saw an average gain of about one month of learning in each subject area of science and social studies. The authors went on to further suggest that these results should be used to guide future policymaking (Fitzpatric, 2018).

The Effects of Summer Break on Engineering Student Success in Calculus

The authors of this study found that "summer break sets students in grades K-12 back by at least one month of instruction and has the strongest impact on mathematics retention." They investigated how the summer gap impacted postsecondary students enrolled in an engineering program. Over five years, "the final course grades for students who took the summer off between the first two courses in the Introductory Calculus for Engineers course sequence were compared with grades of students who took both courses in the same academic year." The results showed "that university students who take the summer off lose the equivalent of about half a course grade more than do students who take the two courses in the same academic year" (Van de Sande, 2018).

Using a Balanced School Year to Improve Student Achievement. A White Paper of the Stark Education Partnership

This white paper details the differences between research done by researchers and practitioners. The meta-analysis of Cooper and Associates as well as the work of von Hipple corroborate that balanced calendars have been shown to have a positive effect on student achievement, although the latter finds the effects less impactful. However, results from dissertations show even greater gains for students with balanced calendars. The authors speculate that balanced calendars are an instructional tool, "that in the hands of skilled educators, balanced calendars produce results" (Entwistle, 2018).

2019

Impact of a Four-Day School Week on Teacher Preparation

This study used interviews with Missouri public school elementary building principals to determine if the four-day school week impacted teacher preparation. The researchers examined how teacher preparation was affected in the four areas of "time management, curriculum awareness, collaboration, and teacher morale." According to the conclusions of the study, "teachers were happier, had better attendance, were able to spend more quality family time, and seemed to be a bit more well rested. Students also were observed to be happier in a four-day school week" (Schultz, 2019).

The Impact of Continuous Learning Calendars on Student Learning

The author of this research looked to understand some of the academic effects of summer learning loss and "the impact [of] continuous learning calendar schools had on student learning." Teachers shared that they believed the year-round calendar as "a positive change that allows students remediation and enrichment during breaks, a more consistent schedule where breaks are given to reduce teacher burnout, and a creative way in which to reach the whole child." The researcher also concluded that the year-round calendar was a positive intervention that motivated students and teachers (Powell, 2019).

How Do Summer Youth Employment Programs Improve Criminal Justice Outcomes and for Whom?

The paper details how a summer youth employment program in Boston was used as an intervention to address positive behavior among adolescents. In this experimental design, the findings showed that "the program reduces violent crime by 35 percent." The author stated that the results suggest that summer youth programs can provide positive community outcomes (Modestino, 2019).

An Intervention Study to Prevent "Summer Reading Loss" in a Socioeconomically Disadvantaged Area with Second Language Learners

In this study, 120 second-grade students and 115 students in third grade from lower socioeconomic groups were provided a summer reading intervention program. These students were then compared to their peers from the same areas who did not receive the summer program. The results showed "that the largest effect sizes between groups (intervention and control) were observed for word decoding in Grade 2 and word comprehension in Grade 3 where the intervention group improved more than the control group" (Faith, 2019).

Retention of Reading Intervention Effects From Fourth to Fifth Grade for Students With Reading Difficulties

This study examined a fourth-grade reading intervention targeting students who had reading challenges. This randomized sample was then provided with a multicomponent reading intervention, where the students received daily intervention in small-group instruction. Students in the treatment group continued to show a marked improvement and "maintained the higher levels of reading comprehension from the end of the 4th-grade intervention to the beginning of 5th grade" (Wanzek, 2019).

Single-Track Year-Round Education for Improving Academic Achievement in U.S. K–12 Schools: Results of a Meta-Analysis

In this meta-analysis, it was found that "students at single-track YRE [year round education] schools show modestly higher achievement in both math and reading—by a magnitude similar to estimates of summer learning loss—but comparable proficiency." The researchers used, "twenty-two online databases in summer 2017 yielded 494 de-duplicated results; 81 warranted full-text examination." The results also yielded the revelation that, "schools that shortened summer to the fewest weeks showed the largest effects in both subjects" (Fitzpatrick, 2019).

Examining the Effectiveness of Year-Round School Calendars on Improving Educational Attainment Outcomes Within the Context of Advancement of Health Equity: A Community Guide Systematic Review

This article focused on the learning losses that students accumulate over summer break. A Community Guide Systematic Review method was used to study evaluations published from 1965 to 2015. The research showed that students lost academic skills over the summer and that children from lower socioeconomic backgrounds fared worse than their peers (Finnie, 2019).

Single-Track Year-Round Education for Improving Academic Achievement in U.S. K–12 Schools: Results of a Meta-Analysis Department of Educational Administration, College of Education, Michigan State University Research

This meta-analysis showed that over summer break, students forget approximately one month of learning in math and reading. The article further states that some of the studies that were part of this research also found that low-income students consistently underperform compared to their more affluent peers. The researchers searched multiple online databases to yield thirty studies of single-track calendar schools. The results showed that "students at single track YRE schools show modestly higher achievement in both math and reading" (Fitzpatrick, 2019).

Preventing a Summer Slide in Reading—The Effects of a Summer School

This study examined children in "a three-week summer intervention to address summer slide with a group of low socioeconomic students in New Zealand." The experiment used a one-to-one intervention approach. The results found that "the summer school group had higher word reading scores than the control group." In addition, these improvements also included, "phonological recording ability, word reading, spelling, and passage reading accuracy" (Nicholson, 2019).

The Keeping in Schools Shape Program: How to Maintain Skill Practice over School Breaks

The authors of this article explained that cognitive skills need to be used consistently or they will diminish over some time. Their research explored what they called the *summer gap effect*. This intervention is "a mobile, engaging, innovative, cost-effective, and flexible program that was designed for the very purpose of helping students stay fresh on prerequisite mathematics skills and concepts." At the end of the program, by sending students text messages with math problems, the researchers were able to decrease summer loss (Van De Sande, 2019).

2020

Teachers' Perspectives on Extended Learning Activities during a Balanced Calendar in a Rural Setting by Charlene Lovette Isom, Liberty University, Lynchburg, Virginia

This study was completed in a rural school district in Virginia with a year-round school calendar. The author found that the schedule change produced some positive reactions from the teaching staff that were sampled. One teacher even explained that they "felt that the extended learning activities influenced student achievement in numerous ways. Teachers believed the extended learning activities provided great opportunities for students as an enrichment effort" (Isolm, 2020).

The Impact of a Year-Round School Calendar on College and Career Readiness as Measured by the SAT Scores of Urban High School Seniors

In this study, Scholastic Aptitude Test (SAT) scores were measured for students attending year-round school with those from a traditional calendar. The author chose to focus on how urban students from both of those schedules fared in terms of the College Board results. The results of the study

> revealed the suitability of year-round school calendars in the preparation of students for career and college readiness . . . this study concludes that the traditional school calendar is likely to prove ineffective insofar as SAT scores and preparation of students for career and college are concerned. (Grant, 2020)

Academic Impact of Rural Idaho Schools on the Four-Day School Week: A Quantitative Research Study

The author of this research studied the test scores of students who had four-day school weeks and five-day school weeks in rural Idaho schools (Barzee, 2020). In comparing the scores of both sets of students, it was found that there was "no significant impact on the academic performance, as determined by the previously mentioned standardized metrics."

The Impact of Summer Programs on the English Language Scores of Migrant Children

This study examined Children of Migrant and Seasonal Farmworkers and the challenges they have in English acquisition. This quasi-experimental design, "[utilized a] pretest/posttest study investigated whether summer Migrant Education Programs (MEP) could help prevent summer learning loss in English proficiency." The researchers used kindergarten through fourth-grade students. The data showed that modest gains of those students who were in the treatment program were evident as compared to their peers who did not receive the intervention (Scmitt, 2020).

Preventing Summer Reading Loss for Students in Poverty: A Comparison of Tutoring and Access to Books

This study investigated students from high-poverty areas and academic interventions to address summer learning loss. The researchers selected

> 100 at-risk youth who participated in tutoring (n = 45) or received self-selected books (n = 55) indicated significant gains for students in both groups in contextual reading fluency, gains only for the books group in word reading fluency, and no gains for either group in reading comprehension.

The researchers felt that this data supports other findings on summer learning loss and highlights the need for academic interventions to address this deficit (Bell, 2020).

Summer Reading Program with Benefits for At-Risk Children: Results from a Freedom School Program

A six-week reading program was designed to maintain students' reading levels during their summer break. Over 400 African-American and Hispanic students from low-income backgrounds were assessed before the implementation of the intervention and then one week before the completion of the program. The results suggest "that this brief summer reading program helped children improve over time, with improvement most notable in children in higher grade levels and those most vulnerable" (Lara-Cinisomo, 2020).

School's Out: The Role of Summers in Understanding Achievement Disparities

The researchers for this study examined data sets from over 18 million students in 2008 through 2016 in every state across the United States. The data was collected from the Northwest Evaluation Association (NWEA)'s Measures of Academic Progress (MAP) assessment to determine summer learning loss. The results found that students "on average, do indeed lose meaningful ground during the summer period in both math and ELA." The authors detail that their data show that summer learning loss is a real occurrence and recommend that educators take the necessary means to address it (Atteberry, 2021).

Four-Day School Week Overview

According to the National Conference of State Legislatures in 2020, districts implementing a four-day week could potentially achieve cost savings ranging from 0.4% to 2.5%, with a maximum of 5.43%. While these changes have mainly occurred in smaller, rural districts, there is potential for positive implications in larger, urban districts as well (Four Day School Week, 2024).

Effects of a Summer Reading Intervention on the Reading Performance of Elementary Grade Students from Low-Income Families

The study aimed to investigate the impact of a summer reading initiative on third-grade students from low-income backgrounds, who were reading below grade level. Rising second graders were divided into two groups: one receiving the reading program and the other not. The findings revealed that students in the intervention group achieved significantly higher scores compared to those in the control group (Beach, 2018).

Children's Development of Semantic Verbal Fluency During Summer Vacation versus During Formal Schooling

The authors of this paper based their research on the work of previous studies of summer learning losses in math, reading, and writing. They investigated how "lexical organization and retrieval, assessed by a semantic verbal fluency task, develops during a lengthy summer vacation versus formal schooling." They examined 68 elementary aged children with pre- and post-assessments. The results found that test scores decreased following summer vacation and corroborate other studies regarding summer learning loss (Rosqvist, 2020).

2021

A Quasi-Experimental Study of the Impacts of the Kids Read Now Summer Reading Program

The researchers from this study examined three schools in two Midwestern school districts to analyze "the literacy impacts of a replicable summer reading program, *Kids Read Now*." Their results showed that "the Kids Read Now participants outperformed comparison group students." The article adds that students who participated in this intervention "equaled over 2 months of learning, or greater than 23% of the learning that takes place over a typical 9-month school year" (Borman, 2021).

Year-Round Education and Student Learning: A Case Study of Stakeholders' Perceptions

In this 2018 qualitative study, perceptions of the year-round calendar from teachers and administrators in a Michigan school district were examined. This particular school district implemented the year-round schedule in 1983. The researcher determined "that participants have an overall positive perception of student learning within a year-round education calendar" (DeLeon, 2021).

A Mechanism to Increase Literacy and Math Skills and to Reduce Summer Learning Loss

In this study, the scores of students who participated in a Summer Academy are discussed. The findings of this research indicate that the students who participated in Summer Academy grew in reading almost double compared to those students that did not participate in Summer Academy. The findings suggest that the students who participated in Summer Academy regressed in math almost double compared to those students who did not participate in Summer Academy (Reynolds, 2021).

A Comparison of the Four-Day School Week to the Five-Day School Week and Reading Achievement of Third, Fourth, and Fifth Graders

This research study compared the reading achievement of four-day school calendars with the traditional five-day school calendars. The MAP reading proficiency mean scores compiled during the years of 2017–2019 from these students were then compared. The results showed "no significant differences in reading proficiency mean scores between any of the matched four-day and five-day school districts." This further suggests that one day less of instruction does not seem to lessen or worsen student achievement (Streeter, 2021).

Modernizing the School Calendar to Fit the Needs of the 21st-Century Student

In this dissertation, the MAP of middle school students for schools with four and five-day school weeks were compared. The study's findings revealed that the achievement scores from both calendar cohorts were insignificant. Therefore, based on these results, four-day school weeks produce similar results to five-day school weeks. In addition, "the perceptions of principals and teachers indicated the four-day school week was an overall benefit to the school climate" (Baker, 2021).

How Teachers Feel Missouri School Schedules Affect Teachers Morale: A Qualitative Descriptive Case Study

Teachers from Missouri elementary schools volunteered to participate in the study "to understand how different types of school schedules and calendars can affect teacher's morale." The data included interviews and surveys and was collected from the teachers. The results showed that teachers from the year-round schedules had increased employee morale and retention (Smith, 2021).

Stakeholder Beliefs, Satisfaction, and Assessments of School Climate after Implementation of a Year-Round Calendar

A Tennessee public K–12 school implemented a year-round calendar over a six-year period and found that the students, parents, and teachers had "satisfaction levels increased after the implementation of YRS and school climate improved" (Adams, 2021).

COVID-19 School Closures and Educational Achievement Gaps in Canada: Lessons from Ontario Summer Learning Research

This study explored the effects of the pandemic on student achievement in cohorts of over 12,000 students from Canadian elementary students to research the effects of COVID-19 in the areas of literacy and numeracy skills. A meta-analysis was conducted and found "learning losses of 3.5 and 6.5 months among typically-performing and lower-performing students respectively, and achievement gaps that grow up to 1.5 years among same grade peers." The authors recommended summer learning programs to address these losses and ameliorate learning loss (Aurini, 2021).

Young African American Scholars Make Reading Gains at Literacy-Focused, Culturally Relevant Summer Camp that Combats Summer Reading Loss

A study was conducted at a summer camp aimed at helping students recover from learning setbacks. The effectiveness of the camp was evaluated, with students taking part in the "Children's Defense Fund's Freedom Schools, [which was] a free, six-week, literacy-focused, culturally relevant summer camp [to address] summer reading loss." The program included more than 100 students in Grades 3–5 who took part in three distinct summer programs. They underwent both pre- and post-tests, with the results indicating "that the literacy-focused summer camp provides students with an academically enriching opportunity that may help prevent summer reading loss, particularly for students in Grades 3–5, who experienced small gains on average in vocabulary, fluency, and comprehension" (Mesa, 2021).

Extended Calendar Model versus Traditional Calendar Model: A Descriptive Analysis of Student Performance Over Time

This study sought to examine the disparities in academic performance between English Language Learners (ELLs) and students eligible for free and reduced lunches (F&RLs) under an extended calendar model compared to a traditional calendar system. Conducted between 2011 and 2018, the research focuses on a single urban/suburban school within the Kansas City, Missouri metro area. The study acknowledges the limited research in this area; it underscores the importance of educational institutions exploring alternative calendar models to better accommodate diverse student needs, moving away from the conventional 180-day school year structure with a three-month summer break (Camburn, 2021).

2022

A Comparison of Academic Achievement for the Four-Day and Five-Day School Week in New Mexico

This study tracked student scores in English and math from two districts in New Mexico—one operating on a four-day school week and the other on a five-day schedule. The research involved 89 public schools in the state. Interestingly, the results revealed no statistical difference in the performance of students from the two cohorts, indicating that the four-day school week was just as effective as the traditional five-day model (Whipple, 2022).

A Qualitative Study Examining the Perceptions of Special Education Team Members Regarding the Impact of the Four-Day School Week on Students Who Receive Special Education Services Data

This researcher examined the impact of four-day and five-day school schedules on Special Education in a Midwestern state. The study involved collecting surveys and conducting interviews with special education staff and administrators. The findings indicated that "the four-day school model was also perceived by special education team members as positive in association with student achievement" (Mitchell, 2022).

Extended Calendar Model versus Traditional Calendar Model: A Descriptive Analysis of Student Performance over Time

This study aims to investigate the academic performance of ELLs and students eligible for F&RLs who participated in an extended calendar model compared to those in a traditional calendar setting. The research spans from 2011 to 2018, with a focus on a school in an urban/suburban area of the Kansas City, Missouri metro region, that adopted the extended calendar in 2015. By analyzing data from this period, the study seeks to uncover any differences in English Language Arts (ELA) and math achievement between students in the extended and traditional calendar models. The key factor under examination is the additional learning time provided by the extended calendar. The findings aim to offer valuable insights into student achievement when allowed extended learning periods (Wallace, 2022).

The Four-Day School Week as a Path for Principal Attraction: Perceptions of Elementary Principals in Missouri

This study aimed to investigate whether significant differences existed between principals working in public elementary schools in Missouri with traditional, five-day schedules and those with alternative, four-day schedules in terms of their perceptions of work–life balance, time for self-care, work-related stress, self-efficacy, and overall job satisfaction. An electronic survey was distributed to public elementary schools in Missouri utilizing both types of calendars, covering areas such as work–life balance, self-care time, stress levels, self-efficacy, job satisfaction, and demographic details. The results indicated that principals with five-day work weeks tended to express higher levels of anxiety regarding work, whereas those with four-day work weeks reported a greater sense of meaning in their work. These findings provide valuable insights for district administrators and school boards when making decisions about school week calendars in efforts to attract and retain staff (Weber, 2022).

Engaging Native American High School Students in Public Health Career Preparation Through the Indigenous Summer Enhancement Program

A summer health program was studied for Native American high school students pursuing health careers with a 1-week summer training program. A qualitative questionnaire from the students reported that they had positive perceptions of the overall program and appreciated "culturally relevant learning experiences in both virtual and in-person environments." The results also suggest that student knowledge on the subject had increased, seeing the entire population attaining the learning objectives of the program (Dreifuss, 2022).

2023

Reproducing or Reducing Inequality? The Case of Summer Learning Programs

This study looked at four summer programs from an Ontario school district using over 10,000 students in a quantitative analysis. The results found that "all summer programs successfully recruited disadvantaged students without stigmatizing them, and raised their average achievement without widening pre-existing gaps." The various programs were also shown to recruit students from a wide variety of socioeconomic backgrounds, thus strengthening the implications of the results (Davies, 2023).

The Impact of Summer Programs on Student Mathematics Achievement: A Meta-Analysis

The authors produced a meta-analysis of 37 studies of summer math programs in mathematics, ranging in grades from pre-K to 12. The focus of this analysis sought to determine if student achievement was found in summer math initiatives. The results showed that "children who participated in summer programs that included mathematics activities experienced significantly better mathematics achievement outcomes compared to their control group counterparts." This study also revealed that achievement was found in different social-economic settings. Finally, their findings suggest that "summer programs are a promising tool to strengthen children's mathematical proficiency outside of school time" (Lynch, 2023).

School's Out: How Summer Youth Employment Programs Impact Academic Outcomes

This study looked at how summer employment influences academic achievement. The authors used a lottery system to select students for the Boston Summer Youth Employment Program. Their research showed that a student who was in this program was "4.4 percentage points more likely to graduate from high school on time and 2.5 percentage points less likely to drop out of high school during the four years after participating in the program relative to the control group" (Modestino, 2023).

Examining the Impact that a Modified School Calendar Had on Teacher Attendance in a Rural Mississippi School District

The objective of this study was to evaluate the influence of implementing a revised school timetable with scheduled breaks after each quarter on teacher attendance in a rural Mississippi school district. Data from the 2022–2023 school year, the inaugural year of the revised calendar, were juxtaposed with data from the 2018–2019 school year, the final full year before the onset of the COVID-19 pandemic. The results revealed that teachers in both academic years had higher rates of absenteeism under the modified school schedule than on the traditional schedule. However, factors such as the COVID-19 pandemic and influenza strain may have influenced these results, highlighting the need for further research to understand the long-term effects of a modified school calendar on teacher absenteeism (Carlisle, 2023).

Best Practices to Improve Summer Reading Growth: A Qualitative e-Delphi Study

The e-Delphi study aimed to establish consensus on best practices for enhancing summer reading growth. Results highlighted four key practices for improving summer reading growth in a southern region school district with a rural, low-SES population. These findings are crucial for developing effective summer reading curricula applicable to similar school districts (Flores-Carter, 2023).

Nonacademic Research

Not a great deal of comprehensive research has been conducted regarding the nonacademic effects of implementing calendar reform. Of course, districts have reported their own financial implications of moving to a balanced calendar but that does not always provide concrete evidence. Over the last 20 years, only a few writers have reported on them.

For example, in 2013, the University of Michigan partnered with the Tourism Center to study the effects of year-round calendar schools on summer travel (Mykerezi, 2016). Based on their findings at the time, the researchers found that the "use of YRE at the state level does not appear to be correlated with travel patterns among households with children." They did establish that most families took their vacation time during the summer, but it did not seem to have much effect on students who attend year-round schools.

Nancy Flanagan wrote an Op-Ed piece in 2015 entitled, "Kids Who Take Vacations in the Middle of the School Year" (Flannagan, 2022). In her article, she explores the increasing phenomena of parents who pulled their children out of school for vacations while school was in session. She posed the question of why so many families were taking upon themselves to "deserve a vacation on their own terms." Meanwhile in Europe, in Lancashire County in England, parents were fined if their children missed five days of school. One of the political leaders at the time stated, "Holidays must not be taken during term time and government legislation prevents schools from granting leave of absence unless there are exceptional circumstances" (Burt, 2019). More recently, parents have found that taking vacations during peak summer months is too expensive and causes them to vacation when school is in session (Kim, 2022).

There have also been some studies on how the summer months cause some health concerns for children. One 2018 study in the Journal of School Health found "that elementary students gain[ed] weight over the summer." A year later, Mary Ann Liebert published an online article examining the impact of Year-Round and Traditional School Schedules on Summer Weight Gain and Fitness Loss (Brusseau, 2019). She found that, "shorter summer breaks appear to have a protective effect on summer weight gain when compared with a traditional 12-week break." She went on to add, "schools might consider a year-round school calendar for its potential to protect against summer weight gain." The International Journal of Behavioral Nutrition and Physical Activity also studied "the impact of summer vacation on children's obesogenic behaviors and body mass index" (Weaver, 2020). The results from their research showed that "children's BMI [Body Mass Index] gain accelerates during summer." Lastly, in 2019, the Sleep Journal studied changes in children's sleep and physical activity during a 1-week versus a 3-week break from school (Weaver, 2019). The results indicated "that during breaks children shifted bed and wake times by more than 1 hour on a 1-week and 3-week break. Further, this study showed that the children slept for approximately 20 to 30 minutes more during breaks from school."

In "The Dynamic Effects of a Summer Learning Program on Behavioral Engagement in School" (Pyne, 2023), the Center for Policy Analysis published a study on how a summer social-emotional curriculum benefits students during the regular school year. This program was implemented with, "low-income middle school students and features an unusual academic breadth and a social-emotional curriculum with year-to-year scaffolding." Their results showed that their intervention "led to substantial reductions in unexcused absences, chronic absenteeism and suspensions and a modest gain in ELA test scores." Meanwhile, in "The Effect of School Summer Holidays on Inequalities in Children and Young People's Mental Health and Cognitive Ability in the UK Using Data From the Millennium Cohort Study" (Kromydas, 2022), the BioMed Central from the UK published a study investigating "inequality changes in children's mental health and cognitive ability across the summer holidays." Using linear and logistic regression analysis, the researchers interviewed students before and after the summer holiday. The research "found inequalities in mental health and cognitive ability according to maternal education, and some evidence of worsening mental health and mental health inequalities across school summer holidays."

NOTE

1. https://onlinelibrary.wiley.com/doi/full/10.1111/1744-7941.12395

Chapter 7

Case Studies in Washington State

Across the state of Washington, more than 45 districts have studied some form of balanced calendars that spread school breaks more evenly across the school year. The primary aim that they all seem to embrace is that a balanced calendar will reduce the number of consecutive days or weeks in a row that students are out of school, as well as reduce the well-documented summer learning loss, while increasing student learning. This redesigned school year was also part of State Superintendent Chris Reykdal's long-term vision for one of several reforms for Washington's K–12 public schools.

DISTRICTS MOVE TO IMPLEMENTATION

During the 2022–2023 school year, five school districts in the state of Washington implemented a version of a balanced calendar. They secured funding through a competitive grant administered by the OSPI.

Each of the five districts responded to the following items as part of the grant application:

1. Please attach your district's modified school year calendar.
2. Describe how the modified calendar will address the unique needs of your student population, for example, low-income children or students, children with disabilities, English learners, racial and ethnic minorities, students experiencing homelessness, and foster care youth.
3. Who is part of your guiding team (administrators, certificated staff, classified staff, union representatives, parents, community members, and others)?

4. If you are awarded this grant, do you agree to participate in OSPI convenings? Select Yes No
   Do you have School Board approval/support? Select Yes No
   If No, how do you intend to inform your School Board and acquire approval?
5. A steering committee will be established consisting of personnel from OSPI and K–12 associations. What support can these organizations provide?
6. Please outline your spending plan below and describe the expenditures. Expenditures can be for various activities, including but not limited to stipends for personnel, contracting with an agency, travel, professional development, release time, and surveys (Note: each entity submitted a proposed budget).

These five state school districts then implemented a modified school year calendar and provided feedback about their experiences in the fall of 2022. The following case studies detail the responses from those school districts and should prove to be helpful to other districts looking to implement their own calendar reform. Each district was asked to respond to the following questions:

What model calendar are you operating on?
How long has your calendar been adopted for?
Why did you want to initially explore a balanced/modified calendar model?
What were some of the obstacles?
What were your solutions?
What lessons were learned and what advice would you provide to a district interested in exploring a modified/balanced calendar model?

CASE STUDY 1

Winlock School District—Superintendent, Dr. Garry Cameron

Winlock is a district located in Lewis County. During the 2022–2023 school year, Winlock's Board of Directors adopted a three-year calendar seen below.

Winlock's student enrollment at the time of this study was 865, with 54 classroom teachers whose average years of teaching experience were 10.3 years. The demographics of the district based for the school year above show 50.1% female, 0.8% Gender X, and 49.1% male. The predominant race is White with 70.5% and the next is Hispanic/Latino at 21.3% followed by Two

Case Studies in Washington State 145

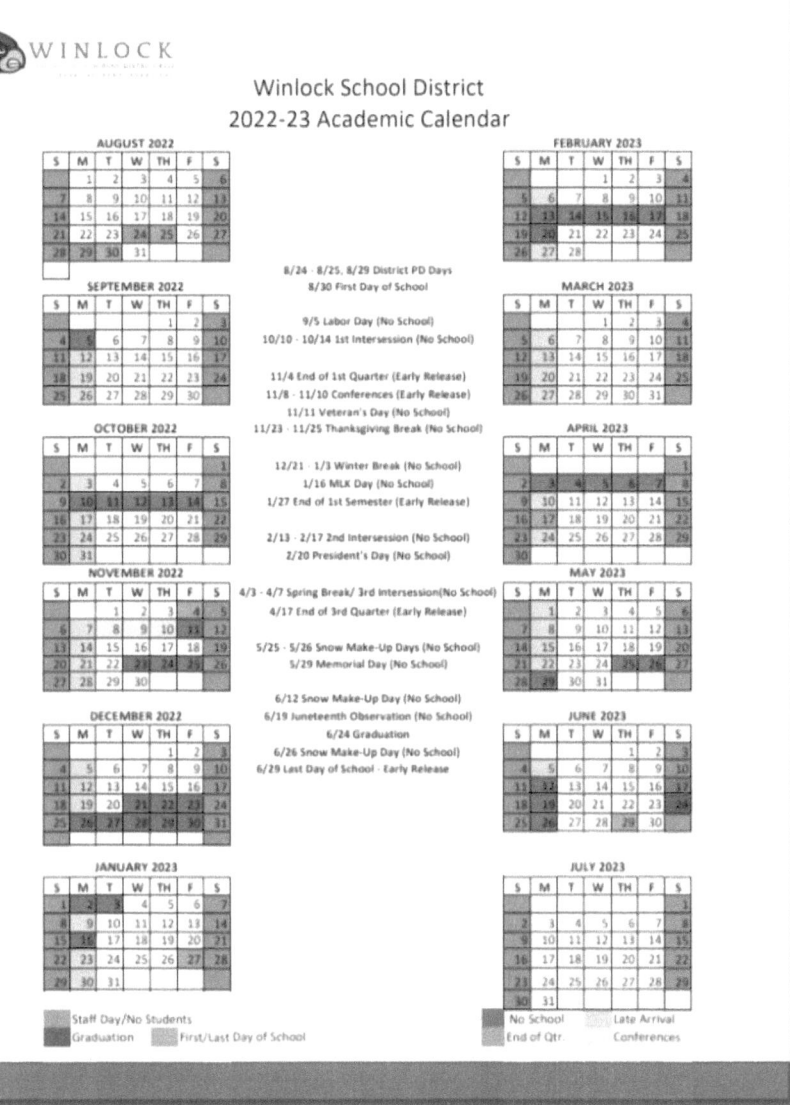

Figure 7.1 *Winlock School District 2022–2023 Academic Calendar.*

or More Races at 5.5%. American Indian/Alaska Native is a 1%, Asian is at 0.9%, and Black/African American is at 0.7%.

The Winlock School District wanted to initially explore a modified/balanced calendar model to reduce summer learning loss, provide extra learning opportunities through intersessions, be able to feed students/families during the intersessions, and allow staff to have breaks after six weeks instead of

11–13 weeks. The district indicated that their initial obstacle to implementation was getting support from stakeholders because they did not anticipate the level of difficulty gaining community support. They addressed this by allowing for additional input before the final implementation.

Some of the lessons learned from this district included having a smaller balanced calendar committee. The smaller size allows for more in-depth discussion where people can fully express complex thoughts. Setting some tentative agreements or consensus on which weeks are off and how many weeks to take off in the summer can be difficult was critical to early successes. Unlike a bond referendum that focuses on construction, calendar reform is more complex. Unlike other districts that had as many as 40–50 committee members, Winlock started small and saw much more success at a faster pace.

CASE STUDY 2

Union Gap School District—Superintendent, Lisa Gredvig

The Union Gap School District is located in Yakima County and serves the towns of Union Gap in Grades K–8. Union Gap's Board of Directors adopted a one-year calendar seen below.

During the 2022–2023 school year, Union Gap's enrollment was 578, with 37 classroom teachers (21–22 data). Average years of teaching experience was 10.6 years. The demographics of the district based for the school year show 46.4% female and 53.6% male. The predominant race is Hispanic/Latino at 85.3%, followed by White at 12.5%. Two or More Races is at 12.5%. American Indian/Alaskan Native is at 0.5%, followed by Asian which is 0.3%, and followed by Black at 0.2%.

Union Gap initially wanted to explore a modified/balanced calendar to help with burnout from students and staff. The district indicated that their obstacles to implementation were getting the community to understand that a balanced calendar did not include anything virtual. The staff also noted an obstacle with getting feedback on possible calendars and did not like having to start school early and end later than it has had for decades.

The solution for this district was to start small and slowly build on more complex components of their plan. The breaks they added are only five days compared to two to three weeks used in other places. The community further disclosed that there was not an interest in going year-round based on the surveys. Their comments also indicated that they wanted smaller breaks but still wanted at least six weeks of summer, which also includes summer school and migrant camp. Migrant camp is one of the activities students identified for migrant services can participate in.

Case Studies in Washington State 147

Union Gap School District
2022-2023
Academic Year Calendar

Green - Conference Week
Red - No School
Blue - Intersession/No School
Highlighted - Snow Make-ups

Events	
Aug 1	School Office Opens
Aug 11	First day of classes
Sept. 5	No School - Labor Day
Sept. 23	No School - 1/2 PD Day
Sept. 26-30	Conference Week
Oct 7	Individual Pictures
Oct 14	PD - No School
Oct 17-21	Intersession
Nov 11	No School-Veterans Day
Nov 15	Picture Retakes
Nov 23-25	Thanksgiving Break
Dec 19-30	Winter Break
Jan 2	New Year Holiday
Jan 16	MLK Day
Feb 15	Class Pictures
Feb 20	Presidents' Day
Feb 21-24	Intersession
Mar 10	PD Day
Mar 13-17	Conference Week
April 3-7	Spring Break
April 10-14	Intersession
April 13-14	Snow Days, if needed
May 29	Memorial Day
Jun 14	Kindergarten Graduation
Jun 14	8th Grade Promotion
Jun 15	Last Day
July 10-21	Summer Intersession
1st Qtr	Aug 11 - Oct 13 (44 days)
2nd Qtr	Oct 21 - Jan 13 (45 days)
3rd Qtr	Jan 17 - Mar 24 (43 days)
4th Qtr	Mar 27 - Jun 15 (48 days)

Figure 7.2 *Union Gap School District 2022–2023 Academic Year Calendar.*

This district officials said that they learned to start small and commit to at least two years with their new calendar. They disclosed that utilizing data was critical in choosing the right direction for their schools. Their initial goal of 20% student participation in the first intersession actually hit 40% participation rate.

CASE STUDY 3

Toppenish School District—Superintendent, John Cerna

Toppenish is located in Yakima County and serves the city of Toppenish and the surrounding areas, including the members of the Yakama Nation. Toppenish's Board of Directors decided to adopt a one-year calendar seen below:

During the 2022–2023 school year, Toppenish's student enrollment was 4,783, with 242 classroom teachers. The average years of teaching experience was 10.2 years. The demographics reported 48.4% female, 0.4 Gender X, and 51.2% male. The Hispanic/Latino is the predominant race at 72.5%, followed by White at 11.6%, American Indian/Alaska Native at 7.3%, Black/African American at 6.2%, Asian at 1.3%, and Two or More Races at 1.1%.

Toppenish wanted to initially explore the modified/balanced calendar because district leadership saw a need for intervention, which had been traditionally done during the summer. But the students and the community viewed summer school as a punishment, not as an intervention. They had already added days off at Thanksgiving and during some three-day weekends, which were based on poor student and staff attendance.

Toppenish indicated that some of the obstacles included working around the state testing schedule, end-of-year reporting dates, and grant releases. As more districts move to this model, they hope that changes occur. Locally, they are still working on custodial/maintenance of buildings. Cost can still be an obstacle as intersessions, buses, and incentives are more costly than running a two-to-four-week summer program.

The solutions to the obstacles included getting creative with braiding federal and state funding with what they used to set aside for summer. Using Title IV, Gear Up, CTE, and Title I funds for intersessions, the district reported that including unions and school board members were very helpful in the planning and implementation of their calendar reform. Notifying families about the dates of upcoming intersessions was also very helpful.

Toppenish School District No. 202
2022-2023 School Calendar

		August 2022				
S	M	T	W	T	F	S
	1	2	3	4	5	6
7	8	9	10	11	12	13
14	15	16	17	18	19	20
21	22	23	24	25	26	27
28	29	30	31			

		September 2022				
S	M	T	W	T	F	S
				1	2	3
4	5	6	7	8	W9	10
11	12	13	14	15	W16	17
18	19	20	21	22	W23	24
25	26	27	28	29	30	

		October 2022				
S	M	T	W	T	F	S
						1
2	3	4	5	6	7	8
9	10	11	12	13	W14	15
16	17	18	19	20	W21	22
23	24	25	C26	C27	28	29
30	31					

		November 2022				
S	M	T	W	T	F	S
		1	2	3	W4	5
6	7	8	9	10	11	12
13	14	15	16	17	18	19
20	21	22	23	24	25	26
27	28	29	30			

		December 2022				
S	M	T	W	T	F	S
				1	W2	3
4	5	6	7	8	W9	10
11	12	13	14	15	16	17
18	19	20	21	22	23	24
25	26	27	28	29	30	31

		January 2023				
S	M	T	W	T	F	S
1	2	3	4	5	W6	7
8	9	10	11	12	13	14
15	16	17	18	19	W20	21
22	23	24	25	26	W27	28
29	30	31				

		February 2023				
S	M	T	W	T	F	S
			1	2	W3	4
5	6	7	8	9	W10	11
12	13	14	15	16	17	18
19	20	21	22	23	24	25
26	27	28				

		March 2023				
S	M	T	W	T	F	S
			1	2	W3	4
5	6	7	8	9	W10	11
12	13	14	15	16	W17	18
19	20	21	22	23	W24	25
26	27	28	C29	C30	31	

		April 2023				
S	M	T	W	T	F	S
						1
2	3	4	5	6	7	8
9	10	11	12	13	W14	15
16	17	18	19	20	W21	22
23	24	25	26	27	W28	29
30						

		May 2023				
S	M	T	W	T	F	S
	1	2	3	4	W5	6
7	8	9	10	11	W12	13
14	15	16	17	18	W19	20
21	22	23	24	25	26	27
28	29	30	31			

		June 2023				
S	M	T	W	T	F	S
				1	W2	3
4	5	6	7	8	9	10
11	12	13	14	15	16	17
18	19	20	21	22	23	24
25	26	27	28	29	30	

		July 2023				
S	M	T	W	T	F	S
						1
2	3	4	5	6	7	8
9	10	11	12	13	14	15
16	17	18	19	20	21	22
23	24	25	26	27	28	29
30	31					

Kinder Academy & WA Kids	August 3, 4, 5	
6th & 9th Grade Academy	August 3, 4, 5	
Optional Day	August 9 - 10	
District Staff Preservice	August 11	
First Day of School	**August 15**	
Early Release	August 22	
Labor Day Break	September 2 & 5	
Early Release	September 19	
Fall Break	October 3 - 7	
Early Release	October 17	
Conferences	October 26 & 27	
No School	October 28	
Veterans' Day Break	November 11	
Thanksgiving Holidays	November 21 - 25	
Early Release	December 5	
Holiday Break	December 19 - 30	
New Year's Holiday	January 2	
M. L. King Holiday	January 13 & 16	
91st Day	January 25	
Early Release	February 6	
100th Day of School	February 8	
Winter Break	February 17 - 24	
Early Release	March 13	
Conferences	March 29 & 30	
No School	March 31	
Spring Break	April 3 - 7	
Early Release	April 17	
Early Release	May 15	
Memorial Day Break	May 26 & 29	
Treaty Day Commemoration	June 9	
Graduation	June 16	
Juneteenth Holiday/No School	June 19	
Last Day of School	**June 22**	

Adoption Date: 4/26/2022

Teacher Days: 180
Student Days: 176
Snow Days= Remote Learning

Figure 7.3 *Toppenish School District 2022–2023 School Calendar.*

CASE STUDY 4

Mount Adams School District—Superintendent, Dr. Curt Guaglianone

The Mount Adams School District is located in Yakima County and serves the community of White Swan. The Mount Adam's Board of Directors adopted a one-year calendar. See below for the 2022–2023 adopted school calendar.

Mount Adam's student enrollment during the 2022–2023 school year was 889, with 63 classroom teachers. The average years of teacher experience was 7.6 years. The demographics for the district based on the school year above show 48.9% female and 51.1% male. American Indian/Alaska Native was the predominant race at 50.4%, followed by Hispanic/Latino at 41.6%. Two or More Races is 4.7% and White is 3.3%.

The administration's desire to lengthen the school year to decrease learning loss was the initial reason for exploring the balanced calendar model. Mount Adams indicated that administration work during the breaks to offer intersessions and transportation for Yakima Valley Technical School students during traditional school breaks were obstacles.

Mount Adams stated that they struggled and did not have any really good solutions. They did alternate administration during intersession one day a week. Their school officials reported the importance of getting the community's input, creating a calendar based on students' needs and communicating to staff and the community.

CASE STUDY 5

Highland School District—Superintendent, Mark Anderson

The Highland School District is located in Yakima County and serves the community of Cowiche, Washington. The Highland's Board of Directors adopted a one-year calendar below:

During the 2022–2023 school year, Highland's enrollment was 1,094 with 91 classroom teachers with the average years of teaching experience at 10.6.

The demographics for this district based on the school above show 47.3% female, 0.1% Gender X, and 52.6% male. Hispanic/Latino is the predominant race at 75.6%, followed by White at 22%. Two or More Races is at 1%, followed by Black/African American at 0.6%. American Indian/Alaskan Native is at 0.5% and Asian is at 0.3%.

Case Studies in Washington State 151

Mt. Adams School District #209
2022-23 School Calendar

August-2022

S	M	T	W	T	F	S
	1	2	3	4	5	6
7	8	9	10	11	12	13
14	15	16	17	18	19	20
21	22	23	24	25	26	27
28	29	30	31			

August
- 10 New Staff Orientation
- 11 Building PD
- 15 District Directed Day
- 17 First Day of School (No Early Release)

February
- 13-16 Parent Conferences
- 17 Snow Day (make-up if needed)
- 20 Presidents Day
- 21-24 Winter Break

February-2023

S	M	T	W	T	F	S
			1	2	3	4
5	6	7	8	9	10	11
12	13	14	15	16	17	18
19	20	21	22	23	24	25
26	27	28				

September-2022

S	M	T	W	T	F	S
				1	2	3
4	5	6	7	8	9	10
11	12	13	14	15	16	17
18	19	20	21	22	23	24
25	26	27	28	29	30	

September
- 5 Labor Day

March
- 9 End Tri 2 (120 days)
- 10 Snow Day (make-up if needed)

March-2023

S	M	T	W	T	F	S
			1	2	3	4
5	6	7	8	9	10	11
12	13	14	15	16	17	18
19	20	21	22	23	24	25
26	27	28	29	30	31	

October-2022

S	M	T	W	T	F	S
						1
2	3	4	5	6	7	8
9	10	11	12	13	14	15
16	17	18	19	20	21	22
23	24	25	26	27	28	29
30	31					

October
- 3-7 Fall Break - No School
- 14 STEM Profession Development
- 24-28 Conferences

April
- 3-7 Spring Break

April-2023

S	M	T	W	T	F	S
						1
2	3	4	5	6	7	8
9	10	11	12	13	14	15
16	17	18	19	20	21	22
23	24	25	26	27	28	29
30						

November-2022

S	M	T	W	T	F	S
		1	2	3	4	5
6	7	8	9	10	11	12
13	14	15	16	17	18	19
20	21	22	23	24	25	26
27	28	29	30			

November
- 11 Veteran's Day
- 18 End of Tri (60 days)
- 21-25 Thanksgiving Holiday No School

May
- 5 District Directed Day
- 29 Memorial Day

May-2023

S	M	T	W	T	F	S
	1	2	3	4	5	6
7	8	9	10	11	12	13
14	15	16	17	18	19	20
21	22	23	24	25	26	27
28	29	30	31			

December-2022

S	M	T	W	T	F	S
				1	2	3
4	5	6	7	8	9	10
11	12	13	14	15	16	17
18	19	20	21	22	23	24
25	26	27	28	29	30	31

December
- 21-30 Christmas Break

June
- 9 Treaty Days
- 16 Last Day of School (End of Tri 180)
- 19 Juneteenth

June-2023

S	M	T	W	T	F	S
				1	2	3
4	5	6	7	8	9	10
11	12	13	14	15	16	17
18	19	20	21	22	23	24
25	26	27	28	29	30	

Total:

January-2023

S	M	T	W	T	F	S
1	2	3	4	5	6	7
8	9	10	11	12	13	14
15	16	17	18	19	20	21
22	23	24	25	26	27	28
29	30	31				

January
- 2 New Years Observed
- 16 Martin Luther King Day

July
- 4 4th of July

July-2023

S	M	T	W	T	F	S
						1
2	3	4	5	6	7	8
9	10	11	12	13	14	15
16	17	18	19	20	21	22
23	24	25	26	27	28	29
30	31					

LEGEND

- First/Last Day of School
- Holiday/No School
- Early Release
  - White Swan 1:00 pm
  - Harrah 1:30 pm
- District Directed Day/PD for Staff - No School for Students, Staff Only
- Trimester Ends
- Early Release - Parent Conferences
  1:00 pm - White Swan; 1:30 pm - Harrah

Revised 4/19/22

Figure 7.4 *Mount Adams School District 2022–2023 School Calendar.*

HIGHLAND SCHOOL DISTRICT
School Calendar
2022-2023

Approved by Highland School District Board of Directors on May 2, 2022

"A QUALITY EDUCATION FOR ALL STUDENTS"

Significant Dates:
July 4   4th of July Holiday
Aug. 16-18 PLD
Aug. 22 First Day of School
Aug. 25 First Day of Kindergarten
Sept. 5 Labor Day-**No School**
Oct. 3-7 **Intersession**
**Oct. 14 Early Release: HJH & HHS ONLY
Oct. 21 Teacher Grading Day/Conf. Prep-**Early Release All Schools**
Oct. 24-28 Conference Week-**Early Release each day MWC & TIS**
**Oct. 24-25 HHS & HJH Full Days of Class
Oct. 26-28 Conferences-**Early Release-HJH & HHS**
Oct. 27 NO LATE START
Nov. 11 Veterans Day-**No School**
Nov. 23 School Break-**Early Release**
Nov. 24 Thanksgiving Day-**No School**
Nov. 25 Native American Heritage Day-**No School**
**Dec. 8 Conferences for HHS and HJH only
**Dec. 9 Early Release: HJH & HHS ONLY
Dec. 16 Winter Break-**Early Release**
Dec. 19-30 Winter Break - **No School**
Jan. 2 New Year's Day-Observed **No School**
Jan. 16 MLK Jr Day-**No School**
Jan. 27 Teacher Grading Day/Semester End-**Early Release**
Feb. 13-17 **Intersession**
Feb. 20 President's Day - **No School**
Feb. 21 PLD-**No School**
Mar. 24 Teacher Grading Day/Conf. Prep-**Early Release: All Schools**
Mar. 27-31 Conference Week-**Early Release each day**
Mar. 30 NO LATE START
April 3-7 Spring Break - **No School**
May 22-26 **Intersession**
May 29 Memorial Day-**No School**
June 16 Grading Day-HHS Graduation-**Early Release**
June 19 Juneteenth/Emancipation Day - **No School**
June 23 Last Day of School-**Early Release**

Legend
- = School Begins/Ends
- = Half-day, note: ** = Half-day for HJH/HHS only
- = Holidays - School Break/Closed
- = School Break-No School
- = Intersession Instruction
- = Conferences, Note: ** = Conferences for HJH/HHS only
- = Certificated Professional Learning Day
- [ ] = Early Release Days for Students

BOLD = Thursdays in **bold** are **not** Late Start Days

Figure 7.5 *Highland School District 2022–2023 School Calendar.*

Highland initially indicated that they wanted to explore the model to better meet student needs. Funding, serving meals during additional learning days, and adjusting the state testing window to accommodate a longer school year were obstacles. The solution to the meal issue was to work with OSPI to assist in funding meals.

The lessons learned included clear communication, especially, communicating to the staff and community that student needs come first. Additionally, creating a calendar based on students' needs is vital.

To break down the questions for better understanding, a comparison table summarizing the responses to the questions below is detailed for each district:

Why did you want to initially explore a balanced/modified calendar model?
What were some of the obstacles?
What were your solutions?
Lessons learned (the advice you would provide to a district interested in exploring a modified/balanced calendar model).

Funding was secured to issue grants for the 2023–2024 school year. However, due to legislative action, the balanced calendar project was terminated. The decision to cut funding for the project did not come lightly. During the most recent Spring 2023 legislative session, the state legislature redirected $55 million of ESSER funding that was already either expended through various programs or obligated to partners with OSPI through grants and contracts. Unfortunately, that created a backfill issue, which required OSPI to redirect much of the ESSER III state set-aside funding—a large portion of which was already committed to programs and had extensive plans to spend—in order to satisfy these payments and obligations. Regrettably, the agency has had to reduce/terminate funding from important programs resulting from these legislative decisions. The balanced calendar project is one of the projects that had to be terminated.

Although funding was terminated, the balanced calendar steering committee continued to provide support through synchronous meetings, where best practices and opportunities for technical assistance were provided. Dr. Pedersen and Dr. Hornak continued on as consultants for the state, continuing their work supporting local education agencies. The various partner agencies representing school staff, including school administrators, and central office staff continue their advocacy and support. Additionally, Education Service Districts (ESDs) 105, 113, and 123 offered support, including the hiring of support hub personnel.

This grassroots support is indicative of the innovative approach Washington state takes when it comes to serving students. Even in the face of adversity, there is an all-hands-on deck approach.

The funding loss provided an opportunity to reach back to the aforementioned implementor districts to ask them what they needed to do to continue the work in light of funding loss. Another unique factor is that two districts, Toppenish and Winlock, had a superintendent transition mid-year.

Table 7.1

	Winlock	Union Gap	Toppenish	Mount Adams	Highland
Objectives	Reduce learning loss, extra learning opportunities for students, and provide meals in a more consistent basis	Mitigate student and staff burnout	Provide timely intervention for students instead of waiting until summer and view intersession as an opportunity, not a punishment	Reduce student learning loss	Meet the needs of students
Obstacles	Getting input from all affected groups	Communication, seeking, and understanding	State testing schedule, state reporting deadlines, maintenance, facilities, bussing, and added costs	Admin are always on with students in the building, transportation, and coordinating with other programs, e.g., tech center	Funding, feeding students, and state testing schedule
Solutions	Get support and communicate	Start small	Be creative with braiding and coordinate all funds	Still exploring	Worked with the state about feeding students and came up with a solution
Lessons Learned	Have a small committee and manage change	Set realistic goals and commit to a 2-year calendar	Get union buy-in early and communicate with families about the opportunity	Getting community input, develop calendar based on students' needs, and communicate	Communicate and develop calendar based on students' need

The districts were asked to respond to the following questions:

1. How and what did you do to adjust to the grant funding loss?
2. How were you able to sustain the balanced calendar?
3. Did the regional hubs provide support? If yes, how? If not, what were the barriers?
4. Which supports received during the study and implementation process were most beneficial?
5. Which supports received during the study and implementation were least beneficial?
6. What supports would you suggest are added for entities interested in the balanced calendar model?
7. What support do you need to continue this work beyond the 2023–2024 school year?
8. What scares you the most as you move forward in the process?
9. What excites you the most as you move forward in the process?
10. What impact has the balanced calendar had on student outcomes?
11. What else do you want to share?

The following narrative details their responses. In response to Question 1, how and what did the district do to adjust to grant funding loss, respondents noted that they used Title I funds, ESSER funds, and braided funding with the 21st Century Community Learning Center grant. Additionally, the district either modified or cut planned intersession activities.

For Question 2 regarding the sustainability concern of a balanced calendar, one district noted that their board had to approve the intersession since they lost funding and had to cut $1.8 million. Since they had a healthy fund balance, they were able to continue with the intersession. Another district said that they will use categorical funding after the 2023–2024 school year and restrict the program as needed due to funding.

Question 3 asked people about the regional hub support. As noted, there were hubs assigned to each of the ESD regions to support districts. Respondents noted the hubs supported during the implementation year, but not so much now that they are doing it.

In response to which supports received during the study and implementation process were most beneficial, funding was the main support. Grant funding helped to support travel to other districts, collaboration with others, and paying stipends to staff for their extra work.

Which supports received during the study and implementation process were least beneficial? One district respondent stated the development of the calendar; there was a lack of studies for us to use to help educate our community.

Question 6 asked respondents to share what supports they would suggest are added for entities interested in the balanced calendar model. Calendar options, examples of intersessions classes/models, and guidance on implementation steps were mentioned. Talking points with each group of stakeholders to guide them along the way as well as detailed Q and A and ways to talk with naysayers were also noted.

What support is needed to continue the balanced calendar model beyond this year? Funding and data on the success of the balanced calendar model were noted. One district said that since the balanced calendar is expensive, our Board is considering moving back to a regular calendar after the next school year.

Having enough funding to support the balanced calendar model and not having more schools following along in the state with the model are things that scare these districts the most.

What excites you the most as you move forward in the process? The work that excites me is a response. Another respondent said that they loved learning about other districts and what they are doing. Looking at their district's data for students that attended intersessions, their growth is great! This district would love to see other district intersession plans to help improve theirs.

The impact of the balanced calendar on student outcomes elicited responses, noting that students who attended all three intersessions had great growth data on the district-wide assessment. Other positives noted were student and staff relationships and reduced issues for those students who struggle with school breaks as they attend intersession. One district said that they are not sure how to measure without considering all the other factors.

What else would you like to share was the last question. The district that responded said that they are very excited about the opportunities a balanced calendar brings to a district and would love to learn from others. Concerns noted were that principals are supposed to state two weeks after the last day of school. That puts them into mid-July, and they expect their administration to come back for the school year on August 1. That only gives them a few weeks off. Balancing the calendar with traditional administrative professional growth conferences where conflict occurs was noted as a concern. Also, student attendance at summer camp conflicts was shared.

The author had an opportunity to visit one of the implementing districts to dialogue with staff and parents. Following a recap of the visit, the author met with the administrator overseeing the balanced calendar as well as the superintendent. A series of questions was asked. See the following for the Q and A.

Q: How and what did you do to adjust to grant funding loss?

A: We were able to modify how we were using Title I funds to fund the intersessions since this action aligned with the intent and purpose of Title

1. We also gave up purchasing a communication program to fund the first intersession.

Q: Your district went through a superintendent change last year. How did this affect this project?

A: The School Board had already adopted a three-year balanced calendar so that part was already in place. I oversaw the project, so there was not much impact. When the new superintendent came on board, we proceeded as usual.

Q: What has been the community feedback?

A: About 60% of the folks in the community favor the balanced calendar approach.

Q: Overall, what have been the intersession participation rates?

A: Rates have been higher at the elementary level compared to the secondary level.

At this last session, 40% of enrolled elementary students participated compared to 10% at the secondary level.

Q: Were the assigned ESD hubs helpful?

A: Yes, they were. Our hub was able to provide resources and was always available.

Q: What scares you about the balanced calendar model moving forward?

A: Continue approval of the calendar by the School Board. Additionally, the effort it will take to go back to a traditional calendar.

Q: What excites you about the balanced calendar model moving forward?

A: I am waiting to see results and hope it shows growth. We have added seven weeks of schooling during the year. This is also an opportunity for staff to job swap during the intersessions. Paraprofessionals can step into teaching, teachers can do recess supervision, and elementary teachers can work with secondary students and vice versa.

Q: What lessons have you learned?

A: Get community input early. Share the calendars. Consider all efficiencies and impact.

Q: What else would you like to share?

A: Would like to see collaboration with area districts that want to explore and implement this model. Have a mechanism for continual dialogue with implementor districts.

During the day, the author was able to visit with two parents to discuss their experiences.

- *Q:* How did you feel when the balanced calendar concept was introduced?
- *A:* Really open to it. Liked the idea. Free time during the school year. Families had the opportunity to attend or not. It was a little of an adjustment. Looking for research to see if the model is successful.
- *Q:* What are some challenges?
- *A:* Coordination with the ECEAP program, what to do with children when there is no school.
- *Q:* What do your children share with you about the intersessions?
- *A:* Overall, they have enjoyed it. It is a more relaxed school day. Fun interaction.
- *Q:* What do you think will happen if the model goes away?
- *A:* The kids that need a place to go will not have a place to go. This model has helped with summer learning loss and allowed for soft breaks. We are a high poverty district, worried about what will happen with more breaks.
- *Q:* What else do you want to share?
- *A:* Overall, I am really happy with it. Folks have opinions. I ask that they step back and look at the broader picture.

The interview with the transportation provided insights into the challenges the district is facing overall with the driver shortage. The district's transportation department has met the challenge of transporting students. The director shared that this model is good for kids so we will make it work.

A teacher representative was interviewed next.

- *Q:* At the beginning of the project there were more cons than pros. Why?
- *A:* People are afraid of change. Folks felt this was pushed on us. It was rushed.
- *Q:* Later, there were more pros than cons. Why?
- *A:* A few of us were able to visit Michigan for a visit. We came back and shared and that changed the narrative. Word of mouth was key. Mitigating teacher burnout helped sway opinion.
- *Q:* What would happen if the balanced calendar model went away?
- *A:* We have been at it for 1.5 years. We do not have enough data yet to assess effectiveness. Need more time to study. By keeping this model, we may be

able to pull students from other districts. I see more student and teacher burnout if this goes away. There are natural peaks and valleys during the year and October is one of them. Everyone is tired in October. It is nice to get a break. Everyone comes back with more energy after the intersession/break. Hope adult issues do not get in the way.

Q: What excites you about the balanced calendar?

A: Our district was one of the first to do it in the area. Hope to draw folks to the district. The breaks are incredible.

Q: What scares you?

A: We will take steps backward if we go back to a traditional calendar. We need to look at the positives and not make rush decisions.

Q: What else would you like to share?

A: Hoping in three years other districts will want to do this. With an over 90% poverty rate, I am concerned about the effect going back to a traditional calendar will have on students.

Lastly, an administrator overseeing this intersession was interviewed.

Q: What did you think when the balanced calendar concept was introduced?

A: As a teacher, I did not like the idea. Communication was lacking, more planning was needed, and I thought it would be rough.

Q: What do you like about the balanced calendar?

A: I personally do not like it. Some say behaviors are better after the break. There is a retraining process. Teacher do get a break.

Q: What else would you like to share with me?

A: Number of students who sign up does not match who shows up. It is a challenge. Cost of intersession is high and other things get forsaken.

The following is the Q and A with the other parent.

Q: What were your thoughts when the balanced calendar concept was introduced?

A: It was a whole new concept. After researching, it started to make sense to me. My kids were getting burned out with the traditional calendar. Saw one of my kids retain knowledge.

Q: What do you think will happen if the district went back to a traditional calendar?

A: There would be burnout. I would be fighting my kids to go to school. We use the break to go on vacation. After the vacation, my kids are ready to go back to school.

Q: How do you think the community feels about the balanced calendar?

A: I think it is 50/50.

Chapter 8

Strategies for Implementing a Balanced Calendar

The COVID-19 pandemic forced schools worldwide to transition from traditional in-person teaching to virtual learning. Amidst this upheaval, the concept of the balanced school calendar, established over 135 years ago, gained renewed attention. This chapter explores why schools consider transitioning to and implementing a balanced calendar.

The NAYRE advocates using the 180 allocated school days more efficiently across the calendar year by reducing the lengthy summer break, which tends to negatively impact student knowledge and retention. To identify potential break periods for exchange, schools often analyze attendance rates over five years and consider local traditions, like county fairs to determine when to schedule a break from school. While the 45/15 model is most common, the balanced calendar allows flexibility to tailor a calendar that fits the community's needs, reducing the need for extensive reteaching each fall.

WHY SWITCH?

Administrators and teachers nationwide have been actively seeking solutions to minimize the impact of summer recess on student achievement. Students appear to lose the equivalent of one month of instruction per summer annually (Ferguson, 1999). Hayes and Grether (1983) stated that summer recess equals a three-month achievement loss. Throughout a typical school experience, the gaps identified at the secondary level can be attributed to the negative impact of summer recess on academic achievement (Hayes & Grether, 1983). As a result, school officials have been left with the burden of investigating ways to minimize the annual summer learning loss.

The need to change the structure of the school calendar has been met with resistance in the past due to the shared experience the majority of Americans experienced while attending school (Rury, 2013). The concept of the balanced school calendar dates back to early 1645. However, it was not until the 1980s that the balanced calendar began to be adopted by school districts across the nation.

Although research once considered biased and conflicted, Hornak (2015) demonstrated that the length of summer significantly impacts mathematical learning retention. In 2015, Hornak's study demonstrated that regardless of economic status and gender, children who attend a balanced school calendar with a summer recess of six weeks retain more mathematical knowledge than their counterparts who attend school on the traditional school calendar with a 12-week summer recess. Furthermore, children who received some mathematical instruction while on summer recess retained more mathematical knowledge than their peers who did not receive instruction during summer recess (Hornak, 2015). Finally, the length of summer recess significantly impacted mathematical retention.

There are various reasons schools consider the transition to a balanced school calendar, as noted previously, and several reasons have been identified as perceived barriers to such a transition. First, the amount of time a student is away from school has a negative impact on their ability to retain knowledge. The NAYRE recommends school districts to use their 180 school days more efficiently across the calendar year by reducing the number of weeks a student is off annually in the summer. To do this, school districts look at attendance rates over the past five years to help identify the points in the school year when students are not in school. It is also essential to look at local and community traditions, such as when the county fair is held. By doing so, school leaders can work to exchange a school break at a time when families have demonstrated a desire or a need to be off. While the 45/15 model is the dominant balanced calendar, there is no one-size-fits-all school calendar. This flexibility allows school leaders to co-construct a school calendar that meets the needs of their specific community. The balanced school calendar reduces the required days teachers reteach annually each fall.

Moving to a balanced school calendar also allows school districts to increase instructional time for students through intersession. Intersession is defined as a short period between instructional terms, which sometimes provides for specific students to attend school for real-time remediation or enrichment. While the 180-day school calendar is the most widely used calendar across the nation, schools continue to serve students who only need 150 days of school but are required to attend 180 school days. In addition, schools serve many students who need 180 days of school, which is typically what we offer in the United States. Following a pandemic, schools also have students with a great deal of unfinished learning, who may require 220 days of school annually to complete the unfinished learning that may have occurred during the pandemic.

Unfortunately, the traditional 180-day school calendar often fails to provide time to increase the number of school days for specific students. To that end, when school districts move to the balanced school calendar, intersession allows school districts to offer additional instructional days for remediation and enrichment as needed, thus offering select students the opportunity to attend additional school days to finish the unfinished learning and close learning gaps. Intersession has also been used to extend the learning opportunities of students who desire extensions to the curriculum.

The balanced calendar has many benefits, such as improving staff morale. Balanced calendar educators indicate that the balanced calendar contributes to a more humane life–work balance. Educator burnout has been positively impacted for those working on the balanced calendar, and the need for substitute teachers has been greatly reduced in balanced calendar schools as staff tends to schedule annual dentist and medical appointments during a planned break from school.

So, what does a potential transition look like? The first step in considering a transition is identifying a stakeholder group to study this idea. Next, it is crucial to determine the needs of your learning community. Do most of your students need more time to complete the unfinished learning that may have occurred during the pandemic? Are you attempting to find ways to reduce the stress level of your staff? Do you have periods when illness overtakes your school community and daily attendance is reduced? Are substitutes hard to find? Are your students taking time off each year to attend a local event, such as a county fair? Do certain holidays impact attendance? Do you want to find a way to create a school calendar that is more in line with current lifestyles? If so, it is time to create a steering committee to investigate a balanced school calendar to determine if the alternative calendar is appropriate for your learning community.

While there is not a one-size-fits-all action plan, it is strongly recommended that you call on a local, state, or national expert to support your steering committee. As noted, the balanced calendar concept has been used for over 100 years in schools nationwide. As a result, there are several resources, including NAYRE or school officials, serving on the balanced calendar who can support new school officials and steering committees studying a potential transition.

Schools that have transitioned often start with building capacity and understanding with the staff, as once parents and guardians are informed, they will frequently ask their trusted educator for an opinion. Any potential transition could be jeopardized if the school employee states that they do not know much or are unsure about the idea. Support for any school initiative is relative to a particular school district. In some cases, support is deemed at a little over 50% of the people supporting an initiative. In other cases, school districts target a higher percentage of required supporters before any change will be considered.

The implementation process is also unique to a particular school district. Some school and district leaders have a great deal of support from the learning community, while other leaders may need more time to build capacity. The NAYRE has seen implementation take as little as a semester to as long as three or more years. A proposed implementation plan can be found in Figure 8.2. Schools that attempt to move too quickly may have difficulty in making the transition. With that, the timeline may be different from one district to another.

Once the steering committee has been established and the research has been conducted, it is time to start holding informational meetings to build capacity with a broader audience. In one case, school leaders held multiple informational meetings, mailed home flyers, and polled parents and guardians on how they felt about a potential transition as families finished parent–teacher conferences.

After building capacity and understanding with the greater school community, it is time to connect with business leaders and educational partners external to the district, such as the Boys and Girls Club or the YMCA/YWCA. Community partners tend to start planning programs and staffing levels for school breaks months, if not years in advance. Surprising a community partner will not only jeopardize the partnership but may also place some undue burden on the community partner as they may have increased staff for a typical 12-week summer that has been reduced due to the transition.

During all stages of the planning and research phase, the steering committee should document and respond to the concerns in a timely manner. While many have been discussed in previous chapters, in addition to transportation, athletics, and food, traditions such as the desire for school-aged students to have a long lazy summer as their parents and guardians did and/or the tradition of vacationing in August tend to be used as reasons not to transition to a balanced calendar. The reality is that American children no longer go outside after breakfast in the summer, only to return home when the streetlights come on as they once did. Today, summer tends to be when children connect virtually with friends over a computer, game console, or cell phone rather than playing outside all day. Parents and guardians with children on a balanced calendar have valued the opportunity to vacation when most students across the nation are in session. Including a week-long fall break into the school calendar, taking the entire week of Thanksgiving off, taking a week off in

Strategies for Implementing a Balanced Calendar 165

February for mid-winter break, or adding a second week of spring break allows families to travel or enjoy time without the burden of dealing with crowds.

With any change initiative, the steering committee must be clear on why a school is considering changing the balanced calendar. With an emphasis on improved academic and nonacademic outcomes for students and staff, everyone involved needs to be able to share why this idea is being considered without hesitation. Figure 8.1 illustrates some of the reasons a school district considers a transition to the balanced school calendar.

After capacity and understanding have been reached with school staff, parents, guardians, and members of the learning community, including local, state, and federal lawmakers, a presentation should be made to the school board for approval to consider a transition.

After years of supporting school districts with a transition to a balanced school calendar, NAYRE has identified several important steps to help districts ensure that the study and implementation of the balanced school calendar has been researched and communicated effectively. Figure 8.3 serves as a guide to avoid the pitfalls that other school districts have encountered.

First, while educational leaders and steering committees are not required to know everything about a balanced school calendar, when asked a question about the concept that is unable to be answered on the spot sends a message: if this is such a good idea, why do the people leading this initiative not know the answer to my question. By partnering with a local leader or someone from NAYRE, district leaders and steering committees can listen for pressure points and work to bring clarity to the concerns without being forced

Figure 8.1

First Semester or Year of Study
- Organize a steering committee
- Connect with a local expert or the National Association for Year-Round Education (NAYRE)
- Conduct research
- Prepare presentations and educational resources
- Conduct informational sessions with staff, parents/guardians, and members of the learning community
- Develop surveys
- Conduct a financial analysis
- Conduct site visits
- Update the Board of Education

Second Semester or Year of Study
- Continue to conduct research
- Identify a list of calendar reform supporters
- Analyze five years of student and staff attendance
- Identify non-negotiable break times (county fair or other local tradition)
- Develop draft calendars
- Conduct Intersession research
- Analyze operations; how will this proposed change impact food service, maintenance, transportation, childcare, etc.
- Engage community partners, such as WMCA/YWCA, Boys and Girls Club, etc.

Third Semester or Year of Study
- Present research and findings to the Board of Education
- Seek School Board approval
- Finalize schedules

Launch and Modify as Needed

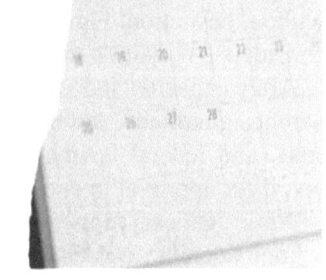

Figure 8.2   *Adapted from Haser & Nasser, 2005.*

to respond in the moment or follow up with a response at a later time. The local expert or the representative from NAYRE should be able to respond to stakeholder questions.

Next, one lesson learned that can be applied to this and almost every other educational initiative is to communicate often. By developing informational materials, and hosting informational sessions for a variety of stakeholders, school districts can build the understanding and capacity of others to help champion this change initiative. Failing to communicate effectively often creates tension and slows the transition.

Local, state, and even federal lawmakers tend to be supportive once they learn about the idea and the reasons why a school district is considering making the change to a balanced school calendar. With that, it is best to connect lawmakers as soon as possible, as in some cases, funding has been set aside to help with this transition. No one likes to be surprised, especially our lawmakers.

Finally, almost everyone attended school and nearly everyone attended school on a traditional school calendar that operated roughly from Labor Day to Memorial Day annually. As such, based on each lived experience, members of your learning community are likely to have some strong feelings about a calendar change. In fact, we predict that you may hear things like "it worked for me, why would we want to change it for our kids" or something similar. Ensuring that all stakeholders, even those without children in school, need to know the way behind this idea and how the school calendar may be changing.

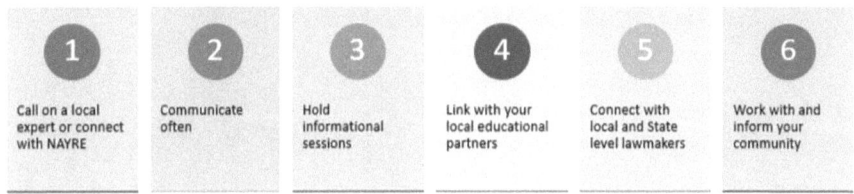

Figure 8.3

CHALLENGES AND CONSIDERATIONS

A balanced calendar benefits staff morale and contributes to a better work–life balance. The balanced calendar can positively impact educator burnout and the nationwide substitute shortage. Implementing the balanced calendar involves building staff capacity and understanding and garnering community support. The implementation process varies but typically includes creating a steering committee, conducting research, connecting with a local expert or someone from the NAYRE, and holding informational meetings to engage with the broader learning community.

Community partnerships are essential, as external partners often plan programs and staffing levels around school breaks. Concerns such as transportation, athletics, and food services need to be addressed, along with traditions like the desire for a long summer break. However, modern lifestyles and the changing nature of summer activities suggest that the traditional long summer break may no longer align with current needs.

In conclusion, transitioning to a balanced school calendar requires thorough planning, community engagement, and a clear understanding of the benefits. By considering the needs of students, staff, and the community, schools can make informed decisions that support improved academic outcomes and overall well-being.

Chapter 9

Questions and Answers

QUESTIONS AND ANSWERS (OSPI, 2024)

Q: What is a balanced calendar?

A: Instead of concentrating 180 school days into 9 months, a balanced calendar spreads them throughout the year. Schools may use the breaks to host "intersessions," where they can provide additional learning experiences.

Q: Does the balanced calendar model work?

A: Schools that follow a balanced calendar tend to have higher achievement scores (Pedersen, 2016). A traditional summer break lasts 10–12 weeks, compared to 5–7 weeks in a balanced calendar. Shorter breaks mean more consistent student–teacher partnerships and less learning disruption. Students need less review time at the beginning of the new school year so that there is an embedded opportunity for expansion of curriculum and learning experiences.

Q: Does it mean more school?

A: Balanced calendars usually keep the same number of school days as traditional calendars, but they add flexibility. With input and feedback from families, education leaders decide what is best for their local community. Teachers who work in a balanced calendar have reported that it is easier to plan instruction in shorter chunks between breaks rather than for a full semester (Pedersen, 2016). In addition, ending the first semester, trimester, or second quarter before winter break creates more energy and readiness for students and teachers when they return (Hasser & Nasser, 2005).

Q: What is an intersession?

A: There are times when additional school days make sense. These additional days, called intersessions, can be added to the school calendar to provide opportunities for more student learning and enrichment. All additional workdays are collectively bargained to determine how the days will be allocated and how teachers and support staff will be compensated.

Q: What about students in foster care or experiencing homelessness?

A: Students in foster care or experiencing homelessness are eligible to receive support through several state and federal programs. These students often have disruptions in their education which can make it difficult for them to be on target for graduation. A balanced calendar can provide additional opportunities for credit accrual and recovery, as well as interrupt the effects of cumulative learning loss in developing individual school graduation plans.

Q: What about students with disabilities?

A: Students with disabilities may not have access to highly specialized resources (occupational therapists, physical therapists, speech and language specialists, and adaptive equipment) during long summer breaks. Transition services, such as job shadows, can take place during intersessions without taking the student out of classroom instruction. When interventions take place at the end of each summative period, there is evidence of a reduction of students needing IEPs or qualifying for special education services overtime (Smith, 2011; Evans, 2007).

Q: What about students who are migratory?

A: When migrant students move between districts with traditional and balanced calendars, the state's Migrant Education program provides supplemental academic help as well as secondary credit accrual and exchange.

Q: What about students in an off-campus program?

A: For students in Running Start (a Washington based program for high school juniors and seniors to take college classes) or who are learning a trade, consider local community college and skills center schedules for potential impact on students participating in those programs part-time.

Q: What about students in advanced programs, like AP or IB?

A: A balanced calendar can provide an opportunity for involvement in special projects and targeted learning opportunities. When considering calendar modifications, schools should take into account the program design and testing schedules for Advanced Placement, International Baccalaureate, and Cambridge International programs.

Q: Does a balanced calendar affect high school credits and graduation requirements?

A: State graduation requirements remain the same. Each school district is responsible for supporting every student to earn necessary credits for graduation, meet their graduation pathway, and complete a High School and Beyond Plan.

What should schools consider when exploring school year calendar change?

Q: What about communication and community engagement?

A: Identify and engage key stakeholders early, including educator groups, families, students, and community partners. Thoughtful communication and engagement can go a long way toward establishing common ground and creating transparency in the process and decision-making. Communicate with families about how changes to the school calendar may affect existing practices and schedules for report cards and student conferences.

Q: What about the use of instructional time?

A: Intersessions can be used to support continuous forward momentum for all students. Schools should consider how to make use of time for supplementary opportunities to learn as intervention or enrichment.

Q: What about collective bargaining agreements?

A: Identify areas that need to be addressed with current local bargaining agreements and work collaboratively to problem-solve and negotiate to reach a consensus with all impacted bargaining units. In general, the school year calendar agreed to during the collective bargaining process will also determine when report cards and student conferences occur.

Q: What about educator and staff support?

A: Transitioning to a balanced calendar requires some rethinking of instructional time and the scope/sequence of instruction and intervention support for students. Throughout the planning and exploration process, districts should work closely with their instructional staff teams to identify where support is needed and proactively factor this support into the transition process and collective bargaining agreements, as necessary.

Q: What about child care, after-school care, and parenting agreements?

A: Connect with families and community partners early, including child care providers.

Gather their feedback about the prospect of a school year calendar change. Some families have shared that it is easier to budget for six weeks of care in the summer with periodic week breaks throughout the school year, than it is to pay for care for 10 to 12 consecutive weeks during a traditional summer break (Flaminio Interview, 2022). Some childcare providers have cited the shift to a balanced calendar has offered a growth opportunity for their business (Ballinger & Kneese, 2006).

In the exploration process, include families who operate under a parenting agreement or who are in single-parent households. In some cases, a balanced calendar may provide more opportunities for equity in shared custody arrangements, especially where one parent has custody during the school year, while the other has custody during summer break.

Q: What about high school sports?

A: High school athletics are often viewed as a barrier due to scheduling challenges, but conflicts can be mitigated. For decades, school districts across the nation have successfully supported interscholastic sports among schools with different school year calendars. In fact, the modern balanced calendar has ties back to the 1890s. Washington Interscholastic Activities Association (WIAA) has successfully navigated a variety of school year calendars. Despite the change in leadership, WIAA has stated their support of allowing districts to determine the right school year calendar for their students and communities.

Q: What about school meals (information is applicable to Washington)?

A: The National School Lunch (NSLP) and School Breakfast Program (SBP) may be operated on planned educational days. Enrolled students attending on-campus educational activities are eligible to participate and may receive breakfast and one lunch daily. Meals must meet the NSLP and SBP meal pattern requirements and are reimbursed at the school's NSLP and SBP rate. Schools must count and claim meals according to a student's approved eligibility status unless they are participating in the Community Eligibility Provision or Provision 2. An application and calendar must be submitted within the Washington Integrated Nutrition System for the participating school and planned educational days at the beginning of each school year. Local Education Agencies should contact their assigned School Meal Program Specialist with any questions.

ANSWERS TO THE COMMON QUESTIONS ABOUT YEAR-ROUND EDUCATION BY NAYRE EXECUTIVE DIRECTOR EMERITUS, DR. CHARLES BALLINGER (NAYRE, 2024)

As school districts consider the move to a modified or balanced calendar, there are common issues that become an integral part of the community discussion that occurs between administrators, school board members, and parents.

The questions are:

1. Does the calendar make a difference in the overall learning of students?
2. Can a nontraditional calendar work on the secondary level?
3. Is there a need for uniformity of calendars?
4. What role does choice in education play?
5. What is the role of NAYRE and how credible is the information it provides?
6. If YRE is such a good idea, why has it not been more readily accepted?

Dr. Ballinger provides his answers to those questions:

1. The first issue is whether there is educational research that shows that calendar arrangements make a difference in the overall learning of students. Yes, there is and it is quite convincing. Interestingly, opponents of modifying and balancing school calendars usually deny that there is such research and are rarely accepting of the available findings.

The research is divided into two parts. The first part deals with summer learning loss. Educational research is very clear that there is summer learning loss because of the long summer vacation of the traditional calendar. That finding is rather consistent across many studies. The largest (and most widely accepted) study in this field of study was done by a team in the psychology department at the University of Missouri, Columbia, headed by Dr. Harris Cooper (the study can be found in the *Review of Educational Research*, Volume 66, no. 3, 1996, and is entitled "The Effects of Summer Vacation on Achievement Test Scores: A Narrative and Meta-Analytic Review"). In layman's language, the study found that summer learning loss is a reality, that all students (including the best) lose in math and spelling skills, and many, though not all, lose in reading skills over the traditional summer. Based on the research about summer learning loss, it is difficult—no, it is impossible—for an educator to defend a calendar which allows so much loss, for any reason other than as a choice for those parents who prioritize lifestyle (10 weeks of vacation) over learning (less learning loss).

The second part of the research is whether doing things differently in calendar arrangements makes a difference. There are two primary studies to look at. The first is one by Dr. Carolyn Kneese, professor emeritus at Texas A&M University, entitled "Year-Round Learning: A Research Synthesis Relating to Student Achievement." Dr. Kneese's conclusion after reviewing six research syntheses and 30 individual studies:

> In summary, one may conclude from this particular review of achievement studies that there is an effective maintenance and improvement of the overall

academic performance of students participating in a year-round education program in comparison to those on the traditional calendar.

Note the two key words: maintenance and improvement. Maintenance keeps what has been learned and improvement adds to it. A second major study was published by a team from the psychology department at the University of Missouri, Columbia, again headed by Dr. Harris Cooper (the article was published in the *Review of Educational Research*, Vol. 73, no. 1, with the title of "The Effects of Modified School Calendars on Student Achievement and on School and Community Attitudes"). After looking at over 400 studies about year-round education, and focusing on 39 school districts, Dr. Cooper's team found that the average effect size for the 39 was small, but nevertheless positive, for those schools with a modified calendar. Also, the team found that parents and staff who participated in modified calendar programs were quite positive about their experiences. That latter finding comports to our knowledge in this office that almost all opposition to a modification of a school calendar comes from those who have not experienced the calendar first-hand.

Opponents of balancing the calendar sometimes will refer to negative studies in their discussion. You should know that such studies just have not been published. More about this later in discussion of whether NAYRE's information is biased.

2. Often there is concern that a balanced (modified, year-round, or nontraditional) calendar may be problematic at the secondary level. While this is sometimes raised in a community's discussion, experience has shown that reorganizing the school year has not been a problem for high school or middle school sports, band, or extracurricular activities in any single-track calendar arrangement (as distinguished from multi-track). Since there have been more than 200 high schools and 300 middle schools in the nation on a balanced or year-round calendar, we have plenty of experience year-round at the secondary level. One has to ask: Why the presumption that there would be a problem? In all 50 states that we are aware of, the state athletic association has language about being "enrolled" in school rather than actually being in school on the day of a game. Those regulations were written so that a basketball game can be played during the winter holidays, between Christmas and New Year's Eve, for example, when school is not in session, or so an athlete who might have reason to be absent during a school day would still be eligible to play in an evening game. Band and extracurricular activities naturally follow whatever the school's schedule might be, so those face no complications at all. As to student employment, a good survey would determine whether any students would be affected by a calendar change.

One large high school in the San Diego area did such a survey and found that fewer than 50% of their students were employed at all, and almost all of that employment was outside of and not affected by the school schedule. In the end, they discovered that fewer than 5% of their student body had jobs that might be affected by a change in the school calendar, and those students could be incorporated within a work-study program during regular school hours. Student summer employment? Again, it will be a very small percentage that would be affected, since most summer employment is for those above 16 and most of those jobs are part-time and flexible. Would a Board ordinarily make a favorable decision for the 10% or so that might be affected in summer employment (an important, but not educational, consideration), or would it consider its primary duty the other 90% for whom summer learning loss is a meaningful issue?

3. Uniformity is almost always more efficient. That is a truism in business, government, religion, and school policies. A cereal company would be far more efficient if the company put out fewer kinds of cereals, but their overall revenue would likely decrease. Every dictator on earth knows that uniformity is to be cherished and enforces uniformity to the greatest degree possible. Religious leaders would like uniformity in doctrine, and fewer houses of worship would cut worship costs considerably. School administrators and school board members have attended seminars that show how uniformity can cut costs. However, there is something to be said for a choice of cereals. There is something to be said for democracy, expensive and messy as it is. There is something to be said for freedom to worship as we choose, expensive though that may be. Of course, uniformity among schools in a district would be cheaper, but there is something to be said for choice even in education, since students do not all learn in the same way.
4. Choice in education is one of the hallmarks of America's stronger school systems. Most of the better systems I have come across over the years offer choices to parents whenever possible. Districts that push uniformity above all else generally decline after a short period of time.
5. The NAYRE is an advocacy group on behalf of rethinking the school year calendar. We are an advocacy group in the same way that the National School Boards Association is an advocate for school boards, the American Association of School Administrators is an advocate for top school administrators, and the National Education Association is an advocate for teachers. All of these groups, though, must maintain credibility while advocating a particular point of view. NAYRE strives to do the same. In the article on modified school calendars mentioned above, Dr. Cooper and team asked both proponents and opponents of

calendar change to send research studies about calendar change (the Cooper team collected over 400 studies). NAYRE sent all of which it was aware.

An opposing group, Time to Learn, which in the past has been funded by the International Association of Amusement Parks and Attractions and which has made claims about negative research on year-round education, sent none. The University of Missouri team, headed by Dr. Cooper, commended NAYRE in its published article for sending a very balanced portrayal of modified school calendars. We stand on our record.

6. Some opponents will say that if year-round is such a good idea, why has it not been accepted more readily? This is an easy one to counter. Try these rebuttals: If democracy, which has about four centuries of existence, is such a good idea, why is it that so few countries in the world have it? Or, why is it that Christianity (or any of the other of the world's religions), with a 2000-year existence, is not universally accepted? The point is quickly made that good ideas do not necessarily achieve universal acceptance, no matter how good they may be.

As a caution, school districts should be aware, however, that opponents of calendar change to benefit student learning are not likely to be swayed by anything I have written, nor by any other factual document that a district might obtain. Year-round parents have experienced what a modified calendar can do. Most of the opponents have not. Therein is part of the problem. Schools are correct, however, to do all they can to support modification of the school calendar. Student learning will benefit because of their efforts.

WHAT ABOUT THE OTHER SIDE OF THE ISSUES— THE CASE AGAINST THE BALANCED CALENDAR?

The information below comes from an article titled, "Busting the Myths About Year-Round School Calendars: 'Balanced Calendars have no academic benefit,'" by Paul T. von Hippel and Jennifer Graves published in Volume 23, Number 2 of *Education Next*.
The authors state,

> Typically, year-round calendars don't increase learning time but rather spread school days more equally across 12 months, with a shorter summer vacation and longer breaks throughout the year. That's the approach in South Carolina, where one quarter of districts will use year-round calendars in 2022–23. In Washington

State, 45 districts have received state grants to assess the potential and practicality of year-round calendars. (von Hipple & Graves, 2023)

The author notes eight myths. Those myths are summarized below:

Myth 1: Year-round schools are open all the time.
Let us start with the name. While it is not technically inaccurate, the term "year-round calendar" can give the impression that children are in school all the time. In fact, the vast majority of schools that use year-round calendars offer 175–180 days of instruction—the same as a traditional nine-month calendar with standard holiday breaks and a 10- or 11-week summer vacation.

Historically, the NAYRE has defined a year-round calendar as one with no break longer than eight weeks. Under that broad umbrella, it is useful to draw a line between "extended-year" calendars, which typically expand instructional time to 200 school days or more, and "balanced" calendars, which have the usual 175–180 school days but rearrange them—shortening the summer vacation and extending fall, winter, and spring breaks.

Extended-year calendars are rare in the United States, where less than one-tenth of 1% of elementary schools offer more than 180 school days. Nearly all year-round calendars in the United States, including those used in South Carolina and under consideration in Washington, are balanced calendars with 180 school days at most.

Myth 2: The main goal of year-round calendars is to help students learn (NAYRE, 2024).
Most public conversation about balanced calendars assumes that they are designed to help students learn. In fact, over the past 50 years, a major reason districts have adopted balanced calendars is to address overcrowding and save money.

Opponents of year-round calendars often have economic motives, as well. Parent groups who oppose year-round calendars often make common cause with summer camps and amusement parks, whose prosperity depends on teenage workers and children being out of school for months in the summer. We were skeptical that summer camps and amusement parks could exert much influence on education policy—until 2011, when an Ohio state legislator contacted one of us to say that Cedar Point, a massive amusement park outside Cleveland that is often called the "roller coaster capital of the world," was lobbying for a bill to effectively outlaw year-round calendars by requiring all Ohio public schools to start after Labor Day. The bill did not come to pass, but similar laws restricting school start and end dates have been passed in 16 other states.

Myth 3: Year-round calendars are new (NAYRE, 2024).

Reporters and advocates often portray year-round calendars as a fresh, untried reform. In fact, various types of extended and staggered calendars were tried throughout the 20th century. A multi-track 45/15 calendar was first adopted in the late 1960s and early 1970s in suburban districts like Hayward, California, and Valley View, Illinois, where enrollments were surging as families left nearby cities and the last cohorts of the baby boom entered elementary school. Meanwhile, educators and representatives from across the United States met in 1968 for the first National Seminar on Year-Round Education. By 1972, the NAYRE had been launched, and more than 900 participants attended the fourth National Seminar on Year-Round Education. A 1973 survey conducted before the fifth National Seminar found that 100 districts with more than 374,000 students were using or planning to use year-round calendars. Most were 45/15 calendars adopted to make better use of space.

Myth 4: Year-round calendars are poised for growth (NAYRE, 2024).

Often, public discussion of year-round calendars implies that they are a new idea and, by extension, are likely to grow in popularity. In fact, until the pandemic, the prevalence of year-round calendars had been declining for 20 years. Nationwide, the percentage of schools using a year-round calendar fell to 3% in 2017–2018 from 6% in 1999–2000 (see Figure 8.2). Much of the national trend was driven by California, where the percentage of K–5 schools using a year-round calendar fell to 7% in 2018–2019 from 26% in 1998–1999. Virtually all of the decline was in schools using multi-track calendars, especially Concept 6 schools. There were especially sharp declines between 2000–2004 and 2011–2012.

Myth 5: Year-round calendars increase learning (NAYRE, 2024).

Proponents often claim that balanced calendars increase learning. For example, an FAQ page published on the Washington State Office of Public Instruction's website claims that "Schools that follow a balanced calendar tend to have higher achievement scores." But claims like that are hard to reconcile with rigorous research. As is often the case in education, you can cherry-pick a study to support any position you like, but a lot of studies are not very good. And for more than 20 years, the most rigorous studies have uniformly found that year-round calendars do not increase learning—and may even, in some cases, reduce it.

Myth 6: Year-round calendars increase summer learning.

The disappointing effects of year-round calendars may seem hard to accept, because there are a couple of common sense arguments suggesting that year-round calendars really should have academic benefits (von Hipple, 2023). But these arguments do not hold up very well when inspected closely.

One argument rests on popular ideas about summer learning. Because year-round calendars shorten summer vacation, the argument goes, they must reduce summer learning loss, which is most acute among disadvantaged students. Therefore, year-round calendars really should boost test scores, especially for the disadvantaged.

There are two weak points in this argument. The first is that popular ideas about summer learning are not consistently supported by recent research (see "Is Summer Learning Loss Real?" feature, Winter 2019). Some recent studies find that children lose very little skill over the summer; other studies find that summer learning losses are no larger among disadvantaged students than among advantaged students.

The second problem is that this argument focuses exclusively on the summer months, while ignoring what happens during the rest of the year. Remember that balanced year-round calendars have no more than the usual 175 or 180 school days, so while they do include more school days during the summer, they also have fewer school days and more vacation days during the fall, winter, and spring.

Myth 7: Year-round calendars help schools supplement instruction.

Another argument for balanced calendars is that they provide more opportunities for supplementary instruction during the "intersessions," or mini-vacations that occur more frequently throughout the year (von Hipple, 2023). Intersession instruction can help catch up students who are behind or offer enrichment to students who are on track or ahead. Or so the argument goes.

However, multi-track calendars that keep classrooms filled cannot easily support intersession instruction, because when students from one track are on break, students from the other tracks are in school, leaving little space free for supplemental instruction. Single-track calendars offer more chances for supplemental instruction because the school is empty during intersessions. But that is not unique to year-round calendars—schools on traditional nine-month calendars have offered summer-school and after-school instruction since year-round calendars were a gleam in reformers' eyes.

Myth 8: Year-round calendars are popular.

Proponents claim that families and kids like year-round calendars, once they realize that they still get vacations (von Hipple, 2023). And in the latest push, year-round calendars are presented as an intervention that teachers will like because intersessions will help them recover from pandemic burnout. But the evidence for these positive attitudes is shaky. In their 2003 meta-analysis, Cooper and his colleagues described opinion polling carried out in more than 50 year-round districts, reporting that "in general, survey respondents felt more positive than negative about modified school calendars." But the data only showed that respondents favored the high end of the rating scale.

For example, when asked to rate the year-round calendar on a scale from 1 to 5, the average response in year-round districts was 3.6. That result is uninterpretable without a comparison group asked to rate their experience on traditional calendars.

The steering committee has held and will continue to hold balanced calendar informational sessions. The feedback below is a summary from the perspective of a PD provider:

Today's session provided valuable insights into the progress and challenges of various districts on their balanced calendar journey. Here are the key takeaways from the discussion:

1. Funding Challenges: Many districts expressed the need to implement changes without additional funding. This highlights the importance of finding cost-effective solutions and sustainable practices.
2. Implementation Status: Some districts have already implemented a modified calendar for the current and upcoming years. Their next step is to secure funding for a February intersession and determine the calendar for 25–26. They are considering whether to revert to the status quo or move further toward a balanced calendar.
3. Support Needs: Districts are seeking additional support beyond funding, including technical assistance, tools such as surveys and intersession program design, and model language for Memorandums of Understanding.
4. Sharing Success Stories: One district reported success in terms of student growth with those who attended all three intersessions. This demonstrates the positive impact of the balanced calendar approach.
5. Willingness to Share: While some districts are not ready to share their experiences, others are open to sharing with colleagues in upcoming networking events. Sharing knowledge and experiences can benefit all districts on this journey.
6. Feedback for Networking Events: Participants expressed interest in a more advanced version (201) led by districts that have successfully implemented balanced calendars. They also suggested facilitating connections between districts at similar stages of implementation or of similar sizes.
7. Student Involvement: Several attendees emphasized the importance of involving high school students in the process, highlighting their valuable perspective.

8. Thoughtful Planning: The need for thoughtful and well-planned intersessions was emphasized as a key factor for success.
9. Investigatory Stage: Some districts are in the early stages of investigation, gathering information and evidence to make informed decisions about implementing a balanced calendar.
10. Community Engagement: Engaging staff, families, and the community was recognized as a crucial step in the process.
11. Student Voice: Acknowledgment of the importance of student voice in the decision-making process was noted.
12. Accessing Funding: Districts are interested in learning about ways to access funding for planning and supporting students during intersession times.

In summary, this session revealed a diverse range of experiences and challenges among participating districts at various stages of the balanced calendar journey. The need for support, sharing of success stories, and gathering evidence to inform decision-making were common themes throughout the discussion. Participants expressed a commitment to continued learning and collaboration in future networking events.

As part of the balanced calendar project, the OSPI and the Washington Association of Education Service District collaborated with various people from varied backgrounds and expertise to develop a question-and-answer document, including a glossary of terms.

Glossary of terms:

Balanced Calendar: The term refers to a variation of the year-round calendar which organizes the school schedule by reducing the summer vacation and redistributing those weeks throughout the year as vacation or intersession. The curriculum and the number of instruction days are generally identical to the traditional calendar (NAYRE, 2000).

Faucet Theory: Faucet theory developed by Entwisle, Alexander, and Olson (1997) is the belief that during the academic school year, the faucet of resources flows for all children; during the summer intermission the faucet of resources is turned off (Rozelle & Mackenzie, 2011).

Intersession: The term refers to intervals of time between instructional sessions used for educational-related services. These might include remedial activities, enrichment activities, and recreational activities or camps (Kneese, 2000).

Multi-track: A multi-track schedule staggers the instructional and vacation/intersession periods of each track throughout the entire year so that some students are receiving instruction while others are on vacation (Kneese, 2000).

Single-track: A single-track schedule generally calls for an instructional year of 180 days, with short breaks (intersessions) interspersed throughout the year (Kneese, 2000).

Summer Learning Loss: Summer learning loss amounts to the amount of educational ground children lose during a summer recess from school (Gordon, 2011).

Summer Recess: Summer recess is the time a student is not in school during the summer months. This break is typically up to 12-weeks annually in the United States (Hattie, 2009).

Track: A track schedule involves a group of students who are assigned to attend school during the same instructional session. These students are on track and off-track at the same time (Kneese, 2000).

Traditional Calendar: The term refers to an academic schedule that usually begins around Labor Day and ends early in the summer, with a winter break, designated holidays, and a long summer vacation of 10 to 12 weeks. (Shields & Oberg, 2000).

Year-Round Education and Year-Round Schooling: The terms are often used interchangeably in the literature, but differ technically. Year-round education means shortening the summer vacation to add more school days to the school year for some students. Year-round schooling, on the other hand, is a change of schedule that does not materially increase the days each child spends in school (NAYRE, 2006b).

Conclusion

So much has changed over the past 135 years, except the dominant school calendar being used across the nation. To that end, while the majority of schools across the nation continue to hold steadfast to the schedule of the traditional school calendar, we hope that this book helps interested parties better understand what a balanced school calendar is and what it could be. Regardless of the reason a district transitions to the alternate calendar, the balanced school calendar offers the flexibility each learning community deeply desires and deserves. This innovative approach to scheduling can lead to improved academic outcomes, enhanced student engagement, and increased teacher retention. By distributing breaks more evenly throughout the year, a balanced calendar helps prevent the "summer slide" and reduces the need for extensive review at the beginning of each school year. This consistency can lead to better retention of information and more effective teaching practices.

Moreover, a balanced calendar can provide opportunities for enriched learning experiences, such as intersession programs, community service projects, and apprenticeships. These experiences can deepen students' understanding of academic concepts and help them develop valuable skills for the future.

Additionally, a balanced calendar can benefit teachers by providing more frequent breaks for rest and professional development. This can lead to greater job satisfaction and improved instructional quality.

Overall, a balanced school calendar has the potential to transform the educational experience for both students and teachers, making it a compelling option for school leaders to consider.

HOW CAN THE INFORMATION IN THE BOOK BE USED FOR REFORM?

This book explains the rationale behind the balanced school calendar, highlighting the benefits for students, teachers, and the community. It can help build support among parents, teachers, students, administrators, and lawmakers. This book provides detailed guidance on how to implement a balanced calendar, including considerations for scheduling, professional development, and communication.

By including case studies from schools that have successfully transitioned to a balanced school calendar, these examples can serve as an inspiration for others considering the change. The book also addressed common concerns and misconceptions about the alternative calendar, such as childcare issues and the impact on extracurricular activities, and provided strategies for mitigating these concerns.

Overall, the research and the lived experiences of the authors have helped shape this guide for schools and districts embarking on the transition to a more innovative and effective school calendar.

WHAT IS THE STATE OF WASHINGTON DOING NOW?

The fall of 2024 will mark nearly five years of comprehensive support for school districts considering a transition to the balanced school calendar in the state of Washington. This is the most comprehensive and sustained effort that NAYRE has been a part of recently. Since 2020, school districts in Washington have accessed technical support, attended conferences, conducted book studies, attended monthly learning sessions, and accessed data and research regarding the balanced school calendar to help make an informed decision. While many school districts have made the transition to a more flexible school calendar, others are still in the process of learning more.

As noted earlier, ESSER funds provided funds for districts to be granted funds for balanced calendar work. The funds were available for two school years. Funding was secured for Year 3, however, due to the Washington State Legislature's re-allocation of those ESSER funds, funding was terminated. Although funding was terminated, the various state partners, consultants, and participating districts continued this innovative work. The momentum continued to carry.

Washington provided us with great lessons on what worked, what did not work, and how to address those areas that did not work. These lessons have been captured and archived for future use. The authors remain committed to supporting anyone interested in learning more.

WHY IS NOW THE BEST TIME?

Perhaps one of the most powerful educational lessons learned from COVID-19 was that how we spend our time should be reimagined. Remote work in the private sector remains popular and many parents desire the same flexibility for their children (Breazeale, 2023). As outlined in previous chapters, the rise of the four day workweek has also inspired the four-day school week. We believe that we will continue to see the private sector more rapidly influencing how we operate our schools. These innovations will mostly continue with additional reforms for school calendars, additional school hours, and virtual learning. Most likely artificial intelligence will also factor into these and other reforms, much like it is changing the shape of many businesses.

Educators have demonstrated that school can be done differently . . . this is the best time to imagine the possibilities!

References

Achor, S., & Gielan, M. (2016, July 13). The Data-Driven case for vacation. https://hbr.org/. Retrieved March 6, 2024, from https://hbr.org/2016/07/the-data-driven-case-for-vacation.

Adams, R. L. (2021). Stakeholder beliefs, satisfaction and assessments of school climate after implementation of a year-round calendar (Order No. AAI28270465). Available from APA PsycInfo®. (2509688015; 2021-27918-257). Retrieved from https://login.delval.idm.oclc.org/login?url=https://www.proquest.com/dissertations-theses/stakeholder-beliefs-satisfaction-assessments/docview/2509688015/se-2.

Addison, J. (2023, November 8). Growing number of American schools shifting to year-round calendars. *Fox News*. https://www.foxnews.com/us/growing-number-american-schools-shifting-year-round-calendars.

ADE Commissioner's Memo. (n.d.). Retrieved March 10, 2024, from https://adecm.ade.arkansas.gov/ViewApprovedMemo.aspx?Id=4989#:~:text=A%20traditional%20school%20calendar%20consists,of%2030%20hours%20per%20week.

Agency of Education. (2020). Extended school year (ESY) services and independent schools. In MEMORANDUM. https://education.vermont.gov/sites/aoe/files/documents/edu-memo-extended-school-year-services-and-independent-schools.pdf.

Agrarian roots? Think again. Debunking the myth of summer vacation's origins. (2014, September 7). *PBS NewsHour*. https://www.pbs.org/newshour/education/debunking-myth-summer-vacation.

Agreement Between the Hawaii State Teachers Association and the state of Hawaii Board of Education. (2023). https://dhrd.hawaii.gov. Retrieved March 12, 2024, from https://boe.hawaii.gov/Pages/Welcome.aspx chrome-extension://efaidnbmnnnibpcajpcglclefindmkaj/https://dhrd.hawaii.gov/wp-content/uploads/2023/04/HSTA-2021-2023.pdf.

Alagoz Ekici, C., Lott, E., Talley, A., Castañeda, S., & Texas Education Agency. (2021). List of Texas public school Campuses on Year-Round Education Calendars, 2020–21. In Texas Education Agency [Report]. Texas Education Agency. https://tea.texas.gov/reports-and-data/program-evaluations/program-evaluations-other-initiatives/yre2020-21.pdf.

Alaska Public Media. (2022, August 1). New K-12 charter school will serve growing Alaska Native population in Mat-Su Borough. https://alaskapublic.org/2022/07/31/new-k-12-charter-school-will-serve-growing-alaska-native-population-in-mat-su-borough/.

Alaska Public Schools Database. (2024). Retrieved March 9, 2024, from https://education.alaska.gov/DOE_Rolodex/SchoolCalendar/.

All Year Montessori - Spruce Tree Montessori. (2024, March 8). Spruce Tree Montessori. https://www.sprucetreemontessori.com/admissions/all-year-montessori/#:~:text=After%20careful%20consideration%20and%20months,academic%20calendar%20for%20all%20ages.

Amending the Calendar. (2021, September). https://www.education.ky.gov/. Retrieved March 12, 2024, from https://www.education.ky.gov/districts/enrol/Documents/Amending%20Calendar%20Guidebook.pdf.

Amestoy, A. (2023, December 22). Public schools test four-day school weeks in response to teacher shortage. https://www.mtpr.org/. Retrieved March 6, 2024, from https://www.mtpr.org/montana-news/2023-12-22/public-schools-test-four-day-school-weeks-in-response-to-teacher-shortage.

Anderson, S. (2014, June). It's About Time. https://wasb.org. Retrieved March 16, 2024, from https://wasb.org/wp-content/uploads/2017/04/time_June-July_2014.pdf.

Andrade, K. G. (2023, April 13). Gov. McKee announces new initiative to increase out-of-school learning. Rhode Island Current. https://rhodeislandcurrent.com/2023/04/12/gov-mckee-announces-new-program-to-increase-out-of-school-learning/.

Annenberg Brown University. (n.d.). National education working paper series. Retrieved April 24, 2024, from https://edworkingpapers.com/.

Anthony, K. (2016). School's out for the summer: Disadvantages of the year-round school calendar on maternal employment. *Chicago Policy Review* (Online), Retrieved from https://login.delval.idm.oclc.org/login?url=https://www.proquest.com/scholarly-journals/schools-out-summer-disadvantages-year-round/docview/1814211708/se-2.

Associated Press. (1993, September 3). Idaho School Districts experiment with Year-Round Schools. https://www.lmtribune.com/. Retrieved March 12, 2024, from https://www.lmtribune.com/education/idaho-school-districts-experiment-with-year-round-schools/article_147ac950-c86c-5dc6-a87a-2f9fcff82a5f.html.

Associated Press. (2023, March 12). Arkansas School District considers 4-day school week. https://www.usnews.com. Retrieved March 10, 2024, from https://www.usnews.com/news/best-states/arkansas/articles/2023-03-12/arkansas-school-district-considers-4-day-school-week.

Atteberry, A., & McEachin, A. (2021). School's out: The role of summers in understanding achievement disparities. *American Educational Research Journal*, 58(2), 239–282. https://doi.org/10.3102/0002831220937285.

Attewell, P., Heil, S., & Reisel, L. (2012). What is academic momentum? And does it matter? *Educational Evaluation and Policy Analysis*, 34(1), 27–44. https://doi.org/10.3102/0162373711421958.

Aurini, J., & Davies, S. (2021). COVID-19 school closures and educational achievement gaps in Canada: Lessons from Ontario summer learning research. *Canadian*

Review of Sociology/Revue Canadienne De Sociologie, 58(2), 165–185. https://doi.org/10.1111/cars.12334.

Baber, E., Petrosky, B. S., Snow, T. M., & Walton III, C. (2021). Sustaining a balanced calendar in Hopewell City Public Schools.

Baker, D. K. (2021). Modernizing the school calendar to fit the needs of the 21st-century student (Order No. 28966248). Available from ProQuest One Academic; Publicly Available Content Database. (2633519717). Retrieved from https://login.delval.idm.oclc.org/login?url=https://www.proquest.com/dissertations-theses/modernizing-school-calendar-fit-needs-21st/docview/2633519717/se-2.

Balanced calendar. (n.d.). https://www.michigan.gov/mde/services/flexible-learning/balanced-calendar.

Balanced School Calendar: Key Considerations for Implementation. (2021, November). www.louisianabelieves.com. Retrieved March 13, 2024, from https://www.louisianabelieves.com/docs/default-source/district-support/staffing-and-scheduling-(balanced-calendar).pdf?sfvrsn=40506418_2.

Ballard, T. (2024, February 19). Senate Bill 2361: Mississippi modified school calendar grant program. *Mississippi First*. https://www.mississippifirst.org/blog/2023-senate-bill-2361/?utm_source=rss&utm_medium=rss&utm_campaign=2023-senate-bill-2361.

Ballinger, C. E. (1995). Prisoners no more. *Educational Leadership*, 53(3), 28–31.

Ballinger, C., & Kneese, C. (2006). *School calendar reform: Learning in all seasons*. Lanham, MD: Rowman & Littlefield Education.

Barrett, M. J. (1990, November). The case for more school days. *The Atlantic Monthly*, 266(5), 78–106.

Barrientos, J. (2024, January 27). 50-State comparison: Instructional time policies. *Education Commission of the States*. https://www.ecs.org/50-state-comparison-instructional-time-policies-2023/.

Barzee, S. (2020, April). Academic impact of rural Idaho schools on the Four-Day School Week: A quantitative research study - ProQuest. Retrieved April 9, 2024, from https://www.proquest.com/openview/58496256144814d59cacf8a73f7ecbdd/1?pq-origsite=gscholar&cbl=18750&diss=y.

Beach, K. D., McIntyre, E., Philippakos, Z. A., Mraz, M., Pilonieta, P., & Vintinner, J. P. (2018). Effects of a summer reading intervention on reading skills for Low-Income Black and Hispanic students in elementary School. Retrieved March 17, 2024, from https://eric.ed.gov/?id=EJ1180023c.

Belay, M. (2023, July 6). Canton charter school first in area to adopt 4-day school week. https://fox8.com/. Retrieved March 13, 2024, from https://fox8.com/news/canton-charter-school-first-in-area-to-adopt-4-day-school-week/.

Bell, S. M., Park, Y., Martin, M., Smith, J., McCallum, R. S., Smyth, K., & Mingo, M. (2020). Preventing summer reading loss for Students in Poverty: A comparison of tutoring and access to books. Retrieved March 17, 2024, from https://eric.ed.gov/?id=EJ1260407.

Bergin, M., Leslie, L., & Zimmer, J. (2023, August 2). 16 school districts in North Carolina defy state law, starting school year earlier than legally allowed. https://

www.wect.com. https://www.wect.com/2023/08/02/16-school-districts-north-carolina-defy-state-law-starting-school-year-earlier-than-legally-allowed/.

Big School System in Kentucky Shifting to Year-Round Classes. (1971, May 27). https://www.nytimes.com/, https://www.nytimes.com/1970/05/27/archives/big-school-system-in-kentucky-shifting-to-yearround-classes.html.

Bill Tracking, 2020 Session Legislation. (2020). https://lis.virginia.gov. Retrieved April 9, 2024, from https://lis.virginia.gov/cgi-bin/legp604.exe?201+ful+CHAP0582.

Black, M. P. W. I. (2023, December 31). Should Black parents worry about a 4-day school week? *AFRO American Newspapers*. https://afro.com/should-black-parents-worry-about-a-4-day-school-week/.

Blume, H. (2023, May 4). School calendar changes spur hot debate in LAUSD - Los Angeles Times. *Los Angeles Times*. https://www.latimes.com/california/story/2023-05-04/mess-with-the-school-calendar-and-youre-messing-with-lives-inside-lausds-hot-debate.

Boner, J. (2023, December 12). Teton 401 passes Four-day school option for 2024-25 school year. https://www.jhnewsandguide.com/. Retrieved March 12, 2024, from https://www.jhnewsandguide.com/this_just_in/teton-401-passes-four-day-school-option-for-2024-25-school-year/article_d1042982-98a5-11ee-8854-57e57182815f.html.

Borman, G. D., Yang, H., & Xie, X. (2021). A Quasi-Experimental Study of the impacts of the Kids Read Now Summer Reading Program. Retrieved March 17, 2024, from https://eric.ed.gov/?id=EJ1312648.

Bowers, L. M., & Schwarz, I. (2018). Preventing summer learning loss: Results of a summer literacy program for students from low-ses homes. https://www.semanticscholar.org/paper/Preventing-Summer-Learning-Loss%3A-Results-of-a-for-Bowers-Schwarz/6589aa70c2b458477709d4be6b355ca30958c21c.

Bracey, G. W. (2002). What students do in the summer. *Phi Delta Kappan*, 83(7), 497–498. https://doi.org/10.1177/003172170208300706.

Breazeale, G. (2023, September 26). The growing popularity of the balanced academic calendar. *Mississippi First*. https://www.mississippifirst.org/blog/the-growing-popularity-of-the-balanced-academic-calendar/.

Brusseau, T. A., Burns, R. D., Fu, Y., & Weaver, R. G. (2019). Impact of Year-Round and traditional school schedules on summer weight gain and fitness loss. *Childhood Obesity*, 15(8), 541–547. https://doi.org/10.1089/chi.2019.0070.

Burke, D. (2023, April 28). New bill could add more days for public schools in Alabama. https://whnt.com/. Retrieved March 9, 2024, from https://whnt.com/news/new-bill-could-add-more-days-for-public-schools-in-alabama/.

Burke, M. M., & Decker, J. R. (2017). Extended school year: Legal and practical considerations for educators. *Teaching Exceptional Children*, 49(5), 339–346.

Burt, S. (2019, January 22). Parents in the UK face heavy fines for taking kids out of school for vacation - travel noire. *Travel Noire*. https://travelnoire.com/parents-in-the-uk-face-hard-fines-for-taking-kids-on-vacation.

Busteed, B. (2021, February 2). The pandemic will obliterate the traditional academic calendar. *And It Can't Happen Fast Enough*. https://www.forbes.com/. Retrieved

March 5, 2024, from https://www.forbes.com/sites/brandonbusteed/2021/02/02/the-pandemic-will-obliterate-the-traditional-academic-calendar-and-it-cant-happen-fast-enough/?sh=7c057726116b.

Camburn, E. M. (2021). Extended calendar model versus traditional calendar model: A descriptive analysis of student performance over time. Retrieved March 17, 2024, from https://mospace.umsystem.edu/xmlui/handle/10355/84170.

Cammarata, G. (1961). Summer programs for students and teachers. *Education Digest,* 27, 26–28.

Caprara, L., & Caprara, C. (2022). Effects of virtual learning environments: A scoping review of literature. *Education and Information Technologies,* 27(3), 3683–3722.

Carlisle, James W. Jr. (2023). Examining the impact that a modified school calendar had on teacher attendance in a rural Mississippi school district. *Theses and Dissertations.* 6007. https://scholarsjunction.msstate.edu/td/6007.

Catteral, C. (2023, April 27). Four-day week proposal OK'd for Little Powder. https://www.gillettenewsrecord.com/. Retrieved March 16, 2024, from https://www.gillettenewsrecord.com/news/local/article_1db3d375-6175-50fc-8d70-3c92badf89a5.html.

Changing the schedule | Ohio Department of Education and Workforce. (n.d.). Retrieved March 13, 2024, from https://education.ohio.gov/Topics/Finance-and-Funding/Finance-Data-and-Information/Guidance-on-Schedule-Change-from-Days-to-Hours/Changing-the-Schedule.

Chasanov, D. (2023, August 3). "It's a big deal": Oklahoma State Department of Education approves four-day school week for two rural districts. *KOKH.* https://okcfox.com/news/local/rural-school-district-districts-four-day-week-weeks-oklahoma-state-department-of-education-osde-waivers-approval-roff-stonewall-public-schools-curriculum-superintendent-morgan-greg-lovelis-ryan-walters-classroom-turnover-retain-talent-employees-learning.

Chipman, D. (2024, February 23). Can a longer weekend increase learning? *News Decoder.* Retrieved March 7, 2024, from https://news-decoder.com/can-a-longer-weekend-increase-learning/.

Clarion-Ledger. (2023, January 1). https://www.clarionledger.com/restricted/?return=https%3A%2F%2Fwww.clarionledger.com%2Fstory%2Fnews%2F2023%2F07%2F20%2Fmississippi-schools-starting-school-earlier-with-modified-calendars%2F70430646007%2F.

Clarey, B. (2023, June 16). Year-round school? Districts around country experiment with more balanced calendar. *Chalkbeat News.* Retrieved March 3, 2024, from https://www.chalkboardnews.com/issues/outcomes/article_f0f7da04-aa71-5b09-a35c-9625c1b2dc8e.html#Signup.

Clark, N. (2024, February 7). Heartland superintendent reacts to research findings on four-day school week schedule. https://www.kfvs12.com. https://www.kfvs12.com/2024/02/06/heartland-superintendent-reacts-research-findings-four-day-school-week-schedule/.

Clarke, K. (2017, July 20). Could longer summer be in store for Indiana families? Year-round schools may be on way out. *Courier Journal.* Retrieved March

12, 2024, from https://www.courier-journal.com/story/news/education/2017/07/19/could-longer-summer-store-indiana-families-year-round-schools-may-way-out/422897001/.

Clifford, K., Christenson, B., & O'Connor, J. (2015). Not getting our money's worth: An outdated school schedule is costing New York $2.3 billion a year more & better learning time can change that. ReadyNation from https://readynation.s3.amazonaws.com/wp-content/uploads/ReadyNation-NY-More-and-Better-Learning.pdf.

CNN News Source. (2023, December 20). Texas schools' four-day week potentially improves student outcomes, attendance. *KABB*. https://foxsanantonio.com/news/local/texas-schools-four-day-week-potentially-improves-student-outcomes-attendance-local-people-education-community-teaching.

Comini, R. (2023, November 16). Principal defends school's transition to four-day week. *CathNews*. https://cathnews.com/2023/11/17/principal-defends-schools-transition-to-four-day-week/.

Commencement of School Term (School Start Date) Information. (n.d.). Wisconsin Department of Public Instruction. Retrieved March 16, 2024, from https://dpi.wi.gov/search/google/year-round.

Conejo, A. (2023, August 4). St. Helena Parish School District gets ready to implement four-day school week and more. https://www.brproud.com/. Retrieved March 13, 2024, from https://www.brproud.com/news/st-helena-parish-school-district-gets-ready-to-implement-four-day-school-week-and-more/.

Cook, B. C. (2016). Missouri School Superintendent Perceptions of Year-Round School Calendars. Retrieved March 17, 2024, from https://eric.ed.gov/?id=ED579555.

Cook, B. M. (2022, July 7). LCPS begins district-wide balanced-calendar. *Las Cruces Bulletin*. https://www.lascrucesbulletin.com/stories/lcps-begins-district-wide-balanced-calendar-classes-begin-july-20-21,12454.

Cook, L. L. (2023, October 25). 4-day school weeks are on the rise in Colorado. https://kdvr.com/. Retrieved March 10, 2024, from https://kdvr.com/news/4-day-school-week-colorado/.

Cooper, H., Nye, B., Charlton, K., Lindsay, J., & Greathouse, S. (1996). The effects of summer vacation on achievement test scores: A narrative and meta-analytic review. *Review of Educational Research*, 66(3), 227–268. https://doi.org/10.2307/1170523.

Cramer, P. (2006). Our poll results: Extended day upsets schedule. Retrieved April 17, 2014, from www.insideschools.org/contact-us/itemlist/category.

Crane, C. (2024, February 2). Surrey school investigating four-day week. minotdailynews.com. Retrieved March 13, 2024, from https://www.minotdailynews.com/news/local-news/2024/02/surrey-school-investigating-four-day-week/.

Cummings, A., & Cardiff University. (2023). Effects of changes to the school year and alternative school calendars: Qualitative research and an updated review of the evidence (No. 90/2023). *Welsh Government*. https://www.gov.wales/sites/default/files/statistics-and-research/2023-10/effects-of-changes-to-the-school-year

-and-alternative-school-calendars-qualitative-research-and-an-updated-review-of-the-evidence_0.pdf.

Dao, E. (2023, June 20). More school districts move to a different calendar model, starting classes early. *ABC15 Arizona in Phoenix (KNXV)*. https://www.abc15.com/news/region-southeast-valley/tempe/more-school-districts-move-to-a-different-calendar-model-starting-classes-early.

Davies, S., Aurini, J., & Hillier, C. (2023). Reproducing or reducing inequality? The case of summer learning programs. *Canadian Journal of Education*. https://doi.org/10.53967/cje-rce.5311.

Davies, S., & Li, A. (2023). Effects of summer numeracy interventions among french-language students in ontario. *Canadian Journal of Behavioural Science/Revue Canadienne Des Sciences Du Comportement*. doi:https://doi.org/10.1037/cbs0000384.

de Bloom, J., Geurts, S. A. E., & Kompier, M. A. J. (2013). Vacation (after-) effects on employee health and well-being, and the role of vacation activities, experiences and sleep. *Journal of Happiness Studies*, 14, 613–633. https://doi.org/10.1007/s10902-012-9345-3.

DeLeon, E. M. (2021). A comparative study of the academic performance of schools on year-round and traditional calendars (Order No. 28866641). Available from ProQuest One Academic. (2617229112). Retrieved from https://login.delval.idm.oclc.org/login?url=https://www.proquest.com/dissertations-theses/comparative-study-academic-performance-schools-on/docview/2617229112/se-2.

Dills, A. K., Hernandez-Julian, R., & Rotthoff, K. W. (2015, October 1). Knowledge Decay between Semesters. *Economics of Education Review*, 50, 2016. Available at SSRN: https://ssrn.com/abstract=2631637 or http://dx.doi.org/10.2139/ssrn.2631637.

Dill, K. (2022). School's out for the summer and many teachers are calling it quits. Retrieved February 12, 2024, from http://www.wsj.com/articles/schools-out-for-summer-and-many-are-calling-it-quits-11655732689.

Davis, J. (2006, February). The promise of extending-time schools for closing the achievement gap. Address given to the *National Association of Year-Round Education*, Boston, MA.

Division of School Business. (2020). Guidance of calendar requirement. In NC Department of Public Instruction. https://files.nc.gov/dpi/documents/fbs/accounting/calendar/sb704-calendar-requirements-052020.pdf.

Dixon, A. (2011). *Focus on the school calendar*. Atlanta, GA: Southern Regional Education Board.

Donis-Keller, C., & Silvernail, D. L. (2009). *Research brief: A review of the evidence on the four-day school week*. Portland, ME: University of Southern Maine, Center for Education Policy. Retrieved from https://usm.maine.edu/.

Dorrn, A. (2023, September 5). Most Americans are not in favor of a 4-day school week: Poll. https://www.newsnationnow.com/. Retrieved March 7, 2024, from https://www.newsnationnow.com/polls/poll-four-day-school-week/.

Dreifuss, H. M., Belin, K. L., Wilson, J., George, S., Waters, A. R., Kahn, C. B., Bauer, M. C., & Teufel-Shone, N. I. (2022). Engaging Native American high school students in public health career preparation through the indigenous summer enhancement program. *Frontiers in Public Health*, 10, 789994. https://doi.org/10.3389/fpubh.2022.789994.

East Orange School District works to prevent the 'summer slide.' (2022, July 4). *Essex News Daily*. Retrieved March 13, 2024, from https://essexnewsdaily.com/news/orange/east-orange-school-district-works-to-prevent-the-summer-slide.

EBA- Term of Instruction: school year — Logan City School District. (2023). *Logan City School District*. Retrieved March 15, 2024, from https://www.loganschools.org/eba-term-of-instruction-school-year.

EdChoice. (2023, December 18). Types of school choice - EdChoice. Retrieved March 16, 2024, from https://www.edchoice.org/school-choice/types-of-school-choice/.

Education - South Carolina Encyclopedia. (2022, July 26). *South Carolina Encyclopedia*. https://www.scencyclopedia.org/sce/entries/education/.

Egbuonu, F. (2023, April 13). Over $4B to go toward New Mexico schools. https://www.koat.com/. Retrieved March 13, 2024, from https://www.koat.com/article/new-mexico-417-billion-schools/43594714#.

Enhancing Summer Learning: The Power of Data-Driven Educational Activities at Camp. (2024, January 4). *American Camp Association*. Retrieved April 25, 2024, from https://www.acacamps.org/blog/sponsored/enhancing-summer-learning-power-data-driven-educational-activities-camp.

Enquirer. (2023, November 24). The case for a 4-day school week: A Q&A with the North College Hill superintendent. *Cincinnati Enquirer*. https://www.cincinnati.com/story/news/education/2023/11/23/ohio-superintendent-says-four-day-week-improved-teacher-wellness/71171570007/.

Entwisel, P., Alexander, K., & Olson, L. (2018). Keeping the faucet flowing: Can a balanced school year sustain student achievement? In *Keeping the faucet flowing: Can a balanced school year sustain student achievement*? (pp. 4–6). Retrieved March 17, 2024, from https://files.eric.ed.gov/fulltext/ED594427.pdf.

Evans, M. (2023, August 3). Georgetown Co. students head back to school on new modified year-round calendar. https://www.wmbfnews.com. https://www.wmbfnews.com/2023/08/03/georgetown-county-students-head-back-school-new-modified-year-round-calendar/.

Extended School Year Services Guidance Manual. (n.d.). https://www.cde.state.co.us/. Retrieved March 10, 2024, from https://www.cde.state.co.us/cdesped/esy_guidelines_rev2017.

Facts About 4-Day Week School & Year-Round School. (2022, May 14). *The Classroom | Empowering Students in Their College Journey*. https://www.theclassroom.com/4day-week-school-yearround-school-16084.html.

Fälth, L., Nordström, T., Andersson, U., & Gustafson, S. (2019). An intervention study to prevent 'summer reading loss' in a socioeconomically disadvantaged area with second language learners. *Nordic Journal of Literacy Research*, 5(3). https://doi.org/10.23865/njlr.v5.2013.

Farbman, D. (2011). Learning time in America: Trends to reform the American school calendar--A snapshot of federal, state, and local action. *Education Commission of the States*. http://files.eric.ed.gov/fulltext/ED521518.pdf.

Ferrarin, E. (2022, August 3). 4 ways transitioning to a 4-day school week impacts districts. K-12 Dive. Retrieved March 7, 2024, from https://www.k12dive.com/news/4-ways-transitioning-to-a-4-day-school-week-impacts-districts/628601/.

Finnie, R. K. C., Peng, Y., Hahn, R. A., Johnson, R. L., Fielding, J. E., Truman, B. I., Muntaner, C., Fullilove, M. T., Zhang, X., & Community Preventive Services Task Force (2019). Examining the effectiveness of year-round school calendars on improving educational attainment outcomes within the context of advancement of health equity: A community guide systematic review. *Journal of Public Health Management and Practice: JPHMP*, 25(6), 590–594. https://doi.org/10.1097/PHH.0000000000000860.

Fischel, W. (2006). "Will I see you in September?" An economic explanation for the standard school calendar. *Journal of Urban Economics*, 59(2), 236–251. ISSN 0094-1190, https://doi.org/10.1016/j.jue.2005.03.006.

Fischel, W. A., Hale, P. F., & Hale, W. B. (2003). Will I see you in September? An economic explanation for the summer school vacation. Retrieved February 24, 2014, from www.dartmouth.edu/~wfischel/.

Fitzpatrick, D., & Burns, J. L. (2019). Single-track year-round education for improving academic achievement in U.S. K-12 schools: Results of a meta-analysis. *Campbell Systematic Reviews*, 15(3). https://doi.org/10.1002/cl2.1053.

Fjeld, J., & Fjeld, J. (2023, October 27). Rio Rancho Public Schools consider 'balanced' calendar. KOB.com. https://www.kob.com/new-mexico/rio-rancho-public-schools-consider-balanced-calendar/.

Flanagan, N. (2022, March 8). Kids who take vacations in the middle of the school year (Opinion). *Education Week*. https://www.edweek.org/leadership/opinion-kids-who-take-vacations-in-the-middle-of-the-school-year/2015/01.

Flores-Carter, G. (2023). Best practices to improve summer reading growth: A qualitative E-delphi study (Order No. 30636075). Available from ProQuest One Academic. (2852505889). Retrieved from https://login.delval.idm.oclc.org/login?url=https://www.proquest.com/dissertations-theses/best-practices-improve-summer-reading-growth/docview/2852505889/se-2.

Fortino, J. (2023, August 21). Independence has switched to a 4-day school week. What do families need to know? KCUR - Kansas City News and NPR. https://www.kcur.org/news/2023-08-21/independence-has-switched-to-a-4-day-school-week-what-do-families-need-to-know.

Four-Day School Week overview. (2024, January 4). Retrieved March 16, 2024, from https://www.ncsl.org/education/four-day-school-week-overview.

Franchi, J. (2023, August 21). Canyons Virtual Academy now offering courses to middle school students. FOX 13 News Utah (KSTU). https://www.fox13now.com/back-to-school/canyons-virtual-academy-now-offering-courses-to-middle-school-students.

Garcia, J. (2023, August 6). Nevada ed board to draft school start time regulation. Serving Carson City for Over 150 Years. Retrieved March 13, 2024, from https://www.nevadaappeal.com/news/2023/aug/06/nevada-ed-board-to-draft-school-start-time-regulation/.

Glines, D. (2009). Grounding calendar change: A call for reimagining continuous learning. In C. E. Ballinger & C. Kneese (Eds.), *Balancing the school calendar: Perspectives from the public and stakeholders* (pp. 131–148). Lanham, MD: Rowman & Littlefield.

Glines, D. (1997). YRE: Understanding the basics. *Educational Resources Information Center.* https://files.eric.ed.gov/fulltext/ED406731.pdf.

Glines, D. (1995). *Year-round education: History, philosophy, future.* San Diego, CA: NAYRE.

Gonzalez, S. (2023, November 8). Schools across the U.S. are trying a 4-day week. Why? To retain teachers. https://www.npr.org/. Retrieved March 6, 2024, from https://www.npr.org/2023/11/08/1211632901/schools-across-the-u-s-are-trying-a-4-day-week-why-to-retain-teachers.

Governor's Summer Fellowship - Governor John Carney - State of Delaware. (2024, March 6). *Governor John Carney - State of Delaware.* https://governor.delaware.gov/governors-summer-fellowship/.

Grant, C. D. (2020). The impact of a year-round school calendar on college and career readiness as measured by the SAT scores of urban high school seniors (Order No. 27958951). Available from ProQuest One Academic. (2406624817). Retrieved from https://login.delval.idm.oclc.org/login?url=https://www.proquest.com/dissertations-theses/impact-year-round-school-calendar-on-college/docview/2406624817/se-2.

Greenman, A. (2014). The effects of experiential, service-learning summer learning programs on youth outcomes. https://www.semanticscholar.org/paper/The-effects-of-experiential%2C-service-learning-on-Greenman/e07c13b9c5eea6a90569498c6253b24e497a8fb4.

Haeberlin, B. (2002). Improving student achievement by balancing the school calendar. *Catalyst for Change, 32*(1), 10–12.

Hackley, J. (2023, September 28). 4-day school week not likely in Highland Co. https://www.timesgazette.com/. Retrieved March 4, 2024, from https://www.timesgazette.com/2023/09/28/4-day-school-week-not-likely-on-highland-co/.

Hanshaw, A. (2024, January 8). Four-day school week faces scrutiny from the Missouri legislature and state education board. *Missouri Independent.* https://missouri-independent.com/2024/01/08/four-day-school-week-faces-scrutiny-from-missouri-legislature-state-education-board/.

Harding, A. (2023, April 24). School district releases 4-day start, end times. https://elkodaily.com/. Retrieved March 13, 2024, from https://elkodaily.com/school-district-releases-4-day-start-end-times/article_e1856fae-e2fd-11ed-8dab-db1ce970ab52.html.

Harris, M. (2023, April 11). State Board of Education green-light4-dayay school week in Piute County. *KUER.* https://www.kuer.org/education/2023-04-10/state-board-of-education-green-lights-4-day-school-week-in-piute-county.

Haser, S. G., & Nasser, I. (2005, February 28). Year-round education: Change and choice for schools and teachers. *Rowman & Littlefield Education.* https://eric.ed.gov/?id=ED489002.

Hazelton, J. (1992). Cost effectiveness of alternative year schooling. *Final Report.* Austin, TX: Educational Economic Policy Center. ERIC Document No. 354629.

Hermansen, K., & Gove, J. R. (1971). *The year-round school*. Hamden, CT: Linnet.
Hess, F. M. (2006). Summer vacation of our discontent. In C. E. Ballinger & C. Kneese (Eds.), *Balancing the school calendar: Perspecitves from the public and stakeholders* (pp. 3–10). Lanham, MD: Rowman & Littlefield.
Heubeck, E. (2023, September 5). Why does the start of the school year vary so much? *Education Week*. https://www.edweek.org/leadership/why-does-the-start-of-the-school-year-vary-so-much/2023/09.
Heubeck, E. (2022, July 6). The latest perk schools are using to attract teachers: 4-Day weeks. *Education Week*. https://www.edweek.org/leadership/the-latest-perk-schools-are-using-to-attract-teachers-4-day-weeks/2022/06.
Horn, M. B. (2022, August 5). More schools should offer Year-Round schooling option. *Forbes*. https://www.forbes.com/sites/michaelhorn/2022/08/05/more-schools-should-offer-year-round-schooling-option/?sh=3684413c4f3c.
Howell, C. (2023, December 25). Analysts examine state schools' calendars. https://www.eldoradonews.com/. Retrieved March 10, 2024, from https://www.eldoradonews.com/news/2023/dec/25/analysts-examine-state-schools-calendars/.
Hornak, D., Mishra, J., & Pedersen, J. (2023). Districts explore balanced school calendars to improve outcomes for students. *Washington State School Directors Association*, 14–15. https://wssda.org/wp-content/uploads/2023/10/Direct-2023-FALL.pdf.
Hornak, D. G. (2018). Decreasing learning loss with balanced calendars. *School Administrator Magazine*. https://www.aasa.org/resources/resource/Decreasing-Learning-Loss.
Hornak, D. G. (2015). Impact of summer recess on mathematics learning retention [Unpublished doctoral dissertation]. Central Michigan University.
Huffman, G. E. (2013). Teacher perceptions regarding the relationship of modified year-round school calendars with student achievement, student behavior, and teacher efficacy. *The Aquila Digital Community*. https://aquila.usm.edu/dissertations/185/.
Hutzell, R. (2023, March 3). Does Maryland's school calendar need to be 180 days? Many school leaders don't think so. *The Baltimore Banner*. https://www.thebaltimorebanner.com/opinion/column/school-days-180-hours-anne-arundel-IBIWZ7PTTFHYNPOOMHM4FE427E/.
Hyun, N. (2024, February 6). Facing $6 million deficit, Coeur d'Alene School District weighs options for next school year. https://www.krem.com/. Retrieved March 12, 2024, from https://www.krem.com/article/news/education/coeur-d-alene-school-budget-deficit-four-day-week/293-f3fc0805-2af4-4681-90f2-a7b76f2ef1d9.
Implications Of Year-Round Education For Hawaii's Public Schools. (1972). LEGISLATIVE REFERENCE BUREAU. https://lrb.hawaii.gov/publications/.
Infoplease. (2023, July 27). School Years around the World. *InfoPlease*. Retrieved March 16, 2024, from https://www.infoplease.com/world/social-statistics/school-years-around-world.
Innovative School Schedules: Recommendations to Enhance Student Achievement. (2017, May). https://www.marylandpublicschools.org. Retrieved March 13, 2024,

from https://www.marylandpublicschools.org/about/Documents/ISSW/ISSWDraftReport052017.pdf.

Instructional Hour Template and Calendar User Guide. (2022, April 5). https://www.sde.idaho.gov. Retrieved March 12, 2024 at https://www.sde.idaho.gov/finance/files/calendar/school/2022-2023/2021-2022-Calendar-Manual.pdf.

Iowa. (2023). Iowa Code 2024, Section 279.10 (38, 1). In Iowa Code (pp. 38, 1). https://www.legis.iowa.gov/docs/code/279.10.pdf.

Isom, C. L. (2020). Teachers' perspectives on extended learning activities during a balanced calendar in a rural setting. *Scholars Crossing*. Retrieved March 17, 2024, from https://digitalcommons.liberty.edu/doctoral/2486/.

Jahal, T., Bardoel, A., & Hopkins, J. L. (2023). Could the 4-day week work? A scoping review. *Asia Pacific Journal of Human Resources*, 62(1). https://doi.org/10.1111/1744-7941.12395.

James, J. (2022, December 9). Nontraditional school calendar not popular in Michigan. https://news.jrn.msu.edu/. https://news.jrn.msu.edu/2022/12/nontraditional-school-calendar-not-popular-in-michigan/.

Jiang, L. G. L. (2024, February 22). The rapid growth of hybrid learning fueled by the pandemic. *Global Focus Magazine*. https://www.globalfocusmagazine.com/the-rapid-growth-of-hybrid-learning-fueled-by-the-pandemic/.

Johnson, A. (2023, July 10). Here's why warm weather causes more violent Crimes—From mass shootings to aggravated assault. *Forbes*. https://www.forbes.com/sites/ariannajohnson/2023/07/06/heres-why-warm-weather-causes-more-violent-crimes-from-mass-shootings-to-aggravated-assault/?sh=1512f5c25ab3.

Johnson, O., & Wagner, M. (2017). Equalizers or enablers of inequality? a counterfactual analysis of racial and residential test score gaps in year-round and nine-month schools. *The Annals of the American Academy of Political and Social Science*, 674, 240–261.

Jones, B. (2023, October 28). Columbus, Lowndes schools host first intersessions for remediation, enrichment. *The Dispatch*. https://cdispatch.com/news/columbus-lowndes-schools-host-first-intersessions-for-remediation-enrichment/.

Jones, H. (2023, June 16). Board OKs modified year-round school calendar for 2024–25. https://www.pmg-sc.com/. Retrieved March 14, 2024, from https://www.pmg-sc.com/the_lancaster_news/article_28af83df-984f-5a9b-91a4-f8a3bbd3dc49.html.

Juhasz, A. (2021, July 16). School is still in session in this Louisiana parish. How is the 'Balance of instruction' going? WWNO. https://www.wwno.org/education/2021-06-22/balanced-calendar.

Karle, I. (2022, December 21). Cut Bank approves four-day school week. https://www.cutbankpioneerpress.com/. Retrieved March 13, 2024, from https://www.cutbankpioneerpress.com/cut_bank_pioneer_press/article_7c038512-8155-11ed-b6bf-073c33d383ca.html.

Kayalar, F. (2016). Views of Teachers on the benefits of after-school programs and summer programs in terms of social emotional learning. https://www.semanticscholar.org/paper/Views-of-Teachers-on-the-Benefits-of-After-School-Kayalar/aa6a40e66b3d9cd264a3e42ba58875a1be282386.

Kazu, I. Y., & Yalçin, C. K. (2022). Investigation of the effectiveness of hybrid learning on academic achievement: A meta-analysis study. Retrieved March 9, 2024, from https://eric.ed.gov/?id=EJ1332714.

Kid's Corner: Colonial Schools. Noah Webster House. (n.d.). Retrieved March 3, 2023, from https://noahwebsterhouse.org/colonial-schools/.

Kim, J. S., Burkhauser, M. A., Relyea, J. E., Gilbert, J. B., Scherer, E., Fitzgerald, J., Mosher; D., & McIntyre, J. (2023). A longitudinal randomized trial of a sustained content literacy intervention from first to second grade: Transfer effects on students' reading comprehension. *Journal of Educational Psychology*, 115(1), 73–98. https://doi.org/10.1037/edu0000751.

Kim, S. (2022, August 4). "Desperate" parent dragged for taking son out of class for cheaper vacation. *Newsweek*. https://www.newsweek.com/family-vacation-school-year-parents-debate-mumsnet-1730965.

King, G. (2023, April 10). 4-day school weeks attracting educators to rural Iowa. The Gazette - Local Iowa News, Sports, Obituaries, and Headlines – Cedar Rapids, Iowa City. https://www.thegazette.com/k/4-day-school-weeks-attracting-educators-to-rural-iowa/.

Kingson, J. A. (2023, May 8). 4-day school weeks are gaining steam, but students are suffering. *Axios*. https://www.axios.com/2023/05/08/4-day-school-week-study.

Kneese, C., & Knight, S. (1995). Evaluating the achievement of at-risk students in year round education. *Planning and Changing*, 26, 71–90.

König, C., & Frey, A. (2022). The impact of COVID-19-related school closures on student achievement—A meta-analysis. *Educational Measurement: Issues and Practice*, 41(1), 16–22. doi:https://doi.org/10.1111/emip.12495.

Korth, B. R. (2022, October 27). Oklahoma lawmakers tried to limit four day school weeks, but they're hanging on in rural communities | StateImpact Oklahoma. *StateImpact Oklahoma | Environment, Education, Energy, Health and Justice: Policy to People*. https://stateimpact.npr.org/oklahoma/2022/10/27/oklahoma-lawmakers-tried-to-limit-four-day-school-weeks-but-theyre-hanging-on-in-rural-communities/.

Kuhfeld, M. (2019, June 6). Rethinking summer slide: The more you gain, the more you lose - Kappanonline.org. kappanonline.org. Retrieved March 4, 2024, from https://kappanonline.org/rethinking-summer-slide-the-more-you-gain-the-more-you-lose/.

Kuhfeld, M., Condron, D., & Downey, D. (2019). When does inequality grow? School, summer, and achievement gaps. (NWEA Collaborative for Student Growth Research Brief). https://www.nwea.org/uploads/2020/03/researchbrief-when-does-inequality-grow-school-years-summers-and-achievement-gaps-2019.pdf.

Kraft, M. A., & Monti-Nussbaum, M. (2017). Can Schools enable parents to prevent summer learning loss? A text-messaging field experiment to promote literacy skills. *The ANNALS of the American Academy of Political and Social Science*, 674(1), 85–112. https://doi.org/10.1177/0002716217732009.

Krejci, C. (2022, March 9). Iowa City district to gather feedback about potential shift to four-day-a-week, year-round school. *Iowa City Press-Citizen*. Retrieved March 12, 2024, from https://www.press-citizen.com/story/news/education/k-12/2022/03

/09/year-round-school-calendar-4-day-weeks-up-discussion-iowa-city-school-district/9433207002/.

Kromydas, T., Campbell, M., Chambers, S., Boon, M. H., Pearce, A., Wells, V., & Craig, P. (2022). The effect of school summer holidays on inequalities in children and young people's mental health and cognitive ability in the UK using data from the millennium cohort study. *BMC Public Health*, 22(1), 154. https://doi.org/10.1186/s12889-022-12540-2.

KY - SB50. (2016). BillTrack50. Retrieved March 13, 2024, from https://www.billtrack50.com/BillDetail/666422.

Lambert, D. (2023, February 3). Four-day school week gaining popularity nationally. Why isn't it happening in California? *EdSource*. https://edsource.org/2023/four-day-school-week-gaining-popularity-nationally-why-isnt-it-happening-in-california/684696.

Lanai High and Elementary. (n.d.). Retrieved March 12, 2024, from https://www.hawaiipublicschools.org/Reports/StriveHILanaiHigh_El21.pdf.

Lane, E. N. (1932). The all-year school: Its origins and development. *Nation's Schools*, 9, 49–52.

Lara-Cinisomo, S., Taylor, D. B., & Medina, A. L. (2020). Summer reading program with benefits for at-risk children: Results from a freedom school program. *Reading & Writing Quarterly: Overcoming Learning Difficulties*, 36(3), 211–224. https://doi.org/10.1080/10573569.2019.1627968.

Laurel School District announces summer intersession. (2022, June 20). https://www.wjtv.com/. Retrieved March 13, 2024, from https://www.wjtv.com/news/pine-belt/laurel-school-district-announces-summer-intersession.

Lee, K. (2022, September 8). Portland school district may consider 4-day weeks for some students. *Press Herald*. https://www.pressherald.com/2022/09/07/portland-school-district-may-consider-4-day-weeks-for-some-students/.

Leone, L. (2023, May 10). Southern Iowa school district finishing out first year with 4-day school weeks. https://www.weareiowa.com/. Retrieved March 12, 2024, from https://www.weareiowa.com/article/news/education/cardinal-school-district-iowa-four-day-school-week/524-a9a6e23d-ddbf-4230-ae40-c22603730234.

Letters to the Editor, The Star-Ledger & Letters to the Editor, editorial@nj.com. (2021, April 4). N.J. should embrace year-'round school use beyond pandemic | Letters. Nj. https://www.nj.com/opinion/2021/04/nj-should-embrace-year-round-school-use-beyond-pandemic-letters.html.

Linder, K. E. (2017). Fundamentals of hybrid teaching and learning. *New Directions for Teaching and Learning*, 2017(149), 11–18. https://doi.org/10.1002/tl.20222.

Li, K. C., Wong, B. T. M., Kwan, R., Chan, H. T., Wu, M. M. F., & Cheung, S. K. S. (2023). Evaluation of hybrid learning and teaching practices: The perspective of academics. *Sustainability*, 15, 6780. https://doi.org/10.3390/su15086780.

Liberty Elementary District transitions to four-day school week. (2023, July 12). The Daily Independent at YourValley.net. https://www.yourvalley.net/litchfield-park-independent/stories/liberty-elementary-district-transitions-to-four-day-school-week,410559.

Lipson, M. (2023, January 17). No more Fridays: A real-world experiment just proved that we should all shift to a four-day workweek. https://www.businessinsider.com/. Retrieved March 6, 2024, from https://www.businessinsider.com/4-day-workweek-successful-trial-evidence-productivity-retention-revenue-2023-1.

Livengood, P. (2023, March 2). The largest DFW district to consider 4-day school week isn't moving forward with it. https://www.wfaa.com/. Retrieved March 4, 2024, from https://www.wfaa.com/article/news/education/schools/mesquite-isd-4-day-school-week-eliminated/287-110600cd-3e8a-453a-99c5-728d884b6754.

Liu, V. Y. T., Community College Research Center, & Teachers College, Columbia University. (2016). Goodbye to summer vacation? The effects of summer enrollment on college and employment outcomes. In *A CAPSEE Working Paper*. https://files.eric.ed.gov/fulltext/ED571649.pdf.

Louisiana Department of Education. (2021, November). Balanced school calendar: Key considerations for implementation. https://www.louisianabelieves.com/.

Luna, J. (2022, September 9). Four-day school weeks: Is the trade-off worth it? *The Thomas B. Fordham Institute*. Retrieved March 18, 2024, from https://fordhaminstitute.org/national/commentary/four-day-school-weeks-trade-worth-it.

Lundstrom, M. (2005). Stop the summer reading slide. *Instructor*, 114(8), 20–26.

Lynch, K., An, L., & Mancenido, Z. (2023). The impact of summer programs on student mathematics achievement: A meta-analysis. *Review of Educational Research*, 93(2), 275–315. https://doi.org/10.3102/00346543221105543.

Lynch, K., & Kim, J. S. (2017). Effects of a summer mathematics intervention for low-income children: A randomized experiment. *Educational Evaluation and Policy Analysis*, 39(1), 31–53. https://doi.org/10.3102/0162373716662339.

MacDonell, S. (2019, April 18). Year-Round school in Michigan. *Metro Parent*. https://www.metroparent.com/education/school-issues/year-round-school-michigan/.

Mackey, M. (2023, February 10). Georgia six-year-old pleads to "government" for four-day school week. *Fox News*. https://www.foxnews.com/lifestyle/georgia-six-year-old-pleads-four-day-school-week.

Massachusetts Department of Elementary and Secondary Education. (n.d.). MA Expanded Learning Time (ELT) - school redesign. Retrieved March 13, 2024, from https://www.doe.mass.edu/redesign/elt/.

Massachusetts passes First Education Law. Native American Writer Born. (n.d.). Accessed on March 3, 2023 at https://www.massmoments.org/moment-details/massachusetts-passes-first-education-law.html.

Mattingly, J. W. (2007). A study of relationships of school climate, school culture, teacher efficacy, collective efficacy, teacher job satisfaction, and intent to turnover in the context of year round education calendars. (Unpublished doctoral dissertation). Louisville, KY: University of Louisville.

McGirl, S. (2021, July 23). New London launches Year-Round School option for kindergarten and first grade. *NBC Connecticut*. https://www.nbcconnecticut.com/news/local/new-london-launches-year-round-school-option-for-kindergarten-and-first-grade/2535300/.

McIntosh, C. E., & Stone, G. E. (2022). Introduction to the special issue: How covid-19 has affected students' health, achievement, and mental health. *Psychology in the Schools*. https://doi.org/10.1002/pits.22820.

Mesa, M. P., Roehrig, A., Funari, C., Durtschi, S., Ha, C., Rawls, E., & Davis, C. (2021). Young African American scholars make reading gains at Literacy-Focused, culturally relevant summer camp that combats summer reading loss. Retrieved March 17, 2024, from https://eric.ed.gov/?id=ED611719.

Means, B., Toyama, Y., Murphy, R., Bakia, M., & Jones, K. (2009). Evaluation of evidence-based practices in online learning: A meta-analysis and review of online learning studies. U.S. Department of Education Office of Planning, Evaluation, and Policy Development, Policy and Program Studies Service. http://www2.ed.gov/rschstat/eval/tech/evidence-based-practices/finalreport.pdf

Mesmer, A. (2022, September 9). Hillsborough school district might consider 4-day school week to address teacher shortage. *FOX 13 Tampa Bay*. https://www.fox13news.com/news/hillsborough-school-district-might-consider-4-day-school-week-to-address-teacher-shortage.

Missouri Department of Elementary and Secondary Education. (n.d.). Summer School Program | Missouri Department of Elementary and Secondary Education. https://dese.mo.gov/. Retrieved April 9, 2024, from https://dese.mo.gov/quality-schools/summer-school-program.

Mitchell, T. G. (2022). A qualitative study examining the perceptions of special education team members regarding the impact of the four-day school week on students who receive special education services (Order No. 29318901). Available from ProQuest One Academic. (2707659445). Retrieved from https://login.delval.idm.oclc.org/login?url=https://www.proquest.com/dissertations-theses/qualitative-study-examining-perceptions-special/docview/2707659445/se-2.

Mo. Code Regs. tit. 5 § 20-100.160. (2024, March 1). https://casetext.com/. Retrieved March 13, 2024, from https://casetext.com/regulation/missouri-administrative-code/title-5-department-of-elementary-and-secondary-education/division-20-division-of-learning-services/chapter-100-office-of-quality-schools/section-5-csr-20-100160-policies-and-standards-for-summer-school-programs.

Modestino, A. S. (2019). How Do Summer Youth employment programs improve criminal justice outcomes, and for whom? *Journal of Policy Analysis and Management*, 38(3), 600–628. https://doi.org/10.1002/pam.22138.

Modestino, A. S., & Paulsen, R. J. (2023). School's out: How summer youth employment programs impact academic outcomes. *Education Finance and Policy*, 18(1), 97–126. https://doi.org/10.1162/edfp_a_00371.

Morse, S. C. (1992). The value of remembering. *Thrust for Educational Leadership*, 21(6), 35–37.

Mykerezi, E., & Qian, X. (2016). Impact of year-round education on travel. https://conservancy.umn.edu/bitstream/handle/11299/176327/Impact%20of%20Year-Round%20Education%20on%20Travel%20FINAL.pdf;Sequence=1. Retrieved March 18, 2024, from https://conservancy.umn.edu/bitstream/handle/11299/176327/Impact%20of%20Year-Round%20Education%20on%20Travel%20FINAL.pdf;sequence=1.

Nachtigal, J. (2023, September 27). District enters year two of four-day venture. *Wise County Messenger.* https://www.wcmessenger.com/articles/district-enters-year-two-of-four-day-venture/.

Napolitano, J. (2022, January 18). Why learning loss is prompting educators to rethink the traditional school calendar: Start earlier, end later, extend breaks for remediation. https://www.the74million.org/. Retrieved March 6, 2024, from https://www.the74million.org/article/why-learning-loss-is-prompting-educators-to-rethink-the-traditional-school-calendar-start-earlier-end-later-extend-breaks-for-remediation/.

National Association for Year-Round Education. (2010). About YRE. Retrieved March 3, 2023, from http://nayre.org/about.html.

NAYRE. (2024). *The National Association for Year-Round Education.* Retrieved February 25, 2014, from http://www.nayre.org.

NEC. (2005). National Education Commission on Time and Learning. *Prisoners of time.* Washington, DC. U.S. Government Printing Office. Retrieved, February 25, 2014 from http://ed.gov/pubs/Prisoners.

National Center for Education Statistics. (n.d.). Table 1.1. Minimum number of instructional days and hours in the school year, minimum number of hours per school day, and school start/finish dates, by state: 2020. Retrieved March 5, 2024, from https://nces.ed.gov/programs/statereform/tab1_1-2020.asp.

National Education Commission on Time and Learning, Robertson, P., Goldberg, M., & Cross, C. T. (1994). Prisoners of time. In *Education commission of the States, report of the national education commission on time and learning* [Report]. Retrieved April 4, 2024, from https://www.ecs.org/clearinghouse/64/52/6452.pdf.

Nebraska Revised Statute 79-503. (n.d.). Retrieved March 13, 2024, from https://nebraskalegislature.gov/laws/statutes.php?statute=79-503.

News Staff. (2023, September 21). The four-day school week: Research shows benefits and consequences. https://www.sansabanews.com/. Retrieved March 6, 2024, from https://www.sansabanews.com/news-newsletter/four-day-school-week-research-shows-benefits-and-consequences.

Nicholas, B., & Harshman. (2013). HOUSE BILL NO. HB0255. In STATE OF WYOMING [Legislation]. https://wyoleg.gov/2013/Introduced/HB0255.pdf.

Nicholson, T., & Tiru, S. (2019). Preventing a summer slide in reading – the effects of a summer school. *Australian Journal of Learning Difficulties*, 24(2), 109–130. https://doi.org/10.1080/19404158.2019.1635499.

Nisbett, R. E. (2009). *Intelligence and how to get it: Why schools and cultures count.* New York: WW Norton & Company.

Nonregulatory Guidance: Extended School Year Services. (2012). In Page 1 of 5. https://osse.dc.gov/sites/default/files/dc/sites/osse/publication/attachments/ESY%20Certification%20Frequently%20Asked%20Questions_Guidance_v.2.2012_0.pdf.

North Dakota Century Code. (n.d.). https://ndlegis.gov/. Retrieved March 13, 2024, from https://ndlegis.gov/cencode/t15-1c06.pdf.

Nwea, E. M. P. R. S. (2023, December 12). Can 4 equal 5? The impact of 4-day school weeks. *eSchool News.* https://www.eschoolnews.com/educational-leadership/2023/12/21/impact-of-four-day-school-weeks/.

Office of Superintendent of Public Instruction. (2023, October 17). Modified calendar supports learning recovery for WinLock Elementary students. *Medium.* https://medium.com/waospi/balanced-calendar-supports-learning-recovery-for-winlock-elementary-students-458653f6b53b.

Oglesby, A. (2023, August 12). What does a four-day school week look like? https://www.kxnet.com/. Retrieved March 7, 2024, from https://www.kxnet.com/news/top-stories/what-does-a-four-day-school-week-look-like.

Oldham, D. & Tennessee Department of Education. (2022). LEA Calendar Approval process 2022–23. https://www.tn.gov/content/dam/tn/education/forms/OGC_2022-23_LEA_Calendar_Approval_Process_Memo.pdf.

Olds, T., Dumuid, D., Eglitis, E. Golley, R., Fraysse, F., Miatke, A., Tomkinson, G.R., Watson, A., Munzberg, M., & Maher, C. (2023). Changes in fitness and fatness in Australian schoolchildren during the summer holidays: Fitness lost, fatness regained? A cohort study. *BMC Public Health,* 23, 2094. https://doi.org/10.1186/s12889-023-17009-4.

OSPI. (n.d.). Office of Superintendent of Public Instruction. Retrieved April 26, 2024, from https://ospi.k12.wa.us/.

Palmer, L. (2024, February 28). MVSD board votes yes to another year of four-day week following survey results. https://www.idahocountyfreepress.com/. Retrieved March 12, 2024, from https://www.idahocountyfreepress.com/community/school-news/mvsd-board-votes-yes-to-another-year-of-four-day-week-following-survey-results/article_df7bf17c-d5a7-11ee-872c-67bec3b6e24e.html.

Park, S. Y., Ahn, J. B., & Pan, B. (2018). Family trips and academic achievement in reading during early childhood: Evidence from a national study. *Scholar Works.* https://scholarworks.umass.edu/cgi/viewcontent.cgi?article=2212&context=ttra.

Parker, L., & Reid, C. (2017). A case study of elementary school parents as agents for summer reading Gain: Fostering a summer leap and holding steady. https://eric.ed.gov/?id=EJ1146496.

Patall, E. A., Cooper, H., & Allen, A. B. (2010). Extending the school day or school year: A systematic review of research (1985–2009). *Review of Educational Research*, 80(3), 401–436. http://www.jstor.org/stable/40927287.

Pennsylvania Department of Education. (n.d.). Glossary of Terms. Department of Education. Retrieved March 14, 2024, from https://www.education.pa.gov/Teachers%20-%20Administrators/Child%20Accounting/Pages/Glossary-of-Terms.aspx.

Pedersen, J. (2012). The history of school and summer vacation. *Journal of Inquiry & Action in Education,* 5(1). https://files.eric.ed.gov/fulltext/EJ1134242.pdf.

Pedersen, J. (2015). Summer versus School: The possibilities of the year-round School, Rowman & Littlefield Publishers. *ProQuest Ebook Central.* https://ebookcentral.proquest.com/lib/delawavall/detail.action?docID=4086136.

Peetz, C. (2024, January 23). The popularity of 4-day school weeks, in charts. https://www.edweek.org. Retrieved March 6, 2024, from https://www.edweek.org/leadership/the-popularity-of-4-day-school-weeks-in-charts/2024/01.

Piedmont Year-Round Education. (n.d.). https://piedmont.kana.k12.wv.us/. Retrieved March 16, 2024, from https://piedmont.kana.k12.wv.us/about.

Pepper, S. (2009). Multitracking in school calendar reform. In C. E. Ballinger & C. Kneese (Eds.), *Balancing the school calendar: Perspectives from the public and stakeholders* (pp. 117–130). Lanham, MD: Rowman & Littlefield.

Powell, S. L. (2019). The impact of continuous learning calendars on student learning (Order No. 22618041). Available from ProQuest One Academic. (2313355464). Retrieved from https://login.delval.idm.oclc.org/login?url=https://www.proquest.com/dissertations-theses/impact-continuous-learning-calendars-on-student/docview/2313355464/se-2.

Prieur, D. (2024, January 22). Florida schools have an absenteeism problem. Here's how two districts are trying to fix it. *WFSU News*. https://news.wfsu.org/state-news/2024-01-22/florida-schools-have-an-absenteeism-problem-heres-how-two-districts-are-trying-to-fix-it.

Prothero, A. (2023, August 24). 4-Day school weeks surge in popularity among American adults. *Education Week*. https://www.edweek.org/leadership/4-day-school-weeks-surge-in-popularity-among-american-adults/2023/08.

Pringle, J. (2023, May 5). Ottawa French Catholic school board forced to scrap four-day school week. *Ottawa*. Retrieved March 4, 2024, from https://ottawa.ctvnews.ca/ottawa-french-catholic-school-board-forced-to-scrap-four-day-school-week-1.6386112.

Public Act 0012 101ST GENERAL ASSEMBLY. (n.d.). Retrieved March 12, 2024, from https://www.ilga.gov/legislation/publicacts/101/101-0012.htm.

Pyne, J., Messner, E., & Dee, T. S. (2023). The dynamic effects of a summer learning program on behavioral engagement in school. Retrieved March 18, 2024, from https://eric.ed.gov/?id=EJ1376853.

Queensland parents reject four day school week. (2024, January 3). *Skynews*. Retrieved March 3, 2024, from https://www.skynews.com.au/australia-news/queensland-parents-reject-four-day-school-week/video/08c45683bcb4980d40c9514593d52629.

Quinn, D. M., & Polikoff, M. (2017, September 14). Summer learning loss: What is it, and what can we do about it? *Brookings*. https://www.brookings.edu/articles/summer-learning-loss-what-is-it-and-what-can-we-do-about-it/.

Radinger, T., & Boeskens, L. (2021). More time at school: Lessons from case studies and research on extended school days. OECD Education Working Papers No. 252. Retrieved February 28, 2024, from https://dx.doi.org/10.1787/1f50c70d-en.

Rahman, K. (2024, February 21). More US Schools moving to four-day week. *Newsweek*. Retrieved March 7, 2024, from https://www.newsweek.com/more-schools-moving-four-day-week-1871966.

Raines, B. (2023, July 24). Perry County students return to class on modified schedule. https://www.wjtv.com/. Retrieved March 13, 2024, from https://www.wjtv.com/news/education/perry-county-students-return-to-class-on-modified-schedule/.

Rakoff, T. D. (1999, April). *Schooltime.* Paper presented at the Annual Meeting of the American Educational Research Association, Montreal, Canada.

Redfield, J. (2023, April 21). Moravia CSD transitions to 4-day school week. *KTVO*. https://ktvo.com/news/local/moravia-csd-transitions-to-4-day-school-week.

Renaud, T. (2024, February 1). Williamsburg County School District adopts modified year-round calendar for 2024–25 school year. https://www.counton2.com/. Retrieved March 14, 2024, from https://www.counton2.com/news/local-news/williamsburg-county-news/williamsburg-county-school-district-adopts-modified-year-round-calendar-for-2024-25-school-year/.

Replogle, C. (2022, June 24). Boys and Girls Clubs of Springfield expanding into Marshfield. https://www.ky3.com. https://www.ky3.com/2022/06/24/boys-girls-clubs-springfield-expanding-into-marshfield/.

Reyez, Z. (2023, June 20). RE-3 School District to officially begin four-day school week in August. *The Fort Morgan Times*. https://www.fortmorgantimes.com/2023/06/20/re-3-school-district-to-officially-begin-four-day-school-week-in-august/.

Reynolds, A. (2021). A mechanism to increase literacy and math skills and to reduce summer learning loss. Retrieved March 17, 2024, from https://eric.ed.gov/?id=ED619136.

Rispens, S., & Rispens, S. (2023, December 19). Changes to four-day school week prompt childcare, hunger concerns. *Montana Free Press*. https://montanafreepress.org/2023/12/19/changes-to-four-day-school-week-prompt-childcare-hunger-concerns/.

Rispens, S., & Rispens, S. (2024, January 15). Montana schools address teacher shortage by adopting four-day weeks to better recruit and retain educators. *Montana Free Press*. https://montanafreepress.org/2023/12/18/montana-schools-address-teacher-shortage-by-adopting-four-day-weeks-to-better-recruit-and-retain-educators/.

Robinson, D. (2023, September 4). Year-round school: Difference-maker or waste of time? https://www.wbtw.com/. Retrieved March 3, 2024, from https://www.wbtw.com/nexstar-media-wire/year-round-school-difference-maker-or-waste-of-time/.

Robles, Y. (2023, November 9). Four-day school week hurt housing market, academics in the 27J district, study suggests. *Chalkbeat*. https://www.chalkbeat.org/colorado/2023/2/7/23588718/27j-four-day-school-week-study-teacher-retention-housing-prices/.

Rogers, T. (2022, June 1). Summer programs expanded at MSD. Milford LIVE! - Local Delaware News, Kent and Sussex Counties. Retrieved March 12, 2024, from https://milfordlive.com/summer-programs-expanded-at-msd/.

Roland, B. (2023, July 24). B22 Fit offering Grant Parish students a place to go on Mondays during the upcoming school year. https://www.kalb.com. https://www.kalb.com/2023/07/24/b22-fit-offering-grant-parish-students-place-go-mondays-during-upcoming-school-year/.

Rosqvist, I., Sandgren, O., Andersson, K., Hansson, K., Lyberg-Åhlander, V., & Sahlén, B. (2020). Children's development of semantic verbal fluency during summer vacation versus during formal schooling. *Logopedics, Phoniatrics, Vocology*, 45(3), 134–142. https://doi.org/10.1080/14015439.2019.1637456.

Russo, M. (2021, December 11). New NYC Schools Chancellor wants longer school days, Saturday and summer classes. *NBC New York*. https://www.nbcnewyork.com/news/local/new-nyc-schools-chancellor-wants-longer-school-days-saturday-and-summer-classes/3445341/.

Sachs, A. (2024, January 28). What's the ideal vacation length for peak relaxation? *The Washington Post.* Retrieved from https://login.delval.idm.oclc.org/login?url=https://www.proquest.com/newspapers/whats-ideal-vacation-length-peak-relaxation/docview/2918837810/se-2.

Sacramento Observer. (2023, September 26). More schools are adopting 4-day weeks. For parents, the challenge is day 5. *The Sacramento Observer.* https://sacobserver.com/2023/10/more-schools-are-adopting-4-day-weeks-for-parents-the-challenge-is-day-5/.

Sanchez, S. (2023, August 4). Back to school four days a week, at least in the San Elizario School District! https://www.elpasoinc.com/. Retrieved March 15, 2024, from https://www.elpasoinc.com/lifestyle/local_features/back-to-school-four-days-a-week/article_29e861d0-3221-11ee-9c06-5f8593d000d7.html.

Sawchuk, S. (2020, March 24). Schools reconsider the calendar as students grow more diverse. https://www.edweek.org/. Retrieved March 5, 2024, from https://www.edweek.org/leadership/schools-reconsider-the-calendar-as-students-grow-more-diverse/2020/03.

Sawyer, D. T., Jr. (2018). Balanced calendar versus traditional calendar: Measuring the difference in reading academic achievement among kindergarten through third-grade students who have been identified as reading below or well-below grade level (Order No. 10929287). Available from ProQuest One Academic. (2090998057). Retrieved from https://login.delval.idm.oclc.org/login?url=https://www.proquest.com/dissertations-theses/balanced-calendar-versus-traditional-measuring/docview/2090998057/se-2.

SBG San Antonio Staff Reports, (2024, February 15). Bandera ISD embarks on the four-day work week experiment. KABB. https://foxsanantonio.com/newsletter-daily/bandera-isd-embarks-on-the-four-day-work-week-experiment-for-teacher-recruitment-local-people-students-jobs-money-community.

Scarbrough, B. (2017). A summer of distinction: Exploring the construction of educational advantage outside the academic year. *Curriculum Inquiry,* 47(5), 481–503. https://doi.org/10.1080/03626784.2017.1398043.

Schmitt, A. M., Horner, S. L., & Lavery, M. R. (2020). The impact of summer programs on the English language scores of migrant children. Retrieved March 17, 2024, from https://eric.ed.gov/?id=EJ1240210.

School Calendars Be in School Every Day! (n.d.). https://mps.milwaukee.k12.wi.us/. Retrieved March 16, 2024, from https://mps.milwaukee.k12.wi.us/en/Families/Resources/School-Calendars.htm.

School calendar Information | Oklahoma State Department of Education. (2017, December 20). Oklahoma State Department of Education. https://sde.ok.gov/documents/2017-12-20/school-calendar-information.

School Finance Manual. (n.d.). https://www.azed.gov/. Retrieved March 9, 2024, from https://www.azed.gov/sites/default/files/finance/files/2020/07/School-Finance-Manual-A-Defining-the-Instructional-Calendar-Posted-7.31.20.pdf.

Schulte, B. (2009). Putting the brakes on summer slide: Modified school calendars build in time to enrich learning and sustain gains. *Educational Digest,* 75(4), 17–22.

Schulz, C. (2023, February 24). Senate Education Committee proposes alternative school schedule. *West Virginia Public Broadcasting.* https://wvpublic.org/senate-education-committee-proposes-alternative-school-schedule/.

Schultz, S. C. (2019). Impact of a four-day school week on teacher preparation (Order No. 27665034). Available from ProQuest One Academic. (2425845428). Retrieved from https://login.delval.idm.oclc.org/login?url=https://www.proquest.com/dissertations-theses/impact-four-day-school-week-on-teacher/docview/2425845428/se-2.

Schumacher, L. E. (2015). Continuous calendar and academic growth: A study of the impact of continuous calendar schools on academic growth of low-socioeconomic-status students (Order No. 3682254). Available from ProQuest One Academic. (1657426701). Retrieved from https://login.delval.idm.oclc.org/login?url=https://www.proquest.com/dissertations-theses/continuous-calendar-academic-growth-study-impact/docview/1657426701/se-2.

Sciullo, F. (2018). Year-Round education and Student Learning: A case study of stakeholders' perceptions - ProQuest One Academic - ProQuest. Retrieved March 17, 2024, from https://www.proquest.com/pq1academic/docview/2089397090/2F4AD269C5E04D5EPQ/3?sourcetype=Dissertations%20&%20Theses.

Sec. 120A.41 MN Statutes. (n.d.). https://www.revisor.mn.gov/statutes/cite/120A.41.

Seamless Summer Option (SSO) | Agency of Education. (n.d.). https://education.vermont.gov/student-support/nutrition/school-meals/seamless-summer-option.

Seamless summer option. (n.d.). Illinois State Board of Education. https://www.isbe.net/sso.

Shammas, C. (2023). The extent and duration of primary schooling in eighteenth-century America. *History of Education Quarterly,* 63(3), 313–335. https://doi.org/10.1017/heq.2023.12.

Shappell, L. (2022, June 23). TUHSD, Kyrene, Tempe El unify school calendars, adopt modified year-round format for 2023-24. *Wrangler News.* https://www.wranglernews.com/2022/06/23/tuhsd-kyrene-tempe-el-unify-school-calendars-adopt-modified-year-round-format-for-2023-24/.

Shepelavy, R. P. (2023, May 30). Is Year-Round schooling the answer we need? *The Philadelphia Citizen.* https://thephiladelphiacitizen.org/year-round-schooling/.

Shinwell, J., & Defeyter, M. A. (2017). Investigation of summer learning loss in the UK—Implications for holiday club provision. *Frontiers in Public Health,* 5. https://doi.org/10.3389/fpubh.2017.00270.

Silva, E. (2007). On the clock: Rethinking the way schools use time. *Education Sector Reports,* 1–9.

Silverman, T. (2023, May 12). Time for a real job. Teen employment teaches responsibility and builds confidence | Opinion. *Pennsylvania Capital-Star.* Retrieved March 4, 2024, from https://penncapital-star.com/commentary/time-for-a-real-job-teen-employment-teaches-responsibility-and-builds-confidence-opinion/#:~:text=It%20may%20be%20surprising%20to,52%25%20of%20all%20U.S.%20teens.

Smith, B. (2022, December 17). WATCH: CMS 4-day week 'transformational,' says principal. https://www.hotsr.com/. Retrieved March 10, 2024, from https://www.hotsr.com/news/2022/dec/17/watch-cms-4-day-week-transformational-says/.

Smith, J. (2023, December 20). When does school end in Hawaii? - Hawaii Star. *Hawaii Star*. https://www.hawaiistar.com/when-does-school-end-in-hawaii/.

Smith, T. (2021). How teachers feel Missouri school schedules affect teachers morale: A qualitative descriptive case study (Order No. 28867115). Available from ProQuest One Academic. (2650005431). Retrieved from https://login.delval.idm.oclc.org/login?url=https://www.proquest.com/dissertations-theses/how-teachers-feel-missouri-school-schedules/docview/2650005431/se-2.

Smithling, C. F., & Swain, C. (2011). *Should school be year-round?* New Rochelle, NY: Benchmark Education.

South Dakota Legislature. (2024). South Dakota Legislature. Retrieved March 14, 2024, from https://sdlegislature.gov/Statutes/13-26.

Spain considering limiting school summer holidays to nine weeks. (2023, August 23). *Canarian Weekly*. Retrieved March 16, 2024, from https://www.canarianweekly.com/posts/Spain-considering-limiting-school-summer-holidays-to-nine-weeks.

Sparks, S. D. (2023, March 7). 4 Studies to know on 4-Day School Weeks. *Education Week*. https://www.edweek.org/leadership/four-studies-to-know-on-four-day-school-weeks/2023/02.

Staff. (2024, February 15). Parents face deadline for input on modified school calendar. https://www.wrdw.com. https://www.wrdw.com/2024/02/15/richmond-county-parents-last-chance-share-modified-school-calendar/.

Star, I. (2023, October 16). Some Indy school districts use fall break for catching up students. Does it work? *Indianapolis Star*. https://www.indystar.com/story/news/education/2023/10/16/indianapolis-school-districts-have-longer-breaks-than-others/71075040007/.

Stark Education Partnership & Stark Education Partnership. (2018). Using a Balanced School Year to Improve Student Achievement. A White Paper of the Stark Education Partnership. Distributed by ERIC Clearinghouse.

Stewart, H., Watson, N., & Campbell, M. (2018). The cost of school holidays for children from low income families. *Childhood*, 25(4), 516–529. https://doi.org/10.1177/0907568218779130.

Stockburger, G. (2023, February 28). Pennsylvania lawmakers pushing four day workweek program. https://www.abc27.com/. Retrieved March 14, 2024, from https://www.abc27.com/pennsylvania-politics/pennsylvania-lawmakers-pushing-four-day-workweek-program/.

Strategic Communication. (2022, December 2). Understanding the rise of the four-day school week: MSU professor discusses the education trend. https://news.missouristate.edu/. Retrieved March 6, 2024, from https://news.missouristate.edu/2022/12/02/four-day-school-week/?utm_source=feed&utm_medium=feed&utm_campaign=feed.

Streeter, Raymond Leffler, II. (2021). A comparison of the four-day school week to the five-day school week and reading achievement of third, fourth, and fifth graders (Order No. 28547962). Available from ProQuest One Academic. (2546662134). Retrieved from https://login.delval.idm.oclc.org/login?url=https://www.proquest.com/dissertations-theses/comparison-four-day-school-week-five-reading/docview/2546662134/se-2.

Stroudmire, E. (2024, January 22). Central Texas school districts report positive results with four day school week. https://www.ktsm.com/. Retrieved March 14, 2024, from https://www.ktsm.com/news/central-texas-school-districts-report-positive-results-with-four-day-school-week/.

Study of the impact of the Four-Day School Week on academic Achievement and Building Growth - January 2024 | Missouri Department of Elementary and Secondary Education. (n.d.). https://dese.mo.gov/media/pdf/study-impact-four-day-school-week-academic-achievement-and-building-growth-january-2024.

Sullivan, E. (2022). Summer learning programs struggle – and Devise solutions – as staff shortages persist. Retrieved from https://www.edsurge.com/news/2022-07-18-summer-learning-programs-struggle-and-devise-solutions-as-staff-shortages-persist.

Superville, D. R. (2022, April 8). Is it time to reconsider the Year-Round school schedule? *Education Week*. https://www.edweek.org/leadership/is-it-time-to-reconsider-the-year-round-school-schedule/2020/06.

Sweetwater County school board agrees to four-day school week in close vote. (2020, May 4). https://www.gillettenewsrecord.com/. Retrieved March 16, 2024, from https://www.gillettenewsrecord.com/news/wyoming/article_46cc23f3-47a2-5f35-afba-3a9994e5d856.html.

Talbot, M. (2000, July 30). The way we live now: School's out for never. *New York Times*. Retrieved from http://www.nytimes.com/2000/07/30/magazine/the-way-we-live-now-7-30-00-school-s-out-for-never.html.

The Academy NJ. (n.d.). The Academy NJ. Retrieved March 13, 2024, from https://theacademynj.org/year-round-calendar.

Thies, B. F. (2024, March 13). Portland, Maine, Schools consider 4-Day week for special ed students. *Breitbart*. https://www.breitbart.com/education/2022/09/09/portland-maine-schools-consider-4-day-week-special-education-students-staffing-shortage/.

Thompson, P. N., Gunter, K., Schuna, Jr., J. M., & Tomayko, E. J. (2021). Are all four-day school weeks created equal? A national assessment of four-day school week policy adoption and implementation. *Education Finance and Policy*, 16(4), 558–583.

Time to Learn / Intersession schools. (n.d.). Retrieved March 9, 2024, from https://www.dallasisd.org/Page/74537.

Title 20-A, §4801: School days. (2023, November 2). Retrieved March 13, 2024, from https://www.mainelegislature.org/legis/statutes/20-a/title20-Asec4801.html.

Tough choices or tough times : The report of the New Commission on the Skills of the American Workforce. (Rev. and expanded.). (2008). Jossey-Bass.

United States. National Commission on Excellence in Education. (1983). A nation at risk : The imperative for educational reform : a report to the Nation and the Secretary of Education, United States Department of Education. Washington, D.C.: National Commission on Excellence in Education : [Superintendent of Documents, U.S. Government Printing Office distributor].

United States. National Education Commission on Time and Learning. (1994). Prisoners of time: Report of the National Education Commission on Time and

Learning. Washington, DC (1255 22nd St., NW, Washington 20202-7591): The Commission: For sale by the U.S. G.P.O., Supt. of Docs.

Unique Setting - Calendars - CBE. (n.d.). Retrieved March 16, 2024, from https://cbe.ab.ca/registration/calendars/Pages/modified-calendar.aspx.

Valle, A. (2023, December 18). More than 100 people voice their opposition to school calendar change. https://www.koat.com/. Retrieved March 3, 2024, from https://www.koat.com/article/new-mexico-oppose-school-calendar-change/46168757#.

Valley, J. (2023, October 5). Could four-day weeks lead to more progress for students? *The Christian Science Monitor.* https://www.csmonitor.com/USA/Education/2023/0920/Could-four-day-weeks-lead-to-more-progress-for-students.

Van De Sande, C., & Reiser, M. (2018). The effect of summer break on engineering student success in calculus. *International Journal of Research in Education and Science*, 4(2), 349–357. https://doi.org/10.21890/ijres.409264.

Van De Sande, C. C. (2019). Keeping in School Shape (KiSS): A program for rehearsing Math skills over breaks from school. *Journal of International Education and Practice*, 2(4), 39. https://doi.org/10.30564/jiep.v2i4.1383.

Vance, T. (2022, July 27). Lt. Gov. Hosemann wants to incentivize school districts to switch to 'modified' calendar. *Northeast Mississippi Daily Journal.* Retrieved March 14, 2024, from https://www.djournal.com/news/state-news/lt-gov-hosemann-wants-to-incentivize-school-districts-to-switch-to-modified-calendar/article_7d44b583-37c6-5ed8-9279-4ed0c3494706.html.

Vollmer, J. R. (2010). *Schools cannot do it alone: Building public support for America's public schools.* Fairfield, IA: Enlightenment Press.

von Hippel, P. T. (2019). Is summer learning loss real? *Education Next*, 19(4). https://login.delval.idm.oclc.org/login?url=https://www.proquest.com/scholarly-journals/is-summer-learning-loss-real/docview/2309281610/se-2.

Von Hippel, P. T., & Graves, J. (2023, April 5). Busting the myths about Year-Round school calendars. *Education Next.* https://www.educationnext.org/busting-the-myths-about-year-round-school-calendars/.

Wahlstrom, K. (2002). Changing times: Findings from the first longitudinal study of later high school start times. *National Association of Secondary School Principals. NASSP Bulletin*, 86(633), 3–21. Retrieved from https://login.delval.idm.oclc.org/login?url=https://www.proquest.com/scholarly-journals/changing-times-findings-first-longitudinal-study/docview/216016019/se-2.

Wallace, D. K. (2022). Extended calendar model versus traditional calendar model: A descriptive analysis of student performance over time (Order No. AAI28541163). Available from APA PsycInfo®. (2578862176; 2021-80515-192). Retrieved from https://login.delval.idm.oclc.org/login?url=https://www.proquest.com/dissertations-theses/extended-calendar-model-versus-traditional/docview/2578862176/se-2.

Wallington, N. (2022, December 16). How will the four-day school week work in Independence?: Here's what we know. https://www.kansascity.com/news/local/education/article270096907.html. Retrieved March 6, 2024, from https://www.kansascity.com/news/local/education/article270096907.html#storylink=cpy.

Walrath-Holdridge, M. (2023, August 13). Homework in August or summer in September? Why back-to-school dates vary so much across US. *USA TODAY*. Retrieved March 5, 2024, from https://www.usatoday.com/story/news/education/2023/08/13/why-us-back-to-school-dates-vary/70532779007/.

Wanzek, J., Petscher, Y., Al Otaiba, S., & Donegan, R. E. (2019). Retention of reading intervention effects from fourth to fifth grade for students with reading difficulties. *Reading & Writing Quarterly: Overcoming Learning Difficulties*, 35(3), 277–288. https://doi.org/10.1080/10573569.2018.1560379.

Warner, A. (2023, March 15). The pros and cons of Year-Round school calendars: A balanced calendar replaces summer with shorter, more frequent breaks. https://www.usnews.com/. Retrieved March 3, 2024, from https://www.usnews.com/education/k12/articles/the-pros-and-cons-of-year-round-school-calendars.

Weaver, E. (2022, December 23). HCS to open first year-round school in 2023. https://www.mydailyrecord.com/. Retrieved March 13, 2024, from https://www.mydailyrecord.com/news/hcs-to-open-first-year-round-school-in-2023/article_f8f2fb50-8224-11ed-9d13-93d5d4e1bf87.html.

Weaver, R. G., Armstrong, B., Hunt, E., Beets, M.W., Brazendale, K., Dugger, R., Turner-McGrievy, G., Pate, R.R., Maydeu-Olivares, A., Saelens, B., & Youngstedt, S.D. (2020). The impact of summer vacation on children's obesogenic behaviors and body mass index: A natural experiment. *International Journal of Behavioral Nutrition and Physical Activity*, 17, 153. https://doi.org/10.1186/s12966-020-01052-0.

Weaver, R. G., Beets, M. W., Perry, M., Hunt, E., Brazendale, K., Decker, L., Turner-McGrievy, G., Pate, R., Youngstedt, S. D., Saelens, B. E., & Maydeu-Olivares, A. (2019). Changes in children's sleep and physical activity during a 1-week versus a 3-week break from school: A natural experiment. *Sleep*, 42(1), zsy205. https://doi.org/10.1093/sleep/zsy205.

Weber, L. E. (2022). The four-day school week as a path for principal attraction and retention: Perceptions of elementary principals in Missouri (Order No. 29993466). Available from ProQuest One Academic. (2774533203). Retrieved from https://login.delval.idm.oclc.org/login?url=https://www.proquest.com/dissertations-theses/four-day-school-week-as-path-principal-attraction/docview/2774533203/se-2.

Weiss, J., & Brown, R. S. (2005). Summer learning: Research, policies and programs. *Teachers College Record*, 107(7), 1429.

Weiss, J., & S., B. R. (2013). *Telling tales over time: Calendars, clocks, and school effectiveness*. New York: Springer.

Wells, J., & Wells, J. (2022, April 19). Four school days in a row is perfect for the average Joe. *NHS Chief Advocate*. Retrieved March 14, 2024, from https://nhschiefadvocate.org/2022/04/four-school-days-in-a-row-is-perfect-for-the-average-joe/.

West, B. (2023, August 14). Rural schools in Montana face uphill battle before start of school year. *KECI*. https://nbcmontana.com/news/local/rural-schools-in-montana-face-uphill-battle-before-start-of-school-year.

West Memphis School District adopts year-round calendar. (2023, March 7). https://www.fox13memphis.com/. Retrieved March 14, 2024, from https://www

.fox13memphis.com/education/west-memphis-school-district-adopts-year-round-calendar/article_3782cb34-bcea-11ed-b99a-7782bcfe010a.html.

West Virginia Department of Education. (2018, May 29). Pre-K school calendar - West Virginia Department of Education. https://wvde.us/early-and-elementary-learning/wv-universal-pre-k/universal-pre-k-collaborative-system/pre-k-school-calendar/.

Why four-day weeks are becoming popular among US schools? Here's all you need to know. (2022, December 28). https://economictimes.indiatimes.com/.

Whipple, M. A. (2022). A comparison of academic achievement for the four-day and five-day school week in New Mexico (Order No. 29326091). Available from ProQuest One Academic. (2701100685). Retrieved from https://login.delval.idm.oclc.org/login?url=https://www.proquest.com/dissertations-theses/comparison-academic-achievement-four-day-five/docview/2701100685/se-2.

White, R. (2023, July 20). Goshen County schools prepare to begin four day school weeks. KNEB-AM 960 AM – 100.3 FM. Retrieved March 13, 2024, from https://ruralradio.com/kneb-am/news/goshen-county-schools-prepare-to-begin-four-day-school-weeks/.

Wildman, L. Arambula, S., Bryson, D., Bryson, T., Campbell, K., Dominguez, T., Flores, R. S., Jackson, S., Killberg, T., Lara, G., Letlow, J. L., Pitts, T. A., Shoop, D. P., Waterman, K. C., and Watkins, M. R. (1999). The effect of year-round schooling on administrators. *Education,* 119(3), 465. https://link.gale.com/apps/doc/A54709073/AONE?u=anon~eebdb3d&sid=googleScholar&xid=6a366428.

WN, NH look at 4-day school week. (2022, January 24). *Nodaway News.* Retrieved March 13, 2024, from https://nodawaynews.com/wn-nh-look-at-4-day-school-week/.

Wilmore, C., & Slate, J. (2012). Texas elementary school academic achievement as a function of school calendar type. *Journal of Education Policy, Planning, and Administration,* 2(1), 24–38.

Woolley-Wilson, J. (2022, October 28). NAEP scores show a long road to academic recovery. Edtech can help shorten it. *EdSurge.* https://www.edsurge.com/news/2022-10-28-naep-scores-show-a-long-road-to-academic-recovery-edtech-can-help-shorten-it.

Wong, A. (2023, January 12). More schools are opting for four-day weeks. Here's what you need to know. *USA TODAY.* Retrieved March 7, 2024, from https://www.usatoday.com/story/news/education/2022/12/28/four-days-learning-more-us-schools-consider-shorter-weeks/10956152002/.

Woulfin, S. L., & Spitzer, N. (2023). Time is ticking: The dynamics of education reform in the Covid-era. *Journal of Educational Administration,* 61(3), 256–271.

Wrigley, M. (2023, November 15). Off on Mondays: How Lincoln High School's first semester with four-day weeks is going. https://www.5newsonline.com/. Retrieved March 7, 2024, from https://www.5newsonline.com/article/news/local/four-day-school-week-lincoln-arkansas/527-a4f0458f-0c75-4965-9c0c-ceeacd3728fb.

Wyatt, D., & Wyatt, D. (2023, January 26). Musd exploring year round education at elementary sites facing growth impacts. https://www.mantecabulletin.com/. Retrieved March 10, 2024, from https://www.mantecabulletin.com/news/

local-news/musd-exploring-year-round-education-elementary-sites-facing-growth-impacts/.

Year-Round Education Calendars. (n.d.). https://www.cde.ca.gov/. Retrieved March 10, 2024, from https://www.cde.ca.gov/ls/fa/yr/yrecal.asp.

Year Round & Extended Year Schools. (n.d.). https://www.doe.virginia.gov. Retrieved March 16, 2024, from https://www.doe.virginia.gov/teaching-learning-assessment/specialized-instruction/year-round-extended-year-schools.

Yellin, D. (2022, May 19). NJ schools under pressure to add religious holidays. But some say it's gone too far. https://www.northjersey.com/. Retrieved March 5, 2024, from https://www.northjersey.com/story/news/2022/05/19/nj-schools-add-diwali-eid-juneteenth-holidays-but-face-backlash/9607168002/.

Zizo, C. (2023, May 19). Year-round school coming to Florida as Gov. Ron DeSantis signs pilot program into law. *WKMG*. https://www.clickorlando.com/news/politics/2023/05/19/year-round-school-coming-to-florida-as-gov-ron-desantis-signs-pilot-program-into-law/.

Zvoch, K., & Stevens, J. J. (2015). Identification of summer school effects by comparing the in- and out-of-school growth rates of struggling early readers. The Elementary School Journal, 115(3), 433–456. https://doi.org/10.1086/680229

About the Authors

Figure C.1   *Dr. David G. Hornak can be contacted at davidghornak@gmail.com.*

David G. Hornak, Ed.D., has lived and worked in Holt, Michigan, for the past 30 years. As an employee of Holt Public Schools, he has taught young fives, kindergarten, first grade, and Reading Recovery. Hornak was promoted 17 years ago, as he became the instructional leader (principal) of Horizon Elementary. Horizon is a YRS, which operates on a balanced school calendar. Hornak has presented hundreds of times to school boards, district officials, community groups, and PTO groups across the world regarding alternative calendar and wellness initiatives such as the *Walking School Bus*. His dissertation titled "The Impact of Summer Recess on Mathematical Learning Retention," which was selected in 2016 as the national dissertation of the year by the National Council of Professors of Educational Administration further supports the need for school officials interested in minimizing the summer learning loss to consider the balanced school calendar. In April 2015, Hornak was named Executive Director of the NAYRE. In July 2015, Hornak was promoted to serve as the superintendent of schools in Holt. He is addicted to serving others, especially his own community as well as those interested in learning more about the balanced school calendar. Hornak and his partner Anne are the proud parents of daughter Olivia and son Maxwell. To connect with David: davidghornak@gmail.com

Figure C.2   *Dr. Jon Mishra can be contacted at jnmishr@aol.com.*

Dr. Jon Ram Mishra currently serves as an assistant superintendent for the OSPI in Washington State. In that role, he provides leadership over elementary, early learning, and federal programs. He has been at the agency since June 2019. Prior to landing at the state agency, Jon has served as a school administrator at all levels in Oregon and Washington state as well as serving at the district level, including a stint as a superintendent of schools. Dr. Mishra has worked in districts ranging in size from less than 300 to greater than 17,000 students in his 33 years of service. Jon has presented at the state and national level on various topics, including the balanced calendar approach, diversity, equity, inclusion, and belonging, instructional best practices, aligning systems for success, emergent technology, and effective implementation of professional learning communities. Jon and his wife, Loreena, have three children, Kaajal, Varsha, and Aakash. Jon is the son of Ram and Bijay Mishra. Jon's parents migrated from the Fiji Islands in 1965 to make a better life for their children. As a servant leader, Jon's hope is his work will leave a legacy of excellence. As an employee of the State of Washington, Jon is prohibited from profiting from the sales of this book.

Figure C.3 *Dr. James Pedersen can be contacted at jamesmpedersen1@gmail.com.*

Dr. James Pedersen is currently the Superintendent for the Essex County Schools of Technology, which is an award-winning school district located in his home state of New Jersey. His career in education spans over 30 years and includes a variety of instructional and administrative positions. He has had the opportunity to teach as an Adjunct Professor at Montclair University, Centenary University, and Delaware Valley University. Pedersen has published and been cited in over 20 articles as well as two books focusing on education, *Rise of the Millennial Parents* (2013) and *Summer versus School: The Possibilities of the Year-Round School* (2015). His research and contributions to the research of school calendars have been a passion of his that was noticed by the educational stakeholders in Washington state who began their work on calendar reform.

www.ingramcontent.com/pod-product-compliance
Lightning Source LLC
Chambersburg PA
CBHW021826300426
44114CB00009BA/337